THE TRINITY AS HISTORY

THE TRINITY AS HISTORY
Saga of the Christian God

Bruno Forte

ALBA · HOUSE　　NEW · YORK

SOCIETY OF ST. PAUL, 2187 VICTORY BLVD., STATEN ISLAND, NEW YORK 10314

Translated from the third Italian edition by
Paul Rotondi, O.F.M.

Originally published by Edizione Paoline under the title
Trinita come storia

Library of Congress Cataloging-in-Publication Data

Forte, Bruno.
    [Trinità come storia. English]
    The Trinity as history: saga of the Christian God / by Bruno
  Forte: [translated from the third Italian edition by Paul Rotondi].
        p.   cm.
    Translation of: Trinità come storia.
    Bibliography: p.
    ISBN 0-8189-0552-2
    1. Trinity.   2. History (Theology)   3. Catholic Church — Doctrines.
  I. Title.
    BT111.2.F6713   1989
    231'.044 — dc20   89-32734
                                          CIP

Designed, printed and bound in the United States of
America by the Fathers and Brothers of the
Society of St. Paul, 2187 Victory Boulevard,
Staten Island, New York 10314, as part of their
communications apostolate.

Printing Information:

Current Printing - first digit 1 2 3 4 5 6 7 8 9 10 11 12

Year of Current Printing - first year shown
  1989   1990   1991   1992   1993   1994   1995   1996

TABLE OF CONTENTS

1.
THE TRINITY AND HISTORY

2.
THE TRINITY IN HISTORY

3.

THE TRINITY AS HISTORY

4.

HISTORY IN THE TRINITY

INTRODUCTION

This book speaks of the Trinity by speaking about history; and it speaks of history by speaking about the Trinity. The history that it recounts is above all that of the paschal event: the history of the death and resurrection of Jesus of Nazareth who rose from the dead and was appointed Lord and Christ with power according to the Spirit of holiness (cf. Rm 1:4). Yet another history is also examined in this work — that of him who in the paschal event is revealed as Love (cf. 1 Jn 4:8, 16), delivering his beloved Son to death and reconciling him, and in him, the world with himself in the power of the Spirit of unity and freedom in love. The account of the paschal event thus unfolds as the story of the Trinity — the eternal event of love — and the history of that eternal love. This book speaks of God by recounting a history of Love.

In speaking of God, the pages that follow speak also of man. In the paschal event, accepted as a Trinitarian event of love, can be read the meaning and the hope of history. As a story thus narrated, the Trinity is not an abstract celestial theorem. Through its salvific self-revelation, the Trinity manifests itself as the origin, the present, and the future of the world — as the adorably transcendent bosom of history.

"Speaking of the Trinity, *'res nostra agitur'* [we deal with our own concerns]. Trinitarian theology must study the Trinity in the light of personal and collective experience, and vice versa" (*First Thesis on FILIOQUE of the 1983 Congress of the Italian Theological Association: Rassegna di Teologia 25* [1984] 87).

Rethought out in this "Trinitarian bosom" are: the human condition, the community of humankind, and the Church in which is already being prepared — through daily gestures of love and the actualizing celebration of the mystery — the future revelation of the glory of love when the history of humankind will converge forever with the eternal history of God, and the Son will deliver everything to the Father, and God will be all in all (cf. 1 Cor 15:28).

This book, like its predecessor to which it is closely connected — *Jesus of Nazareth, the History of God, the God of History: An Essay on Christology as History* — is part of the tradition of Italian, especially southern Italian, historical thought, in the manner of such scholars as Joachim of Fiore and Thomas Aquinas, of Tomasso Campanella and Giordano Bruno, of Giovanni Battista Vico and Alfonsus Liguori, up through Neapolitan Illuminism and the theological school of the eighteenth century, to Benedetto Croce's historicism.

This tradition endeavors to center its thought on the encounter between the world of God and the world of humankind — an encounter that is continually being spelled out in human history and abundantly revealed to us in Jesus Christ. Thus we are permitted to think historically about God and theologically about man, and to think historically about the Trinity and "Trinitarily" about history. At the same time, we come to think about them with life as the starting point. It is the concrete, daily unfolding of history, with its poor "old" and "new" components, its "losses of meaning," personal and collective, with the frequent temptation, especially among the young, of "flights from history" (think of the tragic drama of the chemically-dependent), with so many unavoidable questions and so many insufficient answers which give rise to talk about a "crisis of ideologies" and a "spineless philosophy of life."

The word of theology does not intend to present itself to history as a simple solution to all its problems. Nor does it intend to be the "strong" word that ignores the wearisome historical mediation of love. On the contrary, theology is aware of its weaknesses, even if it is confident. And it cannot be otherwise. In its weakness, the "weakness of God" manifests itself to be a folly wiser than the wise and an impotence more powerful than the strong (cf. 1 Cor 1:25).

In this sense, the divine history of love, which *is* the Trinity, can be proposed to human weariness of life as capable of lighting the way, of giving support on the journey, of spreading hope. Hence, even though the rigor of critical reflection must be used (it expresses a necessary tension toward objectivity), this book does not lack passion. It addresses itself to all (even to those who are not strictly "professional" theologians) by taking a concrete position which encourages others to take concrete positions. Does not telling about love also tend to spread love? And isn't this the way theology ought to transmit saving truth: by becoming itself a kind of salvation event?

I dedicate this book to all those with whom I have been, am now, and will be united in love so that, together, we may always more profoundly walk along the path of unwaning love (cf. 1 Cor 13:8). And, with them, I dedicate it to all "pilgrims" of love: to the many who loved and were loved so that they may render thanks to him who *is* love; to the many who love without being loved, that they may know how to always welcome anew the gratuitous love of him who alone is infinitely capable of it; and, finally, to the many who do not love because they do not know how or wish to know, with the hope that they may meet him who, loving them, will free them from the fear of loving and give them the courage to live the credible proclamation of the good news of the eternal history of love, which came to us in the Jesus event. May he, who is the Christ, see to it that for all those journeying in love this book may be a help for advancing, without tiring, toward their Trinitarian homeland of love.

Bruno Forte
August 15th
Feast of the Assumption of the Virgin Mary

1.

THE TRINITY
AND HISTORY

THE TRINITY AND HISTORY

a) *The Exile of the Trinity*

Is the God of Christians a Christian God?

This question, paradoxical in appearance, arises spontaneously if we consider the manner in which most Christians picture their God. They talk of him by referring to some vague divine "person," more or less identified with the Jesus of the Gospels or with an unidentifiable heavenly being. In prayer they speak to this rather indefinite God while at the same time they find the way the liturgy prays to the Father through Christ in the Holy Spirit a bit strange, not to say abstruse: God is prayed *to*, but not *in*!

It is an undeniable fact that many Christians, "notwithstanding their exact profession of the Trinity, are almost alone as 'monotheists' in the practice of their religious life. One can even risk claiming that if the Trinity should have to be suppressed as false doctrine, a great part of religious literature could still remain unchanged after this occurrence. The suspicion could arise that, for the catechism of the mind and heart (unlike the printed catechism), the representation of the incarnation on the part of the Christian would not have to change at all if ever there were no Trinity."[1]

That the Trinitarian mystery is a theological theorem without practical incidence is a widespread conviction. Kant in his day was convinced of this fact: "From the doctrine of the Trinity, taken literally, it is absolutely impossible to draw anything practical, even if one should pretend to understand it, much less then if we realize that it goes beyond our every concept.''[2]

To the question, ''What is the reason for the fact that in the West the majority of Christians, in their experience and practice of life, are properly only 'monotheists'?'', Moltmann answers by stating: ''In the doctrine of faith and in ethics, it matters little that God is one and three.''[3]

Christian theology has, in fact, more or less reflected — on the theoretical plane — the shortcomings which are observable in the practice, not without negatively affecting the practice itself in so doing. Theological tracts have generally concerned themselves with creation and salvation, anthropology and Christology, revelation and the Church, the sacraments and eschatology without troubling themselves to reflect on these various matters from the point of view specific to the Christian faith: the Trinitarian God. Moral theology developed without any reference whatsoever to this mystery, almost as though Christian activity were not the concrete expression in life (the *Amen vitae!*) of the Trinitarian profession used so frequently at the beginning of a believer's activities: ''In the name of the Father and of the Son and of the Holy Spirit.''

This isolation of the doctrine of the Trinity from the rest of dogma and ethics has not been corrected even in many of the theologies we presently have. Judging from some of the new reformulations of old tracts, of innovative intuitions or investigations in areas ranging from hermeneutics to narrative theology, from political theology to the theology of liberation, it does not seem that the ''Trinitarian Gospel'' enjoys a truly decisive role. It is not an exaggeration to affirm that we are still faced with an exile of the Trinity from the theory and practice of the average Christian. Hopefully, it is precisely this exile which will make us nostalgic and motivate us to a beautiful rediscovery of our ''Trinitarian homeland'' in both theology and in life.[4]

b) *The Return to the "Trinitarian Homeland"*

The beginnings of this Trinitarian neglect, which effectively translates into the non-Christian monotheism of many Christians, can be associated with the preoccupation that the various worlds with which Christianity has come into contact — from the Jewish to the Greco-Hellenistic — have had against the proclamation of the so-called "Christian scandal." We are referring to their "pious" concern to safeguard and defend *the divinity of God*.[5] The Christian faith never ever renounced, it is true, its disturbing and problematic proclamation. It continued to confess — even in the most elaborate forms of theology and dogma — the unheard of *humanity of God,* revealed to us in Christ Jesus. This confession, however, was wed to the "pious" preoccupation of the cultures being evangelized. And it was precisely for this reason that the Christological and Trinitarian "scandal" has always been considered in the light of the mystery of divine unity.

This evolution is particularly apparent in the West where the great theological systems of Augustine, first, and later of Thomas Aquinas depart from the theological contemplation of the one essence of God in order, then, to draw from it the concept of a trinity of Persons. The one God precedes and forms the foundation for the triune God: the divinity of the Absolute comes first and encompasses the personal relativity. The distinction between the two tracts — *De Deo Uno* and *De Deo Trino* — is nothing more than the logical outcome of this approach.

The first tract can well serve anyone who believes in God. It has the force of rationality and universality which could easily threaten to suffocate the second. Not only that. The material proper to the second tract becomes an effort to reconcile the trinity of Persons with the unity of the divine essence, with hardly a reference to the concrete historical revelation of the Three. The Trinity is thus reduced to a sort of celestial theorem within a prior monotheistic doctrine, without effective consequences on the level of the concept of God and the salvation of mankind. The dynamism of the event of revelation is set against a static horizon. The mission of the Son and of the Holy Spirit, as well as the living plurality of the relationships of the Three, are moderated by a metaphysical concept of the immutable and eternal One. The unifying quietude of the Supreme Being reigns over all and absorbs everything in our human discourse about God.

It is not hard to perceive how much this divine quietude contrasts with the physical immediacy of God as related by the testimony of our Christian origins. As soon as one starts to speak in the words of the New Testament (a language which speaks of God as the Father of Jesus Christ[6]), and as soon as one rediscovers the need to think out the history of humanity in the history of the Three, so freely and contagiously narrated in the Easter story, the separation between a discussion of the one and only God and the discussion of the three divine Persons will be seen as untenable.

As is by now more commonly accepted — following the lead of A. Stolz[7] and M. Schmaus[8] — a new rapport between the two areas of thought is being shaped.[9] The one God is being seen above all in the Father and in the unbegun beginning of the Son and of the Spirit in the unity of the Three. This divine unity is no longer being thought of as "essence prior to personal distinction" but as the unity of the reciprocal inhabitation of the Three in the fruitful, inexhaustible circulation of the unique life of eternal love.

The divinity of God — justly at the center of every monotheistic preoccupation — will not be sacrificed on this account. It will be pondered in a Christian way in the light of the humanity of God, of its revelation in the historical terms and activities of Father, Son, and Holy Spirit, in view of the "divinization" of mankind. If, according to some, this causes the loss of "universality" and "rationality" in our Christian-speaking about God, it will at the same time certainly cause it to gain in "singularity" and "wisdom," and hence in authentic universal strength and depth of awareness.

Elevated human speech about God "is like water when compared with the strong theological wine offered by revelation. And then the best critical and obedient disposition of the believer is to have confidence in the *patois de Canaan*, in that language of revelation in which, strangely, people of all times and places succeed in establishing 'youthful bonds' with what is being proclaimed. In this 'Canaanite dialect,' categories and terms, not yet rendered doubtful by identification with *one* culture or one philosophy, are emphasized. And then, one experiences in a lively way — confronted by human feeling — not just *any* kind of anthropomorphism, but precisely that which was concretized in the form of an ontological reality, namely God in human form."[10]

"Minerva's screech-owl cedes its place to the dove of the Holy Spirit."[11] Instead of speaking about God by starting with man, the discussion follows the path of his coming to us, according to that "analogy with Advent" which is the relationship established between God and man by the gift of creation and the grace of redemption.[12] In this light, even the most elevated and sophisticated awareness of the Absolute seems like flimsy "straw" next to the simple yet profound account of the good news. And the Trinitarian scandal proves itself wiser than the wisdom of men.

c) *The Trinity and History*

The Trinity's recall from exile in the concept and practice of believers — their return to the "Trinitarian homeland" — comes about, principally, by means of a return to the history of revelation. This is the deepest meaning of the fundamental axiom formulated by Karl Rahner: "The economic Trinity and the immanent Trinity."[13] The axiom means, above all — *on the plane of one's awareness of God* — that there is no other place from which to proceed less unfaithfully in speaking of the divine mystery than the history of revelation, of the intimately connected words and events by means of which God has narrated his history in our own (the "economy" as the Fathers called it, that "dispensation" of the gift from on high which saves us). The Trinity as it is in itself ("immanent") allows itself to be known in the Trinity as it is for us ("economic").

God in himself and the God who reveals himself is one and the same: the Father through the Son in the Holy Spirit. This correspondence is based on the very mystery of divine fidelity. The Trinity of history manifests itself as the Trinity of glory because "God is faithful and cannot deny himself" (2 Tm 2:13), cannot deceive us in revealing himself to us.

"The reality of God in his revelation cannot be isolated — almost as if there were another divine reality beyond his revelation of himself; rather, the exact same reality which we encounter in revelation is his reality in all its eternal depth."[14]

This correspondence between economy and immanence in the mystery is evident in the figure of Jesus Christ, the Son of God incarnate, the "yes" of supreme divine fidelity (cf. 2 Cor 1:19ff). He is not the personification of some generic "god" in human flesh: He is the Son, the Word of God, the transparent "image of the invisible God" (Col 1:15). The relationship which unites Christ to him who sent him and to the Spirit whom he receives and pours out, reveals a corresponding relationship in the depth of divine life, just as the relationship he establishes with us in the Spirit gives us access to the mystery of the Father at the source and circulation of Trinitarian life. Every abstract hypothesis regarding the Trinity in itself and in its possible activity on our behalf falls before the concreteness of the Christ event, of him known as the Risen One, of his life and deeds to which Easter faith bears witness for us. His singularity is the touchstone of the validity of every doctrine about God!

Without reference to this economy, theology is depleted and exposed to every possible rational trap. For its part, however, the history of revelation must be reflected on and told in an always new way. Without theology, the economy of salvation could remain mute. The economy of salvation is a threshold which refers one, on the one hand, to the profundity of God and, on the other hand, to the actual experience of the mystery. Whoever speaks about God has the task of crossing this threshold in two directions in order to scrutinize in the "Deus revelatus" the "Deus absconditus" and to recount thus in the history of mankind the history of God.

Here is where the axiom's second strong line comes to the fore: "The economic Trinity is the immanent Trinity" *on the plane of the experience of God* (which biblically refers to nothing less than the depth and authenticity of our awareness of him). This means that our encounter with the events of revelation, witnessed to in the living ecclesial tradition of faith under the action of the Spirit, is an encounter with the very mystery of the divinity itself. To have contact with the revelation of the Trinity is to have contact with the eternal history of divine love, and to enter into its mystery. If God in himself were other than the God spoken of in the history of revelation, there would be no way for us to approach the depth of Trinitarian life in spirit and in truth. If the immanent Trinity did not correspond with its economic revelation, no salvation in history would be possible. Humanity would be irrevocably condemned to the human horizon and to the sad experience of our own finiteness. No loophole would remain open. In the end, the inconsistency of nothingness would engulf all.

If, instead, "the sunset of death cannot extend itself over divine things" (Arnobius) and this divine life is made effectively accessible to us in the history of Jesus Christ, then hope in an unfading and full life is given to us, too. In the correspondence between the mystery's economy and its immanence, the Trinity presents itself as the reality of salvation and the experience of grace. In this sense, theological awareness of the Trinitarian mystery from the starting point of economy, even if it is not an immediately practical understanding, is capable of changing more basically the practice of the possible alternatives.

"In fact, the history of Christ with God and of God with Christ becomes, through the Spirit, the history of God with us and in such wise also our history with God. Awareness comes by way of the fact that the knower gets involved in this history which grips him and changes him."[15]

Thinking about God as Trinity from the viewpoint of revelation means — if the mystery's economy corresponds to its immanence — "thinking about God from within God, that is, plumbing the Christian concept of divinization to its foundation. The concept of the triune God is embraced in a vital way by him who believes contextually in the fact of being included in the triune God by the salvific act of the incarnate Word and the divinizing Spirit."[16]

When the Trinity is discussed without separating history from glory, then we are talking about ourselves, *res nostra agitur*, and what are at stake are the destiny and the meaning of all our individual and collective undertakings. It could be said — against the mentioned widespread conviction of abstractness and uselessness of Trinitarian doctrine — that for the Christian nothing is more vital and concrete than faith in the Trinity of Father, Son and Holy Spirit, in whose name, and through whose glory, he is called to be and to fulfill all things. "The Trinity is a confession of soteriological faith!"[17]

The whole of Christian existence is entered into through the Trinitarian mystery — not only on the plane of personal existence but also on that of ecclesial and social life. Not by accident is the exile of the Trinity from the theory and the practice of Christians reflected in the "visibilism" and juridicism which often dominate the understanding of Church[18] and which have had consequences on the socio-political plane.[19] Hence the return to our "Trinitarian homeland" appears as something promising both for ecclesiology and the entire historical situation of Christianity. This return is perhaps the most burning challenge facing the Church and theology in the Church today:

"The greatest ecclesial problem and the greatest task for

theology is that of making the Trinity a spiritually vital thought for the believer and for theology so that faith's whole doctrine and the believer's whole existence may be thought of and lived from the viewpoint of their Trinitarian profession. Consequently, the problem is one of understanding the profession of Trinitarian faith as the permanent beginning of any criticism of ecclesiastical existence, as part of the criticism of worldly existence and of the constant proposition of the eschatological measure of history."[20]

This urgency is equally pressing if one starts from the universal, personal, and collective problem of learning how to love in order to attain, through love, the truth about life. Whoever wants to learn how to love and seeks its strength can no longer tolerate the exile of love from eternal history, which is the Trinity. Kahlil Gibran understood this: "When you love, do not say: I have God in my heart, but rather: I am in the heart of God."[21] Being in the heart of God. Is that not perhaps "remaining" in the Spirit, through the Son, under the loving gaze of the Father?

d) *The Trinity Beyond History*

The thesis about the correspondence between economic Trinity and immanent Trinity, in its twofold revelatory and salvific foundation, is nevertheless not exempt from limits and risks: correspondence cannot be perceived as identity.[22] If from Tertullian on, the need has been felt for formulating the distinction between the economy and the immanence of the Trinitarian mystery, this did not come about without a reason. The economy cannot exhaust God's depth; history cannot — and must not — capture the glory. This is so in the name of divine transcendence and freedom which are also the foundation of the marvelous gratuity of Trinitarian love for us. Precisely because it springs from another and sovereign will, one totally free and not necessitated, the divine initiative of salvation appears to be motivated by nothing other than the gratuity of love! A God settled in history, a divine immanent Trinity totally suitable for its economic self-revelation, would no longer be the Christian God but one of this world's forces, even though the highest and most necessary!

The transcendence and the concealed nature of God in himself in respect to the "Deus pro nobis" can be taken in two ways: on the one hand, in an *apophatical* sense, through the admission of the ineffability of the divine mystery, so totally other, even though it became understood as such wholly within human experience; on the other, in an *eschatological* sense, through a consideration of what is coming and new, precisely of the Christian God as the God of promise.

The *apophasis* speaks of the awe, adoration and silence required in the presence of absolute mystery:"Do not draw near! Remove your sandals from your feet because the place on which you stand is holy ground!" (Ex 3:5).

"God is honored by silence, not because one speaks about or investigates him without reason, but because we are aware of remaining always on this side of an adequate understanding of him."[23]

"We shall place ourselves together on the pathways of charity in search of him of whom it is said: 'Seek always his face.' In this pious and serene disposition of spirit, I should like to find myself joined, before the Lord our God, by the readers of all my books, but especially of this one which inquires into the unity of the Trinity of Father, Son and Holy Spirit, because there is no other argument in regard to which error is more dangerous, research more arduous, and discovery more fruitful."[24]

The investigation of the Trinitarian mystery calls for discretion and humility. The form of thought and expression least inadequate for this would seem, therefore, to be that of the praise and the contemplation of love. In this sense Pannenberg prefers to define human speech about God as "doxologic" rather than "analogic."[25] In it the words evoke what infinitely surpasses them. They do not capture the reality nor do they force it into an ill-fitting straitjacket.

This "adoring" way of speaking about God is, in effect, a theology of response. "The praise that arises therefrom and the awareness of God that such theology acquires is a response to the salvation which is being experienced."[26] The response remains conscious, however, of the infinite transcendence of the gift, and hence of the need to correspond with it, especially with the silence of listening and of lived love. Hence, Trinitarian theology is not opposed to "negative" theology. Instead, it requires it. "Between Creator and creature no likeness can be observed without taking note of the always greater unlikeness."[27] The more awareness of the mystery grows, the more inexhaustible its richness and depth appear. The more silence grows, the more the mystery is seen to be fruitful as well as active.

This inadequacy of the theological word is nourished, however, by hope. The amount already given in the economy is a pledge of what will be fully revealed in the time of glory. The divine promise looks to the end. *Eschatology* offers itself as the transcendence of the present into the future that is coming, guaranteed by the history of revelation as the future of the Trinitarian God with mankind. The relationship between economy and immanence in the mystery thus takes on a dialectic form. Corresponding to the thesis, "The economic Trinity is the immanent Trinity," is the weighty antithesis through which "the immanent Trinity is not the economic Trinity," in the expectation, however, of the eschatological synthesis in which "God will be all in all" (1 Cor 15:28), and history and glory will coexist in fully reconciled diversity. In the face of this "not yet" of the promise, of this ultimate fatherland, "foreseen but not possessed," the theologian knows how to reflect in the shadows of evening — like the sentinel awaiting the dawn (cf. Ps 130:6), when the *cognitio matutina* (morning knowledge) will take the place of the *cognitio vespertina* (evening knowledge) of the time of the wayfarer.[28]

Something of this future light is often given as a clearer reflection in the experience of mystics and spiritual persons in whom the Gospel word is realized: "If one loves me, he will keep my word, and my Father will love him and we will come to him and make our abode in him" (Jn 14:23). In their school, Trinitarian theology is called upon to nurture them in prayer, to endow them with a sense of beauty and to fill them with peace.

At the same time, the Trinity's call to "come back home" reminds one, in thinking about the mystery, of his or her need of permanent reform, of incessant search. In this sense, every word about the Trinity calls forth new words, every silence, new silences that — without denying the richness of past speculations, but gathering them all together into the oneness of an uninterrupted believing search — push beyond and ahead into the profundity of the living God.

This permanent eschatological tension is fraught with critical-prophetic value. It keeps things going. It disenchants every seductive presumption about possession. It questions every possible worldly identification of the Kingdom, freeing the believer from the powers of death so as to open him up, always in a new way, to the future promise of eternal life. The recovery of the "Trinitarian homeland, even if "a dim image in a mirror" (1 Cor 13:12), thus revives the time of exile, unmasks the deceit of every apparent satiety, and stimulates pilgrims in their search for the justice and the peace of the Kingdom. *"Non est status in via Dei: immo mora peccatum est"* (St. Bernard). "There is no standing still on the way to God: indeed, even a delay is culpable."

2.

THE TRINITY IN HISTORY

The centerpiece of the economy of salvation, the ever-living source of the dispensation of Trinitarian love for mankind, is the paschal mystery. Starting with the experience of the Risen One, provided by the first witnesses of the Christian faith, the past is reread, the encounter with the Living One in the Spirit is celebrated in the present, and the future of the Kingdom is announced. The event of the resurrection of Jesus from the dead is the starting point of the Christian movement, the new start which contains in itself all that is specific to faith in Christ in its unheard of singularity.[1] The Trinitarian confession, which is the absolutely proper and original content of this faith, simply makes explicit a truth that is already present in the paschal mystery.[2] The event of the death and resurrection of the Lord is the locus for this Trinitarian faith, the source of the real life that is conveyed by it and a compact synthesis of the ever greater glory made accessible to us in history.

In the perspective of the economy of salvation it can, therefore, be said that the *Trinity*, prior to being an explicit confession of faith, *is an event*. It was in order to communicate the event from which it is derived, namely the story of Easter, that the Christian faith formulated the Trinitarian confession and reread the whole history of mankind in the light of its memory and hope. Thus were the stages by which the Trinity offers itself in history delineated. The Trinitarian event of Easter is linked to a rereading of history in the light of Easter and, therefore, of the confessional development, in time, of faith in the Trinity. More than anything else, Trinitarian theology is shaped in terms of a narrative as well as an argumentative account of these stages.

2.1 THE TRINITARIAN HISTORY OF EASTER[3]

a) *The Easter Experience*

In the beginning there was the experience of an encounter.[4] Jesus showed himself to be alive to those who, cowardly, had abandoned him on Good Friday (cf. Ac 1:3). This meeting was so decisive for them that their existence was totally transformed by it. Courage came in the wake of fear; mission followed abandonment. The fugitives became witnesses and remained such until death in a life given without reserve to him whom they had betrayed in the "hour of darkness." What had happened? There is a hiatus between the sunset of Good Friday and the dawn of Easter Sunday — an empty space of time in which something of such importance took place that it actually gave rise to the Christian movement in history.

Profane history can speak only about this "new beginning," avoiding any attempt to explain its causes after the collapse of various "liberal" interpretations of the birth of Easter faith which tended to make it a purely subjective experience of the disciples.[5] The Christian proclamation, however, recorded in the texts of the New Testament, holds that the encounter with the Risen One is an experience of grace, and that the accounts of the post-resurrection appearances are what give us access to this experience.

The five separate accounts (the Pauline 1 Cor 15:5-8; and those of Mark 16:9-20; Matthew 28:9-10, 16-20; Luke 24:13-53; and John 20:14-29 and 21)[6] are not in agreement in their chronological and geographical details. Nevertheless, they are built on a similar structure which allows the fundamental characteristics of the experience they speak about to show through. There one always finds: (1) *the initiative of the Risen One*, (2) the process of *recognition* on the part of the *disciples*, and (3) the *mission* which makes them witnesses of what they have "heard and seen with their eyes and contemplated and touched with their hands" (cf. 1 Jn 1:1).

The initiative of the Risen One, the fact that it is *he* who shows himself alive (cf. Ac 1:3), who "appears" (the verb used in 1 Cor 15:3-8 and Lk 24:34 is the same as the one used in the Old Testament Greek to describe theophanies such as those described in Gn 12:7; 17:1; 18:1; 25:2), tells us that men's experience of the origins of Christianity had about it the character of "objectivity." It was something that happened *to* them, that "came" to them, not something which "took place" *in* them. It was not a stirring of faith and love which created its object, but the good news which fostered that faith and love in an entirely new way.

Still this does not exclude the spiritual process necessary to the first believers "to believe their own eyes," thus opening them up interiorly to what had taken place in Jesus the Lord. It was what assured a progressive journey — carefully and often underlined in the New Testament to forestall any possible tendencies to excessive "enthusiasm" — and led from awe and doubt to a faith-filled acknowledgment of the Risen One: "Then their eyes were opened and they recognized him" (Lk 24:31).

Process signifies a subjective and spiritual dimension to the basic experience of the Christian faith, thus guaranteeing space for the freedom and uncoerced assent of the believer. The experience of an encounter is thus complete. In a rapport of direct and risky awareness (the word "experience" comes from *ex-perior* and connotes both the direct knowledge of the *peritus* and the risk connected with it, the *periculum*), the Living One manifests himself to his own and offers them a share in his own life. They bear witness to him and to that encounter with him which has marked their existence forever: "Go through the whole world and preach the good news to every creature" (Mk 16:15). "God has raised him from the dead, and of this we are witnesses" (Ac 3:15; cf. 5:31f as also 1:22; 2:32; and 10:40ff).

The Easter experience — at once objective and subjective in virtue of the personal encounter between the Living One and his own — is seen as a transforming experience. The mission of the twelve derives from it. And the movement which will ultimately spread to the farthest ends of the earth likewise draws its impetus from it. It presents itself, therefore, as the experience of dual identities in apparent contradiction: the identity of the risen Christ of glory and the humiliated Christ of the cross; and the identity of the fleeing disciples of Good Friday and the courageous witnesses of Easter Sunday. The Crucified is recognized in the Risen One. And this recognition — which combines supreme shame with supreme exaltation — is such that the disciples' fear is transformed into courage and they become new men capable of loving the new life which they have received as a gift more than life itself, making them ready even for martyrdom.

Why, we might ask, did the experience of an encounter with the Risen One change the disciples' existence so profoundly? An answer to this is possible only if, with them, we leave ourselves open to an ever deeper Trinitarian understanding of the Easter event: the resurrection and the cross, moments in the life of the Galilean Prophet, regarded as acts in which the "God of Abraham, Isaac and Jacob, the God of our fathers" (Ac 3:13), has worked "with power according to the Spirit of holiness" (Rm 1:4), and intervened over him and for his sake. This same God has shown his love in all of this (cf. Rm 5:8), blessing us with "every spiritual blessing in the heavens, in Christ," pouring out on us the "richness of his grace," sealing us in Christ with the Holy Spirit (cf. the hymn of Ep 1:3-14).

The Father's presence and his work in the Spirit are offered as the foundation and ultimate origin both of the identity in contradiction between the Crucified and the Risen One and of the identity in contradiction arising, therefrom, among the "old men" of fear and denial and the "new men" who are willing to witness to the point of giving up their lives. According to the faith of the early Church, Easter is our history because it is the Trinitarian history of God.

b) *The Resurrection as Trinitarian History* [7]

The resurrection of the Crucified is above all Trinitarian history. Ample textual testimony affirms that Christ was raised up.[8] The initiative was God's, the Father's:[9] "God has raised him up" (Ac 2:24 — this formula continually reappears in Acts). The resurrection is the powerful act of God, "Father of glory," who shows by it "the extraordinary greatness of his power," "the efficacy of his strength" (Ep 1:19). In the resurrection the Father makes history because he takes a position regarding the Crucified, declaring him both Lord and Christ: "God has made Lord and Messiah this Jesus whom you nailed to the cross" (Ac 2:36).

In the light of the twofold significance of these titles[10] — theological and soteriological — one understands how the Father's act justifies recognizing in the Nazarene's past the history of the Son of God among men, in his present, the Living conqueror of death, and in his future, the Lord who will return in glory. In the resurrection, God is actively seen as the Father of the incarnate Son who is living for us and will return on the last day.

At the same time, the Father also assumes a position at Easter regarding the history of mankind.

Regarding the past, he judges the triumph of iniquity which took place on the cross of the Humiliated One, pronouncing his "No" to the sin of the world: "And on the cross Christ freed himself from the power of the spiritual rulers and authorities; he made a public spectacle of them by leading them as captives in his victory procession" (Col 2:15).

Regarding the present, he offers himself as the God and Father of mercy, who in the "Yes" to the Crucified speaks his liberating "Yes" to all slaves of sin and death: "But God's mercy is so abundant, and his love for us so great, that while we were spiritually dead in our disobedience he brought us to life with Christ. . . . In our union with Christ Jesus he raised us up with him" (Ep 2:4-6; cf. also Rm 5:8 and Col 2:13, etc.).

Regarding the future, he shows himself as the God of the promise that he has faithfully kept:"What he announced through the mouths of the prophets . . ." and he guarantees "times of consolation, when he will again send his Anointed One, Jesus" (cf. Ac 3:18-20). The resurrection, in the history of the Father, is therefore the great assent that the God of life gives to his Son and, in him, to us prisoners of death. Hence it is the theme of the proclamation of the good news and the basis of our faith, capable of investing our works and days with meaning and with hope: "If Christ is not risen, then vain is our preaching, and vain too is your faith" (1 Cor 15:14).

History of the Father, the resurrection is also the history of the *Son*. This is amply attested to by tradition which affirms: "Christ is risen" (cf. Mk 16:6; Mt 27:64; Lk 24:6-34; 1 Tt 4:14; 1 Cor 15:3-5; Rm 8:34; Jn 21:14, etc.). Prior to the Easter event, Jesus had said: "Destroy this temple and in three days I will raise it up"; and the evangelist comments: "He was speaking of the temple of his body" (Jn 2:19, 21). The Son's active role in the Easter event in no way contradicts the Father's work. If it became the Son's highest obedience that he let himself be raised by the Father, it pertains in equal measure to the fulfillment of this obedience that he allow himself to "be given" by the Father, "to have life in himself" (Jn 5:26). The proclamation that Jesus is Lord is always "to the glory of the Father" (Ph 2:11).

Christ, therefore, rises from the dead, actively taking a stance regarding his history and that of mankind for whom he is offered unto death. If his cross is the triumph of sin, the Law and power because he has been "delivered" from the infidelity of love (the "delivery" of Judas: Mk 14:10), from the hatred of the representatives of the Law (the "delivery" of the Sanhedrin: Mk 15:1), and from the authority of the representative of Caesar (the "delivery" of Pilate: Mk 15:11), his resurrection is the defeat of power, of the Law and of sin. It is the triumph of freedom, grace and love. In him who rises, life conquers death. The abandoned one, the blasphemer, the subversive is the Lord of life (cf. Rm 5:12-17, 25 — the liberation from sin, death and Law effected by Christ).

Regarding the past, the Risen One has confirmed his pre-Easter claim, confounding the wisdom of the wise (cf. 1 Cor 1:23ff) and has leveled the wall of hostility, the result of iniquity (cf. Ep 2:14-18). Regarding the present, he offers himself as the Living One (cf. Ac 1:3) and the giver of life (cf. Jn 20:21). Regarding the future, he is the Lord of glory, the first fruits of a new humanity (cf. 1 Cor 15:20-28). Easter is the history of the Son and, precisely for that reason, it is also our history, because the Risen One has conquered death and given life to us.

The resurrection is, finally, the history of the *Spirit*. It is in his power that Christ has been raised: "Put to death in the flesh, he was given life in the Spirit" (1 P 3:18). Jesus was made by the Father "Son of God in power according to the Spirit of holiness by his resurrection from the dead" (Rm 1:4). The Spirit is above all he who is given by the Father to the Son so that the Humiliated One can become exalted and the Crucified One live the new life of the Risen. And at the same time it is he whom the Lord Jesus gives according to the promise (cf. Jn 14:16; 15:26; 16:7): "God has raised up this Jesus and we are all his witnesses. Exalted at God's right hand, he first received the promised Holy Spirit from the Father, then poured this Spirit out on us" (Ac 2:32ff).

The Spirit is, therefore, part of the Easter event since it is he who establishes the twofold bond between God and Christ and between the Risen One and us. He unites Father to Son, raising

Jesus from the dead. He unites us to the Risen One, making us alive with new life. He guarantees the twofold identity in the contradiction felt by those who lived the Easter experience. He makes the Crucified the Living One and he makes the prisoners of fear and death free and courageous witnesses of life and love. He is not the Father because he is given by the Father. He is not the Son because the Risen One receives and gives him. He is Someone never separated from the other two who is nonetheless distinct and autonomous in his action as the missionary mandate to baptize "in the name of the Father and of the Son and of the Holy Spirit" (Mt 28:19) attests and the greeting — probably of liturgical origin — confirms: "The grace of our Lord Jesus Christ, the love of God the Father and the communion of the Spirit be with all of you" (2 Cor 13:13).

The resurrection of Jesus — history of Father, Son and Spirit — is therefore an event of the Trinitarian history of God. In this event the Trinity is seen in the unified action of the Raiser, the Risen and the Spirit of resurrection and life, given and received. The resurrection reveals the unity of the God of our fathers who gives life in his Spirit to the Crucified, proclaiming him Lord and Messiah, Son of God and the Risen One who, welcoming the Spirit of the Father, gives it to men so that they may have a share in the communion of life in the Spirit with him and with the Father. In the resurrection, the Trinity is seen in the united twofold movement of the Father in the Spirit to the Son, and from the Father, through the Son, in the Spirit to men; in the unity, that is, of the resurrection of Christ and of our new life in him. The Easter event reveals the unity of the Trinity open to us in love. It is the offer of salvation through participation in the life of Father, Son and Spirit. The Trinitarian history of God is revealed in the Easter event. The Trinity *is* the history of salvation; the Trinity is our history.

c) *The Cross as Trinitarian History*[12]

The resurrection is the Living God's viewpoint about his Christ in the Spirit regarding the past of the cross. Without the cross, the event of the Crucified's resuscitation is inconceivable. Without the cross, it can be said that the resurrection is empty. Just as, conversely, without the resurrection, the cross is blind, futureless and without hope. If the resurrection, then, is an event in the history of the Trinity, the cross is no less. The cross, too, is part of the Trinitarian history of God!

The early Christian community very quickly understood the truth of the cross as Trinitarian history. This is apparent not only from the great amount of space accorded the account of the Nazarene's passion in the preaching of the early Church — are not the Gospels "stories of the passion with a detailed introduction" as Kahler's incisive expression puts it? — but also from the precise theological structure which underpins the passion narratives. This structure can be observed in the constant, though certainly not casual, use of the verb "deliver" (*paradidomai*)[13]

In the passion narrative it is possible to distinguish two kinds of consignments. The first is made up of the succession of human consignments made of the Galilean Prophet on the part of others. The betrayal of love consigns him to his adversaries: "Then Judas Iscariot, one of the Twelve, went off to the high priests to *hand Jesus over* to them" (Mk 14:10). The Sanhedrin, custodian and representative of the Law, hands the "blasphemer" over to Caesar's representative: "As soon as it was daybreak, the chief priests, with the elders and the scribes (that is, the whole Sanhedrin), reached a decision. They bound Jesus, led him away, and *handed him over* to Pilate" (Mk 15:1). The latter, though convinced of his innocence — "What evil has he done?" (Mk 15:14) — gives in to the pressure of the crowd instigated by their leaders (cf. 15:11): "After he had had Jesus scourged, he *handed him over* to be crucified" (Mk 15:15). Abandoned by his own, regarded as a blasphemer by the notable men of the Law and as a subversive by the representative of civil power, Jesus moves toward his end. If everything were to stop here, his would be one of the many unjust deaths of history in which an innocent person suffers defeat in the face of the world's injustice.

But the budding community, marked by the Easter experience, knows that it is not such and thus speaks to us of another three mysterious consignments. The first is the one the *Son* makes of himself. Paul makes it clear: "I still live my human life, but it is a life of faith in the Son of God, who loved me and *gave himself* up for me" (Gal 2:20; cf. 1:4; 1 Tm 2:6; Ti 2:14). "Follow the way of love, even as Christ loved you. He *gave himself* for us as an offering to God, a gift of pleasing fragrance" (Ep 5:2; cf. 5:25). Correspondence with Gospel testimony is heard in these expressions: "Father, into your hands I commend my spirit!" (Lk 23:46; also see Ps 31:6). "And bowing his head, he *gave up* the spirit" (Jn 19:30).

The Son consigned himself to God, his Father, for love of us and in our place. The consignment has the aspect about it of a sin offering. In this delivery of self, Jesus' dedication to the Father is accomplished in a supreme fashion and — in the light of Easter — provides us with a glimpse in finite time of the eternal relationship of the infinite gift of self which the Son lives with God his Father. The Son's way to "otherness," his "handing himself over" to death is a projection into the economy of human history of that which takes place in the immanence of the mystery of God.

Through this consignment the Crucified makes history. He takes on himself the burden of sorrow and the past, present, and future sin of the world. He experiences to its full mankind's exile from God, taking on this exile of sinners in his paschal offering and reconciliation:

"Christ has delivered us from the power of the Law's curse by himself becoming a curse for us, as it is written: 'Accursed is anyone who is hanged on a tree.' This has happened so that through

Christ Jesus the blessing bestowed on Abraham might descend on the Gentiles in Christ Jesus, thereby making it possible for us to receive the promised Spirit through faith" (Gal 3:13ff).

Is not the cry of the dying Jesus the sign of the abyss of sorrow and exile that the Son has willed to assume in order to enter fully into the sorrow of the world and to bring it to reconciliation with the Father? "My God, my God, why have you abandoned me?" (Mk 14:34; cf. Mt 27:46).[14]

The *Father's* consignment corresponds to the Son's self-giving. This is already indicated by the so-called "divine passive" formulas: "The Son of man is about to be handed over into the hands of men and they will kill him" (Mk 9:31ff and 10:33-45; Mk 14:41f; Mt 26:45-46). It will not be the men into whose hands he will be delivered who will hand him over. Nor will it be he himself, because the Word is acting passively. The one who will deliver him will be God, his Father: "God, in fact, has so loved the world as to give his only begotten Son so that whoever believes in him may not die but may have eternal life" (Jn 3:16). "He did not spare his own Son, but *handed him over* for us all. How will he not give us everything together with him" (Rm 8:32). It is in this consigning that the Father does of his own Son for us that the depth of his love for us is revealed: "Love then consists in this: not that we have loved God, but that he has loved us and has sent his Son as an offering for our sins" (1 Jn 4:10; cf. Rm 5:6-11).

The Father, too, makes history at the hour of the cross. By sacrificing his own Son, he judges the gravity of the world's sin — past, present, and future — but he also shows the greatness of his merciful love for us. The consignment out of anger — "God *delivered them up* in their lust to unclean practices . . ." (Rm 1:24) — is followed by this consignment of love! The offering of the cross shows the suffering Father to be the giver of the greatest of all gifts, in time and in eternity, by revealing that "God (the Father) is love!" (1 Jn 4:8-16).

The suffering of the Father — which corresponds to that of his crucified Son's sacrificial gift and offering of himself and brings to mind the suffering of Abraham in the offering of Isaac, his "only begotten" son (cf. Gn 22:12; Jn 3:16 and 1 Jn 4:9) — is nothing less than another name for his infinite love. This supreme, sorrowful consignment is — on the part of the Son as well as on the part of the Father — the sign of that supreme love which changes history: "No one has greater love than this, to lay down one's life for one's friends. You are my friends. . . . I call you friends because I have made known to you all that I heard from my Father" (Jn 15:13).

History of the Son and history of the Father, the cross is equally the history of the *Spirit*. The supreme act of consignment is to be found in the sacrificial offering of the Spirit, as the evangelist John concluded: "Bowing his head, *he handed over* his spirit" (Jn 19:30). It is "with one eternal Spirit" that Christ "offered himself up without blemish to God" (Ep 9:14). He who offered himself on the cross is on the other hand the Anointed of the Father: "God consecrated, in the Holy Spirit and in power, Jesus of Nazareth. . . . They killed him, hanging him on a cross, but God raised him up on the third day" (Ac 10:38-40).

The Crucified, in the hour of the cross, consigns to the Father the Spirit which the Father had given him — the Spirit which will be given back to him in fullness on the day of the resurrection. Good Friday, the day on which the Son hands himself over to the Father and the Father consigns the Son to death on behalf of sinners, is the day on which the Son consigns the Spirit to the Father, remaining thus alone, abandoned, far from God and in the company of sinners.[15] It is the hour of death *in* God, of the abandonment of the Son on the part of the Father in the context of their ever greater communion of eternal love, an event which was consummated in the consignment of the Holy Spirit to the Father that rendered possible the supreme exile of the Son into the "otherness" of the world, enabling him to become a "curse" in the land of those accursed by God in order that they, along with him, might enter into the joy of Easter reconciliation.

Without the consignment of the Spirit, the cross would not appear in all its radicalness as a Trinitarian and salvific event. If the Spirit had not allowed itself to be given over in the silence of death, with all the abandonment that death brings with it, the hour of darkness could have been mistaken for an hour of the obscure death *of* God,[16] of an incomprehensible extinguishing of the Absolute. But it would not have been understood, as it truly is, as the act which unfolds *in* God, as the event in the history of the love of the immortal God through which the Son, out of obedience to the Father, plumbs the deepest depths of "alienation" from the Father — there where he encounters sinners. And the Father consigns the Son, out of love, to this supreme exile so that, on the eschatological day of Easter ("the third day"), those exiled from God might return with the Son, in him and through him, to communion with the Father: "He who did not know sin God made sin for us so that we might become, through him, the very justice of God" (2 Cor 5:21ff; cf. Rm 8:3).

"Whatever the distance separating sinful man from God, it will always be less than that which separated the Son from the Father in the former's kenotic self-emptying (cf. Ph 2:7) and in the utter and absolute poverty of his 'abandonment' (Mt 27:46). This, in the economy of redemption, is precisely the aspect of the distinction of persons in the Holy Trinity who otherwise are perfectly united in the identity of the same nature and of an infinite love."[17]

The handing over of the Spirit signifies the exile of the Son in obedience to the Father's consignment and, hence, the salvation made possible for those afar in the company of the Crucified.

In the hour of the cross, then, the Spirit itself makes history — history in God because, handed over to the Father, the Spirit makes possible the Son's "otherness" from the Father in solidarity with sinners while still enjoying the infinite communion expressed by the sacrificial obedience of the Crucified. It is our history, too, because in this way the Spirit brings the Son even closer to us, agreeing — for the sake of those far off — to open up in exile the way with the Son to the homeland of the Trinitarian communion of Easter.

History of Father, Son and Holy Spirit, the cross is the Trinitarian history of God. "In the cross erected on Golgotha, the eternal heart of the Trinity is made manifest."[18] "The theology of consignment can be understood in its depth only in a Trinitarian sense"[19]: "What was traditionally called 'vicarious expiation' must come to be understood, transformed into, and exalted as a Trinitarian happening."[20] The Trinitarian figure is offered on the cross in the unity of the Son who hand himself over, of the Father who hands him over, and of the Spirit who is handed over by the Son and received by the Father:

"If Jesus' cross is understood as an event in the history of God, as a happening involving both Jesus and his God and Father, one would be forced to speak Trinitarily of the Son, Father and Spirit. Trinitarian doctrine, then, is not speculation about God, gratuitous and shorn of every practical application, but only a brief summary of the history of the passion of Christ with all the significance which that history takes on for the eschatological freedom of faith and the life of oppressed nature. . . . The content of Trinitarian doctrine is the real cross of Christ. The model of the Crucified is the Trinity."[21]

The cross, therefore, tells us that the Trinity has made its own the exile of the world subjected by sin so that the exiled may, at Easter, enter into the homeland of Trinitarian communion.

The cross is our history because it is the Trinitarian history of God. It does not proclaim the blasphemy of a death *of* God which makes room in the life of man, prisoner of his self-sufficiency,[22] but the good news of death *in* God so that man may live the life of the immortal God, by participation in the communion of the Trinity, made possible thanks to that death. *On the cross, our "homeland" goes into exile so that the exiled may come "home"*: this is the key to history! The "story of God," made concrete in Jesus' death on the cross on Golgotha, contains all the breadth and depth of human history and can be understood as the history of history. Every human story, insofar as it is marked by guilt and death, is caught up in this "story of God," that is, in the Trinity, and integrated in the future of the "story of God."[23]

The cross thus defers to Easter. The hour of the hiatus remands us to that of the reconciliation; the dominion of death, to the triumph of life! The "otherness" of the Son from the Father on Good Friday, which terminated in the sorrowful handing over of the Spirit — his "descent among the dead" in solidarity with all those who were, are or ever will be prisoners of sin and death — is aimed, in its union with the paschal mystery, at the reconciliation of the Son with the Father which was fulfilled on "the third day" through the gift which the Father makes of the Spirit to the Son and, in and through him, to those at a distance who are thus reconciled: "In Christ Jesus you who once were far off have been brought near through the blood of Christ. It is he who is our peace, who has made the two of us one by breaking down the barrier of hostility that kept us apart. . . . Through him we both have access in one Spirit to the Father" (Ep 2:13-18). The distancing of the cross is followed by the communion of the resurrection: and that in God and for the world!

"Only if we acknowledge from the beginning the Trinitarian dimension of the event can we speak in an adequate way of the 'pro nobis' and of the 'pro mundo.' On the one hand, in the counterpoising of the two wills of the Father and the Son in the Garden of Olives and in the Father's abandonment of the Son on the cross, the economic opposition among the divine persons is made visible. On the other, for him who reflects in depth, it is precisely this opposition which constitutes the highest manifestation of the complete oneness of God's salvific action, whose intrinsic consequentiality is shown, in turn, in the inseparable unity of Christ's death on the cross and in his resurrection."[24]

The death in God for the world on Good Friday passes on to

Easter in the life of the world in God. Precisely because it is not the death of sin but death in love, it is the death of death which does not rend but reconciles, does not deny the unity of the divine but affirms it to the highest degree, both in itself and for the world. On the other hand, unity in the strong "otherness" of the two moments is concisely conveyed by the paschal formulas which acknowledge as Lord and Messiah *the same* Jesus who was humbled in the ignominy of the cross: "God has made Lord and Messiah that Jesus whom you crucified" (Ac 2:36; 10:36; 1 Cor 12:3; 2 Cor 4:5; 1 Jn 2:22).

These formulas, of catechetical (cf. 1 Cor 15:3-8; Lk 24:34; Rm 1:3-5) or liturgical origin (cf. Ph 2:6-11; Ep 5:14; 1 Tm 3:16), narrating the two phases of the paschal event — the humiliation and the exaltation — as proper to the one subject, show the identity in "otherness" of the Crucified and Risen One, of the cross and the resurrection, as events of the one Trinitarian history of God.

If on the cross the Son consigns the Spirit to the Father — thus entering into the abyss of abandonment from the Father — in the resurrection, the Father gives the Spirit to the Son, taking up the world in and with him into infinite divine communion. The Trinitarian God who acts through the cross and the resurrection is one and the same. The Trinitarian history of God is one. The design of salvation which is realized in the two moments is one. "In his paschal mystery Jesus gives us the perfect image of the life of the Trinity."[25]

The "otherness" and the communion of the Three are fully resplendent in the events of the cross and the resurrection. The tragedy of sin and the joy of reconciliation are present in the Trinitarian history of separation and communion for love of the world. Cross and resurrection are our history because they are the Trinitarian history of God! Confession of the Trinity in the unity of the mystery becomes, then, like another name for the paschal event of death and life in God, and hence is like another name for our salvation.

2.2 THE TRINITARIAN REREADING OF HISTORY STARTING WITH EASTER

The Easter experience so profoundly marked the life of the people of the early Christian community that they could not do without rereading the past, present and future in its light. Their recollection became the paschal recollection; their awareness of the present, a paschal awareness; their expectation of the future, the hope of Easter. And since the explication of the basic event of the death and resurrection of the Lord is the Trinitarian confession, it can be said that the recollection, awareness and hope of the early Church are properly Trinitarian recollection, awareness and hope.

The paschal rereading of history, witnessed in the New Testament, is in reality a Trinitarian rereading of past events, the community's present state, and the future that will be. From the Trinitarian experience of salvation one moves on to a Trinitarian understanding of the beginning, of the "meantime," and of the goal of the people of God, just as Israel — beginning with the experience of the saving God — confessed God as creator and Lord of history.[26]

a) The "Trinitarian Memory" of the Early Community

In the first place, the community rereads *the event of the Nazarene* in the light of the Trinitarian event of Easter. What is acknowledged about the end of his earthly existence and in his new beginning through his victory over death is recognized as present in the very beginning of his physical life. The mysteries of his infancy correspond, in a Trinitarian interpretation, to the mysteries of Easter. [27] The principal agent, the one who took the initiative, is the same — God the Father. "In the sixth month, the angel Gabriel was sent from God to a town of Galilee named Nazareth, to a virgin betrothed to a man named Joseph, of the house of David. The virgin's name was Mary" (Lk 1:26ff). The one through whom the Father works is the same — the Spirit: "The Holy Spirit will come upon you and the power of the Most High will overshadow you" (Lk 1:35). The one in and for whom the divine work is done is the same — the Son, Jesus: "You shall conceive and bear a son and give him the name Jesus. Great will be his dignity and he will be called Son of the Most High" (Lk 1:35).

Mary, pure and receptive, makes herself the place in which the Trinitarian history of God, the plan of the Father, the sending of the Spirit, and the mission of the Son, pitches its tents in the history of men. The virginal conception — whose historical nucleus is undoubtedly the result of its absolute originality in the cultural-religious context of its time[28] — is but the Trinitarian confession of the beginning of our full and definitive salvation. What Easter proclaims about the end and the new beginning in the events surrounding the Word made flesh, the accounts of the conception of the Lord affirm of his first beginning. Just as the confession of the Trinity expresses the Easter event, so too the infancy narratives express the Trinitarian faith as the key to the reading of salvation history.

Even the account of his baptism in the Jordan — the moment which was so decisive in the life of the Galilean Prophet as to be called the hour of his calling or vocation[29] — contains a clear Trinitarian structure. This pre-paschal event (which cannot be doubted because it would have been difficult for the community to have invented the Nazarene's act of submission to the Baptist) was made explicit by the Easter faith in the complexity of divine relations. The Spirit descends on Jesus as he emerges from the water while the Father's voice proclaims with the prophet's words: "You are my beloved Son. On you my favor rests" (Mk 1:11; cf. 1:9ff; Mt 1:13-17; Lk 3:21ff). "The humiliation of the baptism of John, according to the plan of the passion (cf. Ph 2:5-10), is followed by the exaltation. . . . The synoptic account of the baptism seems like an anticipated Easter message."[30] The history of the Nazarene, therefore, is acknowledged — even in the hour of its most decisive turn of events — as Trinitarian history in which the divine promise of the pouring forth of the Spirit, signalling the beginning of the new creation, comes to its fulfillment.

The Trinitarian confession emerges in the account of the temptation (cf. Mk 1:12ff; Mt 4:1-11; Lk 4:1-13) where it is the Spirit who leads Jesus into battle over his fidelity to God. We find it in the transfiguration (cf. Mk 9:1-8; Mt 17:1-9; Lk 9:28-36) where, once again, we hear the Father's voice and proclamation while the cloud evokes the Spirit's presence, almost as if to give proof that in his hours of trial, as in those of light, the history of the Nazarene has been the history of the Trinity. His whole life unfolded in relation to the Father in the Spirit, so much so that John's Gospel could thus sum up his mission in the words placed on the Baptist's lips:

"I saw the Spirit descend like a dove from the sky, and it came to rest on him. But I did not recognize him. The one who sent me to baptize with water told me, 'When you see the Spirit descend and rest on someone, it is he who is to baptize with the Holy Spirit.' Now I have seen for myself and have testified, 'This is God's chosen One' " (Jn 1:32-34).

"Jesus' history is not understandable to us without taking into consideration the action of the Spirit, just as we do not succeed in understanding that history if we do not take into account the God whom he called 'my Father' and the activity of Jesus which imposed his existence as Son."[31]

The pre-Easter basis of this Trinitarian reading of the whole experience of the Galilean Prophet can be derived from the unique and exclusive relationship he had with the God of the fathers invoked by him in an unheard of manner with the name of *Abba*. Even though this term is found only three times in the New Testament (Mk 14:36; Rm 8:15; and Gal 4:6), the very fact that it is used in texts addressed to Greek and Latin communities shows its singular authoritativeness. It can be supposed, with foundation, that the presence of the Aramaic original, *Abba*,[32] underlies the 170 times that Jesus calls God "Father" or "my Father" in the Gospels: (Mark, 4 times; Luke, 15 times; Matthew, 42 times; John, 109 times).

The originality of this manner of addressing the God of the fathers "is twofold: It is the first time that one encounters an invocation of the Father by means of a personal title in a Palestinian ambient; and it is the first time that a Jew, in addressing God, invokes him under the name of *Abba*, which is characteristic of familiar speech. Jesus addresses God as a baby might address his earthly father."[33]

"Therefore, Jesus produced an absolute innovation. He spoke with God as a child speaks with his father -- with the same simplicity, intimacy, and confident abandon. With the vocative, *Abba*, Jesus showed the very essence of his relationship with God."[34]

This totally original relationship with the Father, this expression of a "filial awareness" which was absolutely unique and exclusive in relation to God,[35] marks Jesus' history in an unrepeatable way as the history of the eternal Son — a history that, from conception to baptism, from preaching to salvific activity, unfolds entirely by virtue of the Spirit, as the word of the prophet which Jesus applies to himself in the synagogue at Nazareth attests: "The Spirit of the Lord is upon me. . ." (Lk 4:18).

The preaching of the Apostles will refer to this experience of the Spirit which the people of Palestine had by coming into contact with the work and life of the Galilean Prophet: "I take it you know what has been reported all over Judea about Jesus of Nazareth, beginning in Galilee with the baptism that John preached; of the way *God anointed him with the Holy Spirit* and power. He went about doing good works and healing all who were in the grip of the devil, and God was with him" (Ac 10:37ff).

It can then be affirmed that "the power which issued from Jesus and which worked almost on its own, corresponds to what the post-Easter Christian experience calls the 'Spirit,' " and that, therefore, "the fundamental Trinitarian structure of the event of salvation was originally founded on the work of the earthly Jesus."[36]

The paschal rereading will make explicit only what was implicit in Jesus' setting himself before the Father and men in works and words in the power of the Spirit. By acknowledging that the entire earthly experience of the Nazarene was Trinitarian history, the faith-recollection of the budding Church will see in it the history of God with us, of the "otherness" and infinite communion of the Father and the Son in the Spirit which, through the solidarity of the Incarnate Word with us, becomes the story of our "otherness" *from* God taken on in communion *with* God.

"The days of the flesh" of Christ (Heb 5:7) are offered in this light as the time of the Trinitarian God with and for us: not in the weak sense of the human adventure of an indeterminate divine figure, but in the strong and pure sense of the history of the Son of God in the flesh, which is related in each instance to the Father in the Spirit and which brings us, of whom he made himself a friend, into the inexhaustibly fruitful dynamism of divine relations.

The Lord Jesus' earthly experience, then, becomes the Trinitarian God's humble and concrete doorway to time and time's doorway to the Trinitarian life of God. That is the reason the early Church felt the need to recount that experience as Gospel. The Easter narration of the history of Jesus is the good news of the Father who through the Son and in the Spirit enters into a relationship with human history so that mankind's time may enter the very life of the Trinity. The "memory" of the Nazarene's life and of the experience shared with him by the disciples becomes — in the light of Easter and on the basis of a solid pre-Easter foundation — the Trinitarian Gospel and hence the Gospel of our salvation through participation in the divine life. Is it not this "Trinitarian memory" that is promised with the gift of the Paraclete by the Johannine Christ? "This much I have told you while I was still with you: the Paraclete, the Holy Spirit whom the Father will send in my name, will instruct you in everything and remind you of all that I told you" (Jn 14:25ff).

The "Paschal-Trinitarian" memory of the life of Jesus is also linked with the rereading of the experience of Israel. In recalling the history of the fathers, the nascent Church also discovers in it the Trinitarian sign of Easter faith.

The God of Israel was acknowledged as the *Father* of the Lord Jesus, he who raised Jesus from the dead: "The God of Abraham, of Isaac, and of Jacob, the God of our fathers, has glorified his servant Jesus, whom you handed over and disowned in Pilate's presence" (Ac 3:13). This God "in times past spoke in fragmentary and varied ways to our fathers through the prophets; in this, the final age, he has spoken to us through his Son, whom he has made heir of all things and through whom he first created the universe" (Heb 1:1-2). In the resurrection of the Crucified God, "he has fulfilled what he announced long ago through all the prophets" (Ac 3:18; 13:27; 25:22). In Christ Jesus "all God's promises have come true" (2 Cor 1:20).

The Son is, therefore, the one toward whom the whole history of Israel, moved by divine initiative (cf. the account of the history of salvation in Stephen's discourse in Ac 7:2ff) converges. In him the scriptures are fulfilled (cf., for example, Mt 1:22 and the formula "according to the scriptures," in 1 Cor 15:3ff or other places, as in Jn 19:24-36; cf. finally the references to and citations of the Old Testament in the Gospel narratives: 41 times in Matthew alone![37]).

To the men of the Easter experience those scriptures speak as though they had been written for them: "The things that happened to them serve as an example. They have been written as a warning to us, upon whom the end of the ages has come" (1 Cor 10:11; Rm 15:4 and 1 Cor 9:10).

In this light, Christ was viewed as present already in the decisive events of Israel's past history: "Brothers, I want you to remember this: our fathers were all under the cloud and all passed through the sea; by the cloud and the sea all of them were baptized into Moses. All ate the same spiritual food. All drank the same spiritual drink (they drank from the spiritual rock that was following them, and the rock was Christ) . . ." (1 Cor 10:1-3).

The yearning of Israel for Christ and his action in the history of the chosen people are works of the *Holy Spirit*: "This is the salvation which the prophets carefully searched out and examined. They prophesied the divine favor that was destined to be yours. They investigated the times and the circumstances which the Spirit of Christ within them was pointing to, for he predicted the sufferings destined for Christ and the glories that would follow" (1 P 1:10ff; Ac 1:16; 2 Tm 3:16). "Prophecy has never been put forward by man's willing it. It is rather that men, impelled by the Holy Spirit, have spoken under God's influence" (2 P 1:21).

In the memory of the nascent Church, marked by the Easter experience, the story of Israel's salvation reveals, therefore, a clear Trinitarian structure: the God of the fathers guides and orients this history toward Christ his Son, acting — especially through the prophets — in the Holy Spirit! The Trinity is the key to an understanding of the history of salvation!

Does this Easter rereading of Israel's history have a pre-Easter basis? The answer to this question is to be sought not only in the individual events or words of the history of the Old Covenant but also in the ardent longing that Israel (and, therefore, even the early Christian community, the daughter of Israel) felt for its God. This experience is historical in nature. The "God of our fathers" is not, for Israel, some abstract celestial person outside of time and space but the God of the Word who turns to his people in the concrete events of history and demands a response from them, or gives them an answer, "here and now." He is a God who launches into the future, stimulates satisfaction, instills a sense of expectancy, prevents bewilderment, raises hopes, frees from the prison of the present and keeps things moving.

Even after passing from a nomadic to a sedentary lifestyle, the people of Israel never gave in to the tranquilizing fascination of the religiosity of the people among whom they settled — individuals who, in celebrating the repetitive cycle of the seasons, celebrated the eternal return of the identical.[38] Their God remained "Yahweh," the God who is for us, the God of the promise, the God of fidelity. This seems to be the sense of the name ("I am who am!") revealed to Moses in Exodus 3:14-16 as a guarantee of the path to liberation which he would be taking with his people.[39]

The God of Israel is the God of history and not simply the God who makes history by intervening in it: loving and repudiating, rejoicing and suffering, deciding and recanting, capable of hatred and of infinite tenderness, etc. He is also the God who is the Lord of history: immutable in the faithfulness of his love, capable of an eternal election. The God who "loved Jacob and hated Esau" (Rm 9:13) is he in whom are united the most absolute possible transcendence (love of eternal election) and the strongest possible immanence (the taking of sides): the God of concrete positions and eternal fidelity, near and at the same time inscrutable, God of the present and Lord of the future.

In the Old Testament "the tendency becomes ever stronger and more insistent to accentuate — along with the *transcendence* of God, preserved as an intangibly sacred truth — also the *immanence* of God, experienced in an equally vital manner all its own. By means of his *Word*, his *Wisdom* and his *Spirit*, 'notwithstanding' his transcendent superiority, God is actively present in the midst of his people."[40]

This dialectic of "otherness" and "communion" between Yahweh and his people was understood both in the vertical sense of God's absolute superiority to and freedom from the covenant (doxological transcendence) and of his deepest presence among his own (immanence in faith) as well as in the horizontal sense of the infinite ulteriority which he gives history with his promise (eschatological transcendence) and his collaborating nearness in the incessant struggle to open up the present to what is coming and new (immanence in hope and love).

It is at the intersection of all these fixed lines that Old Testament messianism is to be positioned, the "true spine of the Bible"[41]; and it is in relation to these lines that the Easter memory of Israel's past, lived by the newborn Church, was able to reread the chosen people's history as the Trinitarian history of God and the events of Easter as the key to the interpretation of that history.

The doxological, adorable and overwhelming transcendence of the God of the fathers reaches its apex in the infinite separation effected on the cross between the Son, entered into the exile of the Godless, and the Father, totally other in handing over his Only Begotten to death and in accepting — out of love for sinners — his Son's consignment of the Spirit. The eschatological transcendence of the God of the promise is made manifest in the fullest possible way on Easter in the initiative of the Father who, raising his Son in the Spirit, makes resplendent in the shadows of history the long-awaited dawn of glory.

The immanence of the God of Israel reaches its most profound expression in the incarnation of the Son, who allied himself totally with us even to the point of experiencing the exile of the cross, accomplished in virtue of the Trinitarian consignment, and — as immanence in hope and love — in the presence of the Spirit poured out by the Father on the Risen One and by the latter upon us, to open hearts and times ever more and more to the fulfillment of the new and definitive promise. You might say that there is no place where God is farther from the world than on the cross of his Son, companion of sinners. And there is no place where he is nearer — God with us, God with the Godless — than on that same cross.

It is equally possible to affirm that there is no greater "otherness" between God and men than the divine power manifested in the Easter newness, and that there is no greater "communion" than the one realized at Easter with the outpouring of the Spirit. From this exalted perspective all of Israel's past may be understood as the expectation of and preparation for that "first day after the Sabbath." In the history of the people of the promise, it is the Father who in the Spirit prepares for the coming of the Son. In its experience of the "otherness" of and "communion" with its God, Israel was prepared for the experience of the supreme "otherness" of God in the hour of the cross and in the glory of Easter. The same can be said of its supreme "communion" with him in the solidarity of the exile and in the Easter entrance of sinners into their promised homeland together with the Son by the power of the Spirit. The exodus of the new Easter is presented as a compact summary of the ancient Passover. And the Trinitarian history of the Easter event is acknowledged as present, be it even "in mystery," in the history of the people of the Covenant.

Beyond Israel, the paschal memory of the early Church reaches back to the very beginning, to the *protologia* — that is, to God's first words of creation in Genesis — which, read in the light of the experience of salvation, seems to point directly to it. What happened at Easter touches all creation, so much so that, in its light, everything can be understood in a new way from the very beginning. The act of creation itself appears with full evidence as a paschal event and, therefore, Trinitarian. The invisible God creates everything through Christ and in view of him (Col 1:15ff), so much so that in virtue of him "all things exist and we exist for him" (1 Cor 8:6; cf. Heb 1:2-10; Rv 3:14).

This presence of Christ in the creation event sends us back to his pre-existence, to his being with the Father before the world came to be and to his being sent by the Father: "He is the image of the invisible God, begotten before every creature" (Col 1:15), he who "though he was in the form of God . . . did not deem equality with God something to be grasped at. Rather he emptied himself and took the form of a slave, being born in the likeness of men" (Ph 2:6ff). Confession of Christ's pre-existence and of his participation in the act of creation merge: "In the beginning was the Word, and the Word was with God, and the Word was God. He was present to God in the beginning. Through him all things came into being and apart from him nothing came to be" (Jn 1:1-3).

The theology of the Incarnation — "And the Word became flesh" (Jn 1:14) — like that of the mission (cf. Jn 3:17-34; 5:37; 6:40-44; 7:28-33; 8:16-42; 11:42; 12:44ff; 14:24; 16:5; 17:3, etc.) are Easter theologies which convey the eschatological fullness of what has taken place in Christ, making explicit in speaking of ancient history and his pre-existence, the Trinitarian depth of the event of the cross and the resurrection.

It is significant how these affirmations about pre-existence are immediately joined to expressions of Easter faith: "For this reason God has exalted him . . ." (Ph 2:9); "And the Word became flesh and dwelt among us, and we saw his glory . . ." (Jn 1:14); "For the one whom God has sent speaks the words of God; he does not ration his gift of the Spirit" (Jn 3:34).

At the Father's initiative and with the Son's mediation, the early community also confesses the presence of the Spirit in the act of creation. The Easter text of the baptism of Jesus — where we read that upon him who comes up out of the water "the Spirit descends like a dove" (Mk 1:10 and parallels) — recalls the words of Genesis: ". . . a mighty wind swept over the waters" (1:2), thus paralleling the first creation with the new. In one and the other it is the Spirit who acts. Creation is, therefore, understood as a Trinitarian act.

Just as Israel went from the experience of God as Savior to a confession of God as Creator, Lord of the universe,[42] so too the early Christian community went from the salvific experience of the

Trinitarian God to a confession of the *protologia* as Trinitarian history. In this way, the early Church acknowledged that the Trinitarian God is, indeed, the Lord of all things because everything comes from the Father through the Son in the Spirit. Nothing which exists is extraneous to Trinitarian history. Everything comes from the Trinity and celebrates Its gift.

Since creation takes place in view of the Son, and inasmuch as the Spirit pervades the beginning reshaping it to the glory of the Father, it can be said that creation unfolds not "outside" but "within" the Trinity. The Trinity does not transform itself in creation. Created reality is transformed in the Trinitarian mystery of God: "In him, in fact, we live and move and have our being" (Ac 17:28).

The eschatological fullness of Easter thus comes to embrace the whole universe. An event in history, the paschal mystery, reveals history in an event. As the concrete place in which the Trinity manifests itself in time, it is likewise the place in which time is assumed and comprehended, beginning with the act of creation, in the Trinity. The immanence of the mystery is offered in the economy. The fullness of the new creation, like death and life *in* God, evokes the truth of the first creation as an act which is situated in the ineffable relationship of the Father to the Son in the Spirit.

The Trinity is the horizon in which all history is summed up and unified. It is infinitely more and "other" than history, even though it is its place of origin giving meaning to all that is created. The Easter memory of the beginning thus leads to the meaning of the present time and to that of the last things. The *protologia* remands us to an awareness of the significance of present history and to the meaning of eschatology. [43]

The Trinitarian recollection of the early Church, therefore, in referring to the paschal event of the Trinity in order to reread salvation's past, also uses this salvific past to plumb and make explicit the confession of the Trinitarian mystery.

The very names of Father, Son and Spirit are rooted in this

memory. The name Father is founded on a rereading of the absolutely singular way in which Jesus turned to God. The name Son is tied in with this use and, at the same time, with the deepened understanding which Easter provided of the Son's pre-existence and his mission. The name Holy Spirit relates to the Old Testament figure of the *ruach Jahve*, the personal power of the living God whose full outpouring was awaited throughout messianic time (cf. Ezk 36:26ff), and to the new understanding given by this outpouring to the Trinitarian history of the consignment of the cross and of the paschal gift of the Spirit. Event and Easter memory are then strictly bound together. The memory gives a name to the Trinitarian event while the Easter event sheds light on the memory of the history of salvation.

b) *The "Trinitarian Awareness" of the Early Church*

A rereading of the salvific past nurtured a Trinitarian awareness of the present in the early Church, just as the latter was nourished in turn by the former. Even the "today" of salvation is a Trinitarian "today"!

The early community understood itself to be the new "people of God" (cf. 2 Cor 6:16 which recalls Lv 26:12; Heb 8:10 which takes up Jr 31:33), the "Church of God" (Ac 28:28; 1 Cor 10:32; 11:18; Gal 1:13; 2 Th 1:4):

"You, however, are a chosen race, a royal priesthood, a holy nation, a people he claims for his own to proclaim the glorious works of the One who has called you from darkness into his own marvelous light. Once you were no people, but now you are God's people" (1 P 2:9).

This new Israel, the "Israel of God" (Gal 6:16), spiritual and no longer of the flesh (1 Cor 10:18), has been acquired through the blood of Christ (cf. Ac 20:28), as a people of the new covenant, sealed in that blood (Mt 26:28 and parallels; Heb 9:12ff and 10:16).

The Church is the *Body of Christ* (Ep 1:22; 5:23; Col 1:18-24), his spouse (Ep 5:32; 2 Cor 11:2; Rv 21:9-27).

Church of the Father, Church of the Son, it is finally *Church of the Holy Spirit* who dwells within it (1 Cor 3:16; Ep 2:22). The whole experience of the early Church is an experience of the Spirit as Acts, the true "Gospel of the Spirit," attests (consider, for example, Ac 1:8; 2:4; 9:31). The life of the Christian community is born and develops in the power of the Holy Spirit.[44]

People of God, Body of Christ, Temple of the Spirit, the Church born at Easter is presented as the "Church of the Trinity." Hence the event by which one becomes a part of the Church is only understood in an awareness of the origin of Christianity as it relates to the paschal recollection of Jesus' baptism in which the Trinity enters the history of an individual and of a community in order to take possession of them: "Go, therefore, and make disciples of all nations. Baptize them in the name of the Father, and of the Son, and of the Holy Spirit" (Mt 28:19).

A Trinitarian and ecclesial event, *baptism* appears as the locus wherein the Church passes into the Trinity and the Trinity passes into the Church. As a paschal event, in baptism the unique, definitive passage of the Trinity into history and of history into the Trinity — which is the Trinitarian history of the death and resurrection of the Lord — is "re-accomplished." Saying "Baptism" is saying "Easter"; and saying "Trinity" is saying "Church."

It is from the starting point of the unity of the Trinitarian mystery, expressed in the unity of the paschal event with the baptismal event, that the Church, born of baptism, appears as one in a variety of gifts, services and operations: "There are different gifts, but the same *Spirit*; there are different ministries, but the same *Lord*; there are different works, but the same *God* who accomplishes all of them in everyone" (1 Cor 12:4-6).

The unity of the Trinity thus comes to be reflected in the unity of the Church, in ecclesial communion: "That all may be one as you, Father, are in me, and I in you; I pray that they may be one in us, that the world may believe that you sent me" (Jn 17:21). By means of baptism the Trinitarian history of Easter comes to embrace the history of all *redeemed existence*. Celestial life becomes the privileged locus of the presence of Trinitarian history in human history and the access of earthly time to God's "time."

Christian existence shows itself as Easter existence and, therefore, as Trinitarian existence: "In him you are being built into this temple, to become a dwelling place for God in the Spirit" (Ep 2:22; 1 Cor 3:16; 1 P 2:5). "Through baptism into his death we were buried with him so that, just as Christ was raised from the dead by the glory of the Father, we too might live a new life" (Rm 6:4; Col 2:12; 3:3).

And the Spirit received in baptism (Jn 3:5-8) enables us to live in the freedom of sons, made such in the Son: "All who are led by the Spirit of God are sons of God. You did not receive a spirit of slavery leading you back into fear, but a spirit of adoption through which we cry out: 'Abba!' (that is, 'Father!')" (Rm 8:14ff; 2 Cor 3:17).

The Christian life is life according to the Spirit (Rm 8:14), conformity to Christ (Gal 2:20), and participation in the filial experience of the Son in relation to the Father (Gal 4:6). The Christian lives on account of the Trinity! "Clearly you are a letter of Christ which I have delivered, a letter written not with ink but by the Spirit of the living God, not on tablets of stone but on tablets of flesh in the heart" (2 Cor 3:3).

Love is the manifestation of this Trinitarian living: "As the Father has loved me, so I have loved you. Live on in my love . . . This is my commandment: love one another as I have loved you" (Jn 15:9-12). "The love of God has been poured out into our hearts through the Holy Spirit who has been given to us" (Rm 5:5).

This Trinitarian structure of ecclesial existence, founded on baptism, is rediscovered in the commemoration of Easter confided by Jesus to his own. Lived in obedience to his command as the memorial of the New Covenant in his body and blood (Mk 14:22-

24; Mt 26:26-28; Lk 22:19ff; 1 Cor 11:23-25) the *Lord's Supper* is an act of thanksgiving to the Father, along the lines of the paschal prayers of blessing (Lk 22:19 and parallels), which is accomplished in the power of the Spirit: "It is the Spirit who gives life; the flesh is useless" (Jn 6:63 in the context of the discourse on the bread of life; cf. 1 Jn 5:6-8).

Reference to the Trinity thus links baptism to the Eucharist throughout all of redeemed existence, making the "today" of the Church the "today" of the Trinity in history and of history in the Trinity. This is what is expressed in the greeting derived, most probably, from the liturgy of the early Church: "The grace of the Lord Jesus Christ, the love of God and the communion of the Holy Spirit be with you all!" (2 Cor 13:13).

This is the sentiment behind *the prayer of the Christian* who, in obedience to the teaching of Christ, turns to the Father in the power of the Spirit who cries out in believers: "Abba, Father!" (Rm 8:15), "Our Father . . ." (Mt 6:9; Lk 11:2). The Christian does not pray to an abstract divine figure. He does not pray "to" a God, but "in" God, not as a stranger, but as a child of God: "The proof that you are sons is that God has sent forth into our hearts the Spirit of his Son which cries out 'Abba!' ('Father')" (Gal 4:6). In the Spirit, through the Son, prayer reaches the Father and from him obtains the gift: "How much more will the heavenly Father give the Spirit to those who ask him" (Lk 11:13).

To pray is to enter into the Trinity so that the Trinity may enter the believer's heart: "Anyone who loves me will be true to my word, and my Father will love him; we will come to him and make our dwelling place with him" (Jn 14:23). "That is why I kneel before the Father . . . that he will bestow on you gifts in keeping with the riches of his glory. May he strengthen you inwardly through the working of his Spirit" (Ep 3:14-17).

In the Easter awareness of the early Church, to be a Christian was nothing other than living in the Trinity, fulfilling everything "in the name" and "to the glory" of Father, Son, and Holy Spirit.

To be aware of the present was to experience the mystery; it was to anticipate in time the history of what will be fully accomplished in the time of glory. The Trinity, locus of the faith "today," is also the goal of our future hope, our as yet unpossessed promised fatherland.

c) *The "Trinitarian Hope" of Early Christianity*

In the light of Easter, the early Church reread not only the past and present of its faith, but also the future of its hope. Paschal memory and paschal awareness merge in the Trinitarian prophecy of history. Heir to the biblical concept whereby God is "at the beginning" because he is "at the end"[45] that is, because he is the eschatological fulfillment of the promise, the early Christian community, confessing the past and the present to be "Trinitarian history," could not but profess the future to be such as well.

Even the end of history — and, therefore in its light, the period of the "meantime" — stretched out between the "already" and the "not yet," is a paschal event; the history of the Trinitarian God for the world and of the world in the Trinity.

The end-time is principally *the history of the Father*. In continuity with the Jewish expectation of the "day of Yahweh" (Am 5:18ff), the Christians awaited the day established by God "on which he is going to 'judge the world with justice' through a man he has appointed — one whom he has endorsed in the sight of all by raising him from the dead" (Ac 17:31). This day pertains to the times and moments "that the Father has reserved to himself" (Ac 1:7; Mk 13:32). It is the hour of the final coming of the Kingdom of God (cf. Mt 26:29, the parallel of the two cited texts; cf. also 1 Cor 15:24).

The end-time, then, is also *the history of the Son*. It is awaited as "the day of our Lord Jesus Christ" (cf. 1 Cor 1:8; 5:5; 2 Cor 1:14; 1 Th 5:2; 2 Th 2:2, etc.). It is the time of the second coming, the hour of the "parousia," of his new presence among his own: "This Jesus who has been taken from you will return, just as you saw him go up into the heavens" (Ac 1:11; cf. the eschatological discourse and the role of the Son of Man in Mk 13; Mt 24-25; Lk 21; 17:20-37; 2 Th 2:1-12; 1 Th 4:13-18). In that time what the Risen One called "firstfruits" will be accomplished: "It is he . . . who is the beginning, the firstborn of the dead" (Col 1:18; 1 Cor 15:23), in whom all things will be brought into one according to the Father's plan (Ep 1:10).

The end-time is finally *the history of the Spirit*. If he is the "down payment," so to speak, on our future inheritance (cf. Ep 1:13ff), he will also be the one who acts on the day of our final resurrection: "If the Spirit of him who raised Jesus from the dead dwells in you, then he who raised Christ from the dead will bring your mortal bodies to life also through his Spirit dwelling in you" (Rm 8:11).

As the history of Father, Son, and Spirit, the end-time is, therefore, acknowledged by the early Church as the *Trinitarian history of God*. The Father gives the Son the task of judging the world in the Spirit so that the Son may subject everything to himself and himself with all of creation "to the One who made all things subject to him, so that God may be all in all" (1 Cor 15:28; cf. Jn 5:21ff).

That will be the hour of the final Easter, this too marked by the mystery of a supreme consignment: "After that will come the end when . . . he will *hand over* the kingdom to God the Father" (1 Cor 15:24). Then the Father, in response to the Son's handing over everything to him, will pour the Spirit out on all and will rule with the one and the other together in glory: " 'It shall come to pass in the last days,' says God, 'that I will pour out a portion of my Spirit on all mankind . . .' " (Ac 2:17 which cites Jl 3:1 in reference to the eschatological time of the temporal and eternal Passover). Then the "glory of God" will enlighten the heavenly Jerusalem, and "its lamp shall be the Lamb," and from the throne of God and the Lamb will spring "a river of living water, clear as crystal" (an image of the Spirit: Rv 21:22-23; 22:1; Jn 4:1; 7:37-39).

What took place in the temporal Easter will be re-proposed in all its fullness in the light of the eternal Easter: the Trinitarian event of history is the sign and the promise of the Trinitarian event of glory! The handing over of the Son and the outpouring of the Spirit, to and from the Father respectively, will invest the entire universe. In the Trinity will repose the march of time ". . . and there will be no more death or mourning, crying out or pain" and a "new heavens and a new earth" will appear (Rv 21:4-11).

The Father who gives the Spirit and makes us sons of the Son will then be fully revealed as the origin and the goal of history: "I am the Alpha and the Omega, the Beginning and the End. To anyone who thirsts I will give to drink without cost from the spring of life-giving water. He who wins the victory shall inherit these gifts; I will be his God and he shall be my son" (Rv 21:6ff).

The Trinity, therefore, reveals — in the faith of the early Church — the meaning of history. Moving from the Father, through the Son, in the Spirit (*protologia*), the world's experience returns in the Spirit through the Son to the Father (*eschaton*). The compact and concentrated place wherein this dynamism is revealed is Easter. The whole of history is paschal history in this light — a movement which flows from the Trinity, returns to the Trinity, and develops in the bosom of the Trinitarian God who is always infinitely greater. The Trinity is the womb of history, the fatherland of time, the locus of living, dying and conquering death.

Hence the Trinity is the hope of the Church, the good news to be announced to all, the Gospel of hope for the world: "Through him we have gained access by faith to the grace in which we now stand, and we boast of our hope for the glory of God . . . This hope will not leave us disappointed, because the love of God has been poured out in our hearts through the Holy Spirit who has been given to us" (Rm 5:2-4).

The memory, the awareness, and the hope of the early Church

thus come together in a great Trinitarian confession. Past, present, and future find their true significance and value in the light of the paschal event narrated as the Trinitarian history of God. The faith, hope, and love of the Christian stands or falls with the Trinity. Nothing more than faith in the Trinity is specifically and vitally important for the existence of the Church. Far from being an empty heavenly theorem, the Trinity is an event in which — by revealing the very life of God itself — people's works and days find their meaning and their strength.

2.3 THE TRINITARIAN CONFESSION IN TIME[46]

a) *The "Narrated" Trinity*

The faith of the early Church "narrated" the Trinity. By proclaiming the Easter event, it recounted the history of the Trinity. The oldest Christian confessions bring together, in an unheard of identity, the two dissimilar moments of the cross and the resurrection. Announcing that "Jesus is the Lord, the Christ," the early Church relates the history of the humbled Jesus of Nazareth who has been exalted by God and made Lord and Messiah (Ac 2:36). This history of humiliation and exaltation is not only the history of the Son who humbles himself and rises to life but also the history of the Father who consigns him to death and gives him new life, and the history of the Spirit who, handed over to the Father on the cross, is poured out in fullness in the Easter victory. Whoever confesses that "Jesus is Lord" relates the Trinitarian history of God in our midst!

This telling inspires further telling, introducing into the divine life the one who recounts it with faith: "For if you confess with your lips that Jesus is Lord, and believe in your heart that God raised him from the dead, you will be saved" (Rm 10:9). "The word of faith we preach" (Rm 10:8) is nothing else than this. This "narrative" structure of the original Trinitarian confession is extended to the relating of past, present and future history in its totality as Trinitarian history.

The narration of the Trinity is particularly present in the catechesis for baptism and in the liturgical act of baptizing: "Even though one cannot postulate an absolutely uniform Trinitarian formula for the apostolic and the post-apostolic periods, there is nevertheless no doubt that in the baptismal catechesis the truth about the Trinity had its place."[47]

And it is in connection with admission of candidates to baptism that the Trinitarian account began to assume the form of the symbol of faith, especially as a triple response to a triple question in the context of the celebration of the sacrament and then under the form of a confession recited by catechumens before being baptized.[48]

Thus, in its origins and even afterward, notwithstanding the successive extensions of the three articles on the Father, Son and Spirit, the Symbol appears as the account of the Trinitarian history of God for us: the history of the Father whose basic, eschatological primacy over all things is affirmed; the history of the Son, replete with the whole series of events in the life of the Lord; the history of the Spirit, open to embracing the present of the Church and the future of life.[49]

The Symbol's liturgical context, then, shows how the narration of the Trinitarian event is done in such a way as to transmit it. Telling the history of the Trinity draws one into it, thanks to the paschal act of baptism. The account is actualized in the lives of those who have confessed it by telling it. The "narrated" Trinity is a saving confession, a making real through recall of the paschal Trinitarian event which causes the life of the believer to be a Trinitarian life, a paschal existence. *Mystery proclaimed* becomes *mystery celebrated* in order to be in the Church and in history *mystery lived*. The baptized will have to recount with their lives what they have proclaimed with their lips at the moment they received the baptismal gift of new life. By living in the Spirit of God, poured out by the Son, they will be the Church, one and holy,[50] the living memorial of the Trinity: "A people gathered together by the unity of Father, Son and Holy Spirit.''[51] They have entered the Trinity through the grace of baptism after having confessed the Trinitarian history of their God:

"Do you believe in God the Father almighty?
Do you believe in Jesus Christ, the Son of God,
who was born of the Holy Spirit of Mary the virgin,
and crucified under Pontius Pilate,
died and was buried,
and rose on the third day alive from the dead,
and ascended to the heavens and sits at the Father's right hand,
and will come to judge the living and the dead?
Do you believe in the Holy Spirit,
and the holy Church and the resurrection of the body?"[52]

b) *The "Disputed" Trinity*

The dense theological and salvific richness of the narrative confession of the Trinity will be put to the test by its clash with the pre-existing or foreign conception of God as compared to the one conveyed by the Easter message.

Provocation will come especially from the Jewish world whose rigorous monotheism was so open to the idea of God's immanence as proposed by their fathers in the history of their people that they could only find scandal in the identification of this presence with that of the Galilean Prophet, condemned by the Law's representatives as a blasphemer. The doxological and eschatological transcendence of Yahweh seemed threatened by the unheard of confidence with which the Nazarene claimed kinship with God, his Father, and by the paschal proclamation of the coming of the fullness of time in the events of his death and resurrection. Jewish piety felt it had to defend itself against such an attack on divine "otherness" and the inexhaustible excess of the promise in comparison to the present. Assimilated into a Christian ambient, this preoccupation will tend toward *monarchianism*: the affirmation of the oneness of God guaranteed by the exaltation of the absolute primacy of the Father's divinity.

The Trinitarian confession will stir up the Greco-Hellenic world as well. A widely held thesis has been that of the "Hellenization of Christianity"[53] — by which "dogma" would be considered the "result of the Greek spirit ripened on Gospel soil," or the result of a theology which in its turn would have been the "product of the spirit of the time" (Harnack), or the expression of Hellenistic thought infiltrating the Christian faith because of the loss of its original eschatological tension (Werner). Against this, it should be observed that the paschal Trinitarian event, proclaimed in preaching, celebrated in the liturgy, lived in the life of the believer, will constitute the irreducibly subversive Christian nucleus of the faith as far as the Greek conception of history and the divine is concerned.

In place of an idea of time, derived as was the Greek idea of time from the myth of the eternal return of the identical in the framework of cosmic order, the Easter Trinitarian faith will propose an idea of the historical future decidedly oriented toward the fulfillment of the glory promised in the Easter events.

Against a vision of man assimilated into the rhythm of nature, the account of God's history with humankind will affirm the concept of man as the center of personal and individual relationships, enriched by the highest possible dignity, stimulating the elaboration of the concept of "person" according to which the individual goes from being the object to being the subject of history.

In place of the idea of divinity elaborated out of a fascination with the One to whom the fragmentation of the many can be referred, the Trinitarian confession will propose the event of the Three who enter into the division of the many right up to the scandal of the laceration of the cross. The Trinity will take upon itself this exile of the separated, reconciling them in the highest possible degree, and making them fruitful in multiple new relations, on Easter day.

This Greek vision — which taken as a whole appears more static-metaphysical than historical-dynamic — will influence the Christian soul, urging it toward a rigorous affirmation of the divinity of the One, God the Father, in regard to whom the role of the Other is subordinated (as in *Arianism*) or rendered either useless or reduced to a pure formal expression (or mode of revelation) of the one divinity (as in *Sabellian modalism*) right up to the thesis of *patripassianism*, in which it is the Father who suffered and died in the hour of the cross.

Pagan philosophy, with its conception of the One as opposed to the many, makes itself felt in the tendency toward subordinationism. God is pure and untouchable as regards the world. The abyss that opens between him and the creature is the place where Arius believes he can locate the Christian figure of the Son, as an intermediate being between the divine and the human, the "first-born of creation."

The syncretistic fascination of gnosticism — with its accent on the unfathomable depths of the divinity which can, to some extent, be plumbed thanks to the various degrees of knowledge which are connected to differentiated modes of revelation — is perhaps active in the modalist tendency.

Judaism, pagan culture, and gnosticism are therefore the different fronts which pick a quarrel with the Christian Trinitarian scandal to which they oppose — be it even in different forms — the same "pious" objection of safeguarding the transcendent divine One, presenting themselves as the defenders of the divinity of God against the presumed intolerable compromise and diminishment of the divine in the worldly, the mortal and the transient.

Whether it is a case of "monarchical monotheism" of a Jewish-Christian kind or of "monotheistic Christianity," as in the Arian solution where the Christian Trinity is subordinately reduced to the One, or of a pure and simple monotheism with an external Christian coloring, as in Sabellius' concept where the One is garbed in an external Trinitarian form,[54] the argument is basically the same: the concept of the divine is not determined by the Trinitarian event of Easter, and hence by the concreteness of the history of revelation, but is predetermined by a concept of the Absolute specific to the "spirit of the times."[55]

The scandal of the conjunction, possible in the Trinity, between "immanence" and "otherness" in the cross and resurrection of the Nazarene is emptied of all meaning. The Absolute abandons history; the One remains resplendently "other" and alien and tremendously adorable as far as this world is concerned. Man, the multiple, returns to the prison of his fallen state without true redemption, alone on the uncrossable threshold separating him from God. Nor does the figure of the created intermediary who belongs, really, to only one of the two worlds, that of creatures, succeed in reconciling the separation of the world from God. The refusal to face up to the Trinitarian scandal thus resolves itself in a kind of sad denial of the way of salvation offered to those afar; that is, to the many prisoners of sin and death, who are "without hope and without God in this world" (Ep 2:12).

c) The "Professed" Trinity

The Christian faith responds to this dispute over the Trinitarian "scandal" and to its reduction to a worldly concept of the Absolute with an effort to convey the lived and liturgically celebrated experience of the mystery of the Trinity by means of an explicit dogmatic profession.

The most profound motive behind this process of explaining and defending the orthodox position is soteriology. If the revelation of the Trinity in history is denied, the salvific entrance of history into the Trinity is likewise denied. If the Son were not God, cross and resurrection would be human events like so many others and not the locus of salvation, the world's portal and ours to divine life. If the Spirit were not God, his work would not divinize man; and the abyss between history and glory would remain unspanned.

This dense soteriological meaning of the process of dogmatic elaboration explains its spiritual inspiration and vehemence while giving evidence of its permanent value. In the defense of authentic faith, the point at issue is not an abstract theory about God but ''the liberation of prisoners'' and ''the joyful message to the poor'' brought by him on whom rests the Spirit of the Lord (Lk 4:18).

''The soteriological scope of the primitive development of the Trinitarian dogma also reveals at the same time the religious significance of this process. The task of protecting New Testament faith in the redemption by means of the construction of the Trinitarian bulwark could not have been upheld except by religious existential forces and had to seek the release once again of such forces. Thus the Trinitarian mystery during the time of its formation was not felt and developed as a *mysterium logicum* but as an adorable *mysterium salutis*; and this is shown also in the fact that from the beginning the doxology appropriated this mystery.''[56]

Not by chance did the result of this process of dogmatic elaboration flow into the profession of faith proclaimed in the liturgy!

The two great attempts at defining the dogma of the Trinity in response to the attacks on it by different forms which would dilute the so-called scandal of Easter were the Council of Nicea (325) and that of Constantinople (381).

The first took a position against the crisis created by Arius: ''The point at issue is this: Is the figure of Jesus to be determined by the Absolute, and thus as it has come to be thought of philosophically and religiously by Hellenistic culture, or, instead, are the practice and the preaching of Jesus the determinants in the last analysis? The Council of Nicea chose to answer affirmatively to the second horn of the dilemma. It did so by refusing to separate from the historic image of Jesus the bond of Christ with God."[57]

This is the profound sense of the formula of the *homoousios* which in time will characterize the Nicene confession, introduced into the section of the Symbol on the Son. Absent from scripture, passed on from the gnostic to the Christian theological world, especially the Alexandrian, this expression intends to convey, against Arian reductionism, that "the Son is on the same level of being as the transcendent God."[58]

The intention of the Nicene Fathers consists, that is, in shedding light on the way of understanding the relationship between Father and Son: "Openly condemning the errors of Arius and proclaiming in a positive way the true and strict divine filiation of the Word generated by the substance of the Father, thus as his absolute identity of essence with the one true God, the Nicene Symbol proclaimed the divinity of Jesus Christ."[59] The whole series of affirmations introduced into the part of the profession of faith regarding the Son flows in this direction:

"We believe . . . in one Lord Jesus Christ,
Son of God, generated as the only begotten of the Father,
that is, of the same substance as the Father,
through whom all things were created,
those of heaven and those of earth. . . "[60]

These affirmations are followed by the compact yet concrete account of the story of Jesus, present also in the preceding Symbols. Between the "new" ontological things enunciated and those which are historico-salvific, there is no opposition. The former translate into the categories of the Greek world the scandal conveyed narratively by the second. The history of Jesus as Trinitarian history is made explicit in metaphysical language as his consubstantiality with the Father; the "ontology of the mystery" is separately explained in terms of the economy of salvation, but is not opposed to it.[61] Christian faith makes itself "Greek with the

Greeks'' without on this account renouncing its original, subversive identity.

This parity on the plane of divine being between the Son and the Father justifies in ontological categories the salvific worth of the life and deeds of the Nazarene, recalled by the formula "for us men and for our salvation." Jesus is God with us and for us! His identity in being with the Father, expressed by the word *homoousios*, is the aspect of the Trinitarian scandal — based on the paschal event — which the faith of the Church offers in simple opposition to the Arian watering down of the good news.

The defense and clarification of the Nicene faith, the work of Athanasius and the Cappadocians, connected with the inclusion of the question of the divinity of the Holy Spirit (and hence of the three divine Persons) — in a time whose relative brevity shows its full maturity on the level of the living of the faith — merge in the Oriental Synod of Constantinople of 381, later (after the middle of the fifth century) recognized as the Second Ecumenical Council.

The Symbol attributed to this Synod, called afterward the ''Nicene-Constantinopolitan Symbol,'' develops Nicea in the section dedicated to the Holy Spirit, of whom are predicated the divine attributes of "Lord" and "giver of life," while it affirms the procession from the Father and the right of adoration in union with the Father and the Son.[62] The parity of the Three on the level of divine being is clearly professed in this way as is the conception expressed by the Cappadocian Fathers with the formula *mia ousia, treis hypostaseis,* rendered into Latin by means of a terminology which dates from Tertullian's time, as "one nature (substance, essence), three persons."[63]

Against the absorption of Father, Son, and Holy Spirit into the One — as the "spirit of the time" saw it — the Christian faith reaffirms the original stumbling block of the identity in "otherness" of the Three, inserting into the narrative structure of the Symbol categories proper to the world in which it was undergoing inculturation, incorporating the result of the theological debate which had gone on there. In the Nicene-Constantinopolitan Symbol, the "narrated" Trinity is fused with the "argued" Trinity in the continuity of the profession of the true faith.

Thanks perhaps to this equilibrium of fidelity and newness, of continuity in the proclamation of the message and the updating of the argumentation, "the importance of the Nicene-Constantinopolitan creed for the development of the Trinitarian faith of the Church cannot be easily exaggerated. This Symbol, which soon entered the liturgy, has since decidedly determined the faith of the community right up to our own day and age and has provided the definitive interpretation of the faith of the Church."[64]

Having affirmed the value of Nicea-Constantinople in the history of the Trinitarian confession, it is necessary to show its limits as well. The encounter with Hellenistic thought regarding the Absolute could not help but introduce a certain acceptance of the antithesis. As often happens, "superficial antagonism is joined in the synthesis at a deeper level along with the assimilation of the contrary thought; the conquest of the adversary comes about through the fusion of his own elements."[65]

Thus, Christian theology was practiced not only as the deepening and defending of one's own idea of God, but also as the assumption of accents and motives originally absent. This is why the two Councils — keeping the original narrative structure of the Symbol, with its confession of the history of the Father, Son and Spirit — make it explicit by affirming, on the one hand, the parity of being between Son and Father, and, on the other, the parity of the Spirit with them.

Nothing, however, is said about the relationship between divine unity, strongly affirmed in this way, and the Trinity of Persons. Neither are the personal relations of the Son with the Father and that of the Spirit with the Son illustrated. The explication of the narrative Creed, therefore, takes place in the sense of a more marked accentuation of divine unity, passing over in silence the articulation of the relationships among the Persons and the Council's original stands on the one substance.

This privileged attention to the One God is the price paid for the defense of the Triune God in the culture of the Greco-Roman world. What in the kerygma is the paschal event of the Three — caught up in fruitful reciprocal relationships and with the world in the Trinitarian history of the cross and resurrection — becomes, in the dehistoricized prospect in which the dogma is formulated, the unity of divine being in which the Three are seen above all in their substantial equality. This change of viewpoint, even if it be in the continuity of the profession of the same faith, will determine in a relevant manner the successive deepening of the mystery and will penetrate the experience of salvation itself.

d) *The "Reasoned" Trinity*

It is possible to distinguish in the theological study of Trinitarian faith which followed on the decisive dogmatic "episode"[66] three great moments which develop speculation about the mystery in keeping with the proper character of the world of thought in which they were respectively expressed. The Trinity is "reasoned" about from the perspective of the primacy of being or objectivity (the ancient and the medieval worlds), from that of the primacy of subjectivity (the modern and the contemporary epochs), and finally from that of implicit or reflected attention to the interpreted or hermeneutical circularity between subject and object linked to the emergence of historical consciousness.[67]

aa) Thinking about the Trinity *from the viewpoint of the primacy of being* developed in direct connection with the accentuating of the unity of essence or divine substance, hinted at in the course of the Trinitarian controversy in a Greco-Roman ambient under the impulse of the conception of the Absolute understood as One opposed to the many. The great systematizations of this trend are especially Western and are linked with great names like those of Augustine and Thomas Aquinas.

Augustine's Trinitarian doctrine[68] explicitly proposes to "explain, as far as possible, how the Trinity is one and true God and how it is fully exact to say, believe and think that the Father, the Son and the Holy Spirit are of one and the same substance or essence" (*De Trinitate*, 1.2.4).

In conformity with this scope, the fifteen books of Augustine's *De Trinitate* expound above all the reason for the unity and the equality of the Trinity according to the scriptures (Books 1-4), hence the speculative defense of the Trinitarian dogma with the doctrine of the relations (Books 5-7: with the introduction to the mystical knowledge of God in Book 8), and finally the search for the image of the Trinity in man (Books 9-14: Book 15, after a summary of the preceding, offers a meditative reprise of the life of the human spirit and the data of scripture regarding the procession of the Son and the Holy Spirit). The starting point and the permanent hermeneutical viewpoint is the unity of the divine being. Even the historical activity of the Trinitarian God leads back to the oneness of essence because the inseparable Three operate inseparably. Will and action in the Trinity are one and undivided.

How, then, can we explain the personal Trinity attested to by revelation and confessed in the Symbols? It is in response to this question that Augustine introduces the concept of "relation," "the most subtle and delicate line of thought that could ever be traced to show in some way the differences in the divine nature without, however, destroying thereby the unity with strong categories."[69]

In reference to themselves the divine Persons are the one true God and merge together in the divine essence; in reciprocal relation they are distinguished respectively as the Father who generates, the Son who is generated, the Spirit of one and the other. This relationship constitutes the divine Persons as such.

It is legitimate, then, to ask what ontological force this relation has. Is not the relation perhaps a pure accident, lacking real substance? Augustine acknowledges this difficulty and seeks to overcome it by insisting on the immutable character of the divine relations which would be the basis of their ontological reality. An accidental element, the character of immutability, would thus enter to guarantee the reality of the distinctions flowing from the relations (cf. *De Trin*. 5.5.6).

An undeniable difficulty is revealed here: Is not this "accidental" foundation of a "real" distinction too weak? Is not the reality of the divine Persons thus diminished in favor of the unity of their essence?[70] It is also on account of this difficulty that Augustine clearly shows the need to deepen the understanding of the relational life of the Three by starting with the psychological analogy founded on the biblical idea of man as the image of God.[71] The dynamism of the immanence of the Trinitarian life is considered analogous to the immanent process of the human spirit, an analogy whose evident limit lies in the fact that what happens in the inner life of one man is referred to what takes place among the three Persons of the divinity (cf. *De Trin*. 15.22.42).

Just as being, knowing, and willing (*mens, notitia,* and *amor*: cf. *De Trin*. 9.5.8; 9.12.18) or, better yet, memory, intelligence, and will (*memoria, intelligentia,* and *voluntas*: cf. *De Trin*. 10.11.18; 10.12.19; 14.6.8; 15.21.40-41), constitute three distinct poles, reciprocally regulated and co-involved, essentially united and equal, so too the three divine Persons are mutually related within the one divine essence.

And just as the mind knows and loves itself, or latent knowledge (memory) has a self-perception of the spirit (intelligence) and self-love (will), so too, the infinite transcendence of the mystery aside, in the one divine essence the Father generates the Son-Word by way of knowledge and, loving him, with him breathes (spirates) the Holy Spirit by way of the will (cf. *De Trin*. 15.27.50).

Or, according to the analogy of love whose fruitfulness Augustine recognizes but which he acknowledges not having properly developed (cf. *De Trin.* 15.6.10), the eternal Lover loves the eternally Loved and is re-loved by him in the Love eternally received and given: *"Ecce tria sunt: amans, et quod amatur, et amor"* (*De Trin.* 8.10.14; cf. 6.5.7 and 8.8.12: "You see the Trinity if you see love").

The doctrine of relations and psychological analogy permit Augustine to think about the biblical Trinity within the unity of the divine essence from the viewpoint of the primacy of being. Nevertheless, this does not happen without a certain weakening of attention to the history of revelation; that is, to the concreteness of the salvific action of each of the divine Persons.[72]

The Trinity is thought about less in relation to the paschal event and, hence, to the horizon of history than it is in relation to the popular religious fascination with the concept of the divine Absolute, one and unique, other and sovereign, as far as the multiform future of the world is concerned. In this sense the pastoral and spiritual flavor of Augustine's work can best be understood. Faithful to dogma, his work intended to "reason it out" in the most eloquent possible way for the world in which he lived. History, having remained rather out of the limelight in providing material for probing the mystery, asserts its rights on the level of the form of thought. Speaking the language of his time and reasoning from its speculative point of view, Augustine answered the need for interior unity proper to his epoch which was in the throes of a profound process of actual disintegration.

At the same time, he never abandoned reference to him — the Christ — in whom alone it is given to us to "adhere to the One, enjoy the One, persevere in Unity" (*De Trin.* 4.7.11). This explains how "the most immanent of the immanent" Trinitarian doctrines (A. von Harnack) could have exercised such a fascination to say nothing of such a profound influence on the theology and the Christian soul of his time and long thereafter.

The great Scholastic synthesis of *Thomas Aquinas*[73] does not escape this fascination and influence. Even for him, the starting point is the unity and the singularity of the divine being, so much so that, because of this, his systematization of the distinction between the two tracts, "De Deo Uno" and "De Deo Trino," will become commonplace if not traditional. Considering first "that which regards essence" and then "that which regards the distinction of Persons," he makes clear how the decisive problem is that of reconciling the personal Trinity with the essential unity that precedes and establishes it.

Or, situating these concepts historically, he sought to reconcile the God of Christian revelation with the God of Aristotelian metaphysics which triumphantly invaded the culture of his time. Thomas conducted a genial and conciliatory approach by speculatively elaborating Augustine according to his succession of concepts regarding the divine essence (object of "De Deo Uno") and the processions, relations, persons and missions (object of "De Deo Trino").

The processions indicate the intradivine origins. These are the vital, immanent activities (*processio ad intra*) which indicate the dynamism of life in God; that is, in the ambit of the one and unique divinity (cf. *Summa Theol.* I q.27 a.1). The first of these processions is generation by which from the Father, the living principle, proceeds the Son consubstantial to him, by way of the intellect, much the same way the mental word or concept proceeds from the intellect: the generated one is the Word (cf. *ibid.* a.2). The second procession takes place by way of the will and stands in relation to the first as love to knowledge, from which it differs and which it follows (one does not love except what is first known): this is procession by way of love, the procession of the Spirit (cf. *ibid.* a.3).

By studying these intradivine origins before considering the relationships based on them, Thomas can restrict the Augustinian psychological analogy to the simple functions of the intellect and the will, with the dual effect of assuming Aristotelian psychology in full and distinguishing better between the procession of the Word and that of the Spirit:

"The procession of love in the divinity must not be called generation. This is evident if one takes into account the difference between the intellect and the will: the act of the intellect is the act whereby the known object is in the knower according to his likeness. The act of the will, on the other hand, is the act whereby it is not the willed thing that is in the will, but it is the will which has a certain inclination towards that which is willed. Hence the procession that takes place in an intellectual way is according to the likeness of the one knowing and can be called generation insofar as the generator generates another like himself. The procession that takes place by way of the will, though, is not had in likeness but rather in an impulse or movement towards something else. This is why what proceeds in divinity by way of love does not proceed as generated or as the Son but as the Spirit, a name by which is designated a vital motion and an impulse, inasmuch as it is moved or stimulated to do something by love" (*ibid*. a.4).

Four relations in God flow from the two processions because "according to each procession there should be derived two opposite relations — one of him who proceeds in contrast to the principle from which he proceeds; and the other, in contrast to the principle itself" (q.28 a.4). From the four relations — paternity, filiation, active spiration, and passive spiration — only three constitute the Persons because active spiration is an act common to the Father and the Son. In their *esse in* (that is, their being in relation to each other), these relations are identified with the one and unique divine essence (cf. *ibid*. a.2) while in their *esse ad* (that is, their being in relation to the created world) they are really distinguished and establish the Trinitarian reality (cf. *ibid*. aa.1 and 3).

It is here that Thomas for a second time goes further than Augustine. If the latter had used the term "person" without conviction ("more not to remain without saying something than to express that reality" — *De Trin*. 5.9.10), the Angelic Doctor can now use the term in the sense of "subsistent relation," based on the realism of the divine processions: *"Persona igitur divina significat relationem, ut subsistentem"* "Person, as applied to God, does not signify relation, but substance" (q.29 a.4). In this packed definition "*relation* means the individuating element which distinguishes the Person; *subsisting* designates the absolute ontological position of the Person."[74]

When it is opposite and incommunicable, therefore, relation in God constitutes the Persons: "Paternity and filiation, insofar as they are opposite relations, pertain by necessity to two Persons. Subsisting paternity is the Person of the Father while subsisting filiation is the Person of the Son . . . . Spiration pertains to the Person of the Father and to that of the Son, insofar as it is not in a relation of opposition either to paternity or to filiation. Consequently, the procession belongs to another Person who is the Person of the Holy Spirit, proceeding by way of love" (q.30 a.2).

Finally, Thomas — not without first having underlined the mystery's transcendence (cf. q.32 a.1) — bases on the eternal procession even the divine missions that are attested to in scripture: "The mission of one divine Person permits, on the one hand, the procession of origin from him who sends and, on the other, a new mode of existing (in the world)" for him who is sent (q.43 a.1). Implying unity of action *ad extra* (that is, action directed outside) by the Trinity, the missions come together in the Persons through that manifestation, by means of essential attributes, which is appropriation (cf. q.39 a.7): As the Son proceeds in God by way of the intellect, so the work of revealed knowledge, in the economy, is appropriated by him (cf. q.43 a.5 rep. ob. 1). And just as the Father is the absolute principle of intradivine dynamism, so too the work of creation is appropriated by him, and in him is designated the One who sends the Son and the Spirit (who is sent by the Son, or by the Father through the Son) without being himself sent: "Mission requires proceeding from another. . .; because the Father is from no other, it does not become him in any way to be sent" (q.43 a.4). He gives himself to the creature "inasmuch as he freely communicates himself to it" (q.43 a.4 rep. ob. 1), not inasmuch as he is given by another.

Thomas' lucid and coherent system, therefore, speculatively develops Augustine's, working from within the same hermeneutical viewpoint: that of the primacy of being, the fascination of the One. If the relational life of God is better dialecticized thanks to the use of this concept of procession and the more elaborated concept of person, the historico-salvific reality of the action of Father, Son, and Spirit is no less distant.[75] The divine essence is clearly emphasized in the Trinity of Persons. A kind of unitarism, linked to Aristotelian metaphysics and psychology, risks reducing the Persons to "fruits" of the one and unique essence (H. F. Dondaine), while the "missions appear to be the last link in the chain which begins with essence," so much so that "an energetic reminder is needed, a kind of sudden mental jolt, to get us to take into account that their source is instead the Person of the Father."[76]

Moreover, the consequences of the application of the psychological analogy are biblically unsustainable. Even the Father-Son relationship is, for the New Testament, a love relation, while the relationship between the Spirit and the other two Persons can be defined as "volitional" only with difficulty. Thomas himself reveals his uncertainties (think, for example, of the approach of the *Contra Gentiles* IV, 1ff., which is so different from that of the *Summa Theologica*!). If his great merit is having proposed the Trinitarian confession in a language and in a hermeneutical point of view proper to a culture dominated by the primacy of being, nonetheless, the limits cited will open the way to that "extravagant essentialism of Trinitarian theology which has, on its own, penetrated both preaching and catechesis if not the entire Western culture"[77] draining the believer's reflection of the salvific and existential trust proper to the Easter witness to and the liturgical celebration of the mystery.

Even in Thomas, the Trinity is reflected on less from the starting point of the revelatory-salvific event (of Easter) than from that of the Absolute, proceeding less from history than from metaphysics. The dynamism of salvation cedes its place to the seduction of immutable and eternal Being.

This manner of thinking — ever more exclusive in the later Scholastic period — finds its most concise formulation in the principle set forth by the Council of Florence (1442) but going back to Augustine for its original idea, called the "golden rule" of Trinitarian speculation: "In God everything is one where there is no opposition of relation."[78] Affirming the priority of the One in the divine Being, and resolving the dynamism of the Trinity through the doctrine of the opposition of relations — in which the Three are identical to the One as far as their essence is concerned — the principle ratifies the greatest possible reception into the Christian faith of the "pious" idea regarding the unity and singularity of the divine, without compromising the personal Trinity. The price paid, however, is the loss of the effective incidence of the Trinitarian mystery in theology and in practice, the exile of the Trinity from both the theory and the life of Christians.

   bb) Thinking about the Trinity *from the viewpoint of the primacy of subjectivity* developed in connection with the "discovery" of the subject proper to the modern epoch. The disintegrating tendencies which characterized the end of the Middle Ages had their effects on the dissolution of the political (the formation of the national states), the religious (the Reformation and the Counter-Reformation) and the critical syntheses (the decline of Scholasticism and the re-emergence of the subject and its historical dimension).[79]

   If the Cartesian *"cogito"* represents the theoretical triumph of this process, it is German idealism which actually made the effort to "think out" the crisis from which the modern world sprang and to organize a consideration of the real from the starting point of this turnabout from the transcendental, and hence from the evidence provided by subjective reason drawn from its objective and objectifying potential. Even Christian dogma, which pervades the whole of Western thought, is reread from this new hermeneutical viewpoint. The credit for having attempted this new reading, with its far-reaching and absolute consequences, goes to *G.W.F. Hegel*.[80]

It is the concept of God as spirit, as absolute subject living in the dialectic process of self-differentiation and self-identification, that explains the internal origin of the differences in God:

"If, as spirit, God cannot be for us an empty word, he must be conceived of as God, One and Three; this is that in which the nature of God is made explicit. God thus comes to be conceived insofar as he, of himself, makes himself an object in the Son and remains in this object. Moreover, in this distinction of himself from himself, he at the same time overcomes the distinction and loves himself. He is, in other words, identical with himself; he reunites with himself in this love. Only thus is God spirit. . . . Only the Trinity is the determination of God as spirit. Without this determination, spirit is an empty word."[81]

Inasmuch as God is spirit, God is a vital process. He is dynamism personified, history whose truth is arrived at only at the end, in the total self-possession of himself resulting from the distinction from himself and from his return to himself. In this way Hegel rediscovers the eschatological dimension of the Trinity, God's being all in all which comes about only at the end (cf. 1 Cor 15:28) and which can establish the perfect correspondence between the "*curriculum vitae Dei*" and the history of the world. The economy thus reveals its logical foundation: the eternal history of God. Cross and resurrection allow the dialectic of infinite "otherness" and "communion" in the Absolute to shine through:

"God is no more; God is dead: There is no more atrocious thought than this, that all that is eternal and true does not exist; that negation is present even in God. The deepest sadness, the certainty of being irremediably lost, the abandonment of every value all converge here. The process, however, does not stop; rather an inversion takes place. God, in fact, contains this process in himself and it is only the death of death. God rises to life again.''[82]

In the life of Christ, the story of the Absolute is told and the totality of history is revealed:

"That which the life of Christ represents . . . is the process of the nature of the spirit, God in human form. This process is, in its development, the advancing of the divine idea toward the loftiest separation, toward the contrary of sorrow and death which is itself the absolute conversion, the supreme love, the negation of the negative in itself, the absolute reconciliation, the conquest of the opposition of man to God and the end, which comes in that splendor which is the joyful reception of human nature in the divine. The first, God in human form, is real in this process which manifests the separation of the idea and its unification, its fulfillment as truth. This is the totality of history.''[83]

In a process of the spirit similar to that of divine unity and the Trinity of Persons, Hegel — who drew from Father, Son, and Spirit the representation of what is conceptually the process of self-differentiation and self-identification in the life of the spirit — treats the problem of their unity explicitly, the problem of the unity of the Absolute.

His solution, tied in with the concept of person as the recovery of self in the other, can affirm the perfect harmony of the Trinity with divine unity. If love is proper to the person, the renunciation of one's isolation to give oneself totally to the other and to exist in this self-giving, there is no conflict between "otherness" and "communion." Further, the more personal reality is affirmed of the Three, the more it is founded on unity. If love is distinction and the overcoming of the distinct,[84] then personal distinctions are healed in the divine life of love in the highest communion of the three Persons, in their absolute unity.

Hegel has thus expressed the unity of God with an intensity and a lively energy never before reached, not by means of a reduction of the triple personality but precisely through the most acute accentuation of the ideal of the personality of the Father, Son, and Spirit. This idea would represent "the high point of Trinitarian doctrine as regards the relationship between unity and trinity."[85]

We must ask, however, if the affirmation of the double unity of the Absolute in itself and with history — even if it results from a Trinitarian dialectic process — does not undo in reality, not only the "otherness" between God and the world, but even the true personal "otherness" in God.

We cannot escape the strong impression that the Hegelian correspondence of immanent Trinity and economic Trinity, the form of the most general equation between ideal and real, is resolved through the total immanentization of the Absolute in history. The unity of absolute subject does away with the distances between time and eternity. Heaven and earth reach the point of reciprocally assuming one another. The transcendence and the freedom of God begin to be absorbed by the necessity of the one and totalizing dialectical process of the Absolute.

And are not the real distinctions between the divine persons swallowed up in this Trinitarian mediation of the unity of the unique divine subject? Does not the thought of the Trinity from the viewpoint of the primacy of the subjective resolve itself into a new, and much more tragic, form of unitarism where the One, no longer perceived in a static state of being, is represented in the movement of the becoming of the "I" in the "Self," up to the self-identification of the "I" and the "Self"?[86]

If Hegelian reflection has the merit of thinking about God as the living God — taking history up into the Truth and the Idea (thus strongly binding economic Trinity to immanent Trinity) — this does not avoid the final "monism of the Spirit," in which the salvific dialectic of "otherness" and "communion" between God and the world is lost, in which the God settled in the world is no longer able to offer salvation to the world. And God, the one absolute subject, can no longer redeem human subjects, taking them up into a participation in a true intra-Trinitarian personal dialogue.

The charm of the Hegelian God remains immense all the same. The "history of God" and "history in God" appear as concepts whose fruitfulness is no longer negligible. An example of this is the Trinitarian theology of *Karl Barth*.[87] If, by Hegelian reduction, there is a clear denial of the Absolute in history and history is viewed as the undue absolutizing of the act of reason — and therefore as a supreme form of idolatry[88] — the assumption of history in God — whose life is publicly taught, starting with revelation, as the movement of the one divine subject in three distinct manners of being (*drei Seinsweisen*) — has been persuasive.

The Christian God is the Revealer, the Revelation, and the Revealed. In the unique revelation of divine sovereignty, God hides himself, is revealed, communicates and offers himself in the three "modes of being" — hidden, revealed, and participated in; Father, Son, and Spirit: the Father in the hiddenness of the cross, the Son in the light of Easter, and the Spirit in the outpouring of Pentecost; the Father in the initiative of creation and redemption; the Son in the history of revelation and redemption; the Spirit in the sanctifying divine participation. If the Trinity is viewed in the dynamic unity of the event of revelation, if the Christian God is reflected on in history and from the starting point of the history of salvation, the primacy of the unique absolute subject is no less in evidence.

Revelation is God's self-revelation in the Spirit. The absolute subject manifests itself by becoming the object of revelation in order to restore the one and the other to unity in the Spirit of both. But if the Father is the subject of revelation, what personality remains to the Son and the Spirit? Is not the biblical concreteness of the Three lost? Once again it is the paschal event, the compact story of the relating of the Three in the salvific event, which creates a problem in the reading of the mystery in which the stumbling block of the Trinity risks getting lost in the ideal conciliation of the absolute spirit.[89]

"Barth's Trinitarian doctrine attempts, therefore, to express the insuppressible subjectivity of God and thus posits itself as a variation of the modern problematic of subjectivity and its autonomy. The three modes of being in which it is manifested pertain to the self-constitution of the absolute Subject. We thus find ourselves facing a typically modern conceptual image or, better still, a typically idealistic one which, notwithstanding every diversity of the material order, in any event links Barth to Hegel."[90]

If Hegel, with his question about the living God, is the great challenge and the great promise of modern Christian theology, he is no less its great risk.

cc) Third, with respect to Trinitarian speculation carried out under the heading of the objectivity of being and to that conducted along the lines of the subjectivity of the spirit, there is thinking about the Trinity *from the viewpoint of history,* that is, from the viewpoint of the permanent circularity between subject and object.

At a non-thematic hermeneutic level, this viewpoint is met in the great tradition of the Greek Fathers.[91] The starting point in this tradition is the Trinity of the divine Persons which is attested to by the "economy" of salvation. Divine unity is explained as unity of principle, the dynamic unity of the life which flows from this principle and returns to it. The source, the eternal font of divinity, is the Father:

"The active principle is one and the operation is one. In fact, the Father fulfills everything through the Word in the Holy Spirit, and in this way the unity of the Trinity is kept intact."[92]

The Son and the Holy Spirit proceed from the Father, not by temporal procession, but in an *eternal* movement through which each of the Persons exists in the others, in a reciprocal inhabitation and compenetration, the divine "pericoresis," in which Trinity and unity are perfectly reconciled, without either being swallowed up in the other:

"One Person's remaining and residing in another of the three Persons means that they are inseparable and are not to be separated, that they enjoy among themselves a compenetration without confusion, not in such a way that they blend into one another or are mixed together, but in a way that joins them. In other words, the Son is in the Father and in the Spirit, and the Spirit is in the Father and the Son, and the Father is in the Son and the Spirit without any fusion or mixture or confusion. The movement is one and identical because the impetus and dynamism of the three Persons is one, something which cannot be said of created nature.''[93]

Unity of principle thus establishes the unity, ever in motion, of the divine Persons, which is revealed in the missions of Son and Spirit and in the fulfillment, promised in and based on them, of the return of the created to its beginnings in the recapitulation of all things in Christ and in the final handing over of everything and everyone to God the Father. The economy is therefore the threshold of the mystery, the confronting of the immanence of divine life which still remains other and adorable, never reducible to worldly grasp. Eastern speculation thus comes to read immanence and transcendence, human subjectivity and objectivity in God, in a fruitful cycle which does not resolve one or the other, affirming simultaneously the ''otherness'' and the ''communion'' of the Persons in God and of the Trinitarian God with the world.

This rich approach is to be found in a single figure of the Latin Middle Ages whose influence on the later development of these ideas should rightly be emphasized: *Joachim of Fiore*,[94] the Calabrian abbot of the 12th century, who knew how to think historically about the Trinity and ''Trinitarily'' about history.

Joachim thinks about the Trinity in a historical way: the dynamism of the revelation of the divine Persons is for him the manifestation in time of the eternal movement of the immanent divine life. The symbolic dialectic of past-future, prophecy-hope which unites the three ''states'' of the world — that of the Father (or the Law) to that of the Son (grace), and the latter to that of the Spirit (or full freedom in love)[95] — is assumed to signify the relation that joins the divine Persons among themselves:

"Just as at the beginning of the second state (that of grace) the Spirit manifested his glory in part and will manifest it in fullness at the beginning of the third, so he offered an initial understanding which looked to the second state, in the image of his procession from the Father, and he will offer yet another proper to the third state, to the image of his procession from the Son."[96]

The third state which will begin with Elijah refers properly to the Holy Spirit by the fact that he will show his glory in it, as the Father did in the first state and the Son in the second. Since the Holy Spirit, then, does not proceed only from the Son but, as the holy doctors say, principally from the Father, for the purpose of showing his procession with the Son from the same Father, coming with the Son himself at the beginning of the second state, even so, as it clearly appears in the Acts of the Apostles, he has shown his glory in part so as to manifest it in fullness at the coming of Elijah."[97]

It is in history that the dynamism of glory is revealed. What takes place at the time of the divine missions reveals the movement of intratrinitarian life, which from the Father is displayed in the Son and with him in the Spirit, in a circularity that is both one and three, according to the "table of the divine circles" of the *Liber figurarum*.[98] The relationship of likeness ("*similitudo*") between the states of the world and the divine processions does not render either divine "unity" or "otherness" meaningless. The three "*traditiones*" — that of the Old Testament which referred to the Father, that of the New Testament which is linked to the Son, and that of the "*sacramentum Ecclesiae*" (sacrament of the Church), connected to the Spirit — spring from the unity of the Trinity:

"These three traditions proceed equally from the entire Trinity whose works — although under one aspect attributed distinctly to the individual Persons, in confirmation of the truth of the Persons — nevertheless could not in the least be divided because of their supreme unity."[99]

"In fact, the works of the Trinity are inseparable."[100]

"God is one without confusion of Persons: He is three in Persons without division of substance. . . . This substance, which is God, is one and supremely one, and constitutes a unique and most simple nature. In confessing one substance, we do not deny the Trinity; but we abhor portraying it as divided into parts. We piously and faithfully believe that the three Persons are one substance only, which in turn is the three Persons."[101]

The divine Trinitarian life, which is revealed in the dynamism of the "history of salvation," does not end there, remaining adorably transcendent:

"Even though the whole Trinity appeared to Abraham in the form of three men, no one has seen God in the purity of his nature."[102]

"We can understand something about this not so much from being able to know *how* it is but from being able to believe *that* it is."[103]

Reflected on from the beginning of the history of revelation, the Trinity is understood as the fruitful dynamism of the divine Persons in their transcendent unity, welded to history (which finds sense in it) but not resolved in history.

In this light, Joachim seems perfectly orthodox in regard to the Trinity.[104] Western in his terminology and in his defense of the *Filioque*, he nonetheless remains close to the Greek Fathers in starting out from the economy of salvation history and the principality of the Father. He positions himself almost as a meeting point between these two theological worlds, both of them faithful to the original scandal of Christianity, notwithstanding their diversity, in that southern part of Italy which is the land where East meets West and "where everything had its start" in not a few of the decisive turns in the history of thought.[105]

Thinking historically about the Trinity, the Calabrian abbot also thinks Trinitarily about history, and this is perhaps the most original aspect of his message. He sees time unfolding like the unfolding of life within God: there are "three ages as there are three

Persons,"[106] "three states of the world owing to the three Persons of the divinity."[107] In the light of Trinitarian life, he thus scans the times of history:

"The mysteries of the divine Page indicate the three stages of the world to us: the first is that in which we were under the law; the second is that in which we are under grace; the third, still to unfold in the future, is that in which we will be under an even greater grace. . . . The first state was one of knowledge, the second is one of wisdom and the third will be that of the fullness of the intellect. The first was characterized by servile servitude, the second by filial servitude, and the third by freedom. . . . The first was lived in fear, the second in faith, the third in love. . . . The first by the light of the stars, the second in the early light of dawn, the third at high noon. The first in winter, the second in spring, the third in summer. . . . The first state refers to the Father, creator of everything; the second to the Son, who deigned to assume our dust; the third to the Holy Spirit, of whom the Apostle says: 'Where there is the Spirit of the Lord, there is freedom' (2 Cor 3:17)."[108]

The grandiose aspect of this concept is that it brings the human experience to its eternal roots and takes the passing of times not as suspended in nothing and therefore condemned to insensitiveness but as founded in the proceeding of the same divine Persons in a vital movement which comes from what is more of history and tends in history to what overcomes history. The Trinity becomes the sense and strength of human experience, the origin, the place and the goal of history.

In the intensity of his intuition, Joachim will not avoid ingenuity and forced symbols, sometimes seeing the "*vestigia Trinitatis*" (traces of Trinity) even as traces of a divine self-realization scrutinized Trinitarily. Not by chance will Thomas Aquinas invoke against him the principle of inseparable activity of the Three in the one history of salvation.[109]

Nevertheless, the interlocking of the states in the Joachimite vision is indicative of the eternal mutual coinvolvement of the divine Persons. If there is an enthusiastic accentuation of the *"solus Spiritus veritatis"* (the one Spirit of truth) and of the "spiritual good news," this is due both to a reaction against a lack of emphasis on the Christian doctrine of the Holy Spirit throughout the West and to a certain optimistic tension, a lively and (in a very radical sense) well-founded hope in the Trinitarian significance of history.

In this sense it is right to affirm that "Joachimism is a theology of hope under the form of a theology of the Spirit."[110] A text like the following reveals this vision's whole prophetic burden as promoter of the future and, therefore, also challenger of the present:

"If the promise of the reign of Christ made to Abraham was fulfilled after the course of many, many years so that, as the world aged, the synagogue would generate that seed promised to Abraham and to David, why would the Church despair of being able to generate, through the gift of the Holy Spirit, children of adoption who could, with the gift of God, advance as the chosen race and spiritual kingdom?"[111]

But is this hope of the Church Trinitarily founded to the point of being considered divine hope? Is it right to say that "the future *in* God becomes the future *of* God, an awesome turn about of affairs which lies at the heart of yesterday's and today's debates on the orthodoxy or heterodoxy of Joachim"?[112] It is the question of the relationship between historical thought about the Trinity and Trinitarian thinking about history. Several have maintained that the concept of the Trinity depends on a theory of history.[113] The temporal future would absorb the Trinity in a kind of self-divinization. History would become the verification of and the interpreter of dogma. The Trinity would be a function of history! If this were true, however, the profound motivation behind the Joachimite intuition — namely, the transcendent hope which is founded on that which is greater than history — would be diminished. This is why — beyond all our insufficient symbolism and verbal expressions — the formula coined by Karl Barth to summarize the message of Joachim remains true:

"His thought process does not consist in an attempt to explain the Trinity starting from the world, but in the opposite attempt to explain the world starting from the Trinity so as to be able to speak of the Trinity in the framework of this world."[114]

In the thinking of the Calabrian abbot, this circular methodology of interpretation is perfect, even under the rigors of an anticipatory intuition: from the economy of history he proceeds to the immanence of the mystery, to return from the immanence of the divine life to history and there to read its profound sense, Trinitarily based. The history of revelation sends one back to glory, and glory offers the key to a reading of history, of which it is the origin and supreme fulfillment. In Joachim the return to history in thinking on the Trinity causes the rediscovery of existential salvific power, the ultimate dynamic of prophecy in hope.[115]

On the basis of Joachim's intuition — even though much misunderstood — a renewed attempt on the part of Jurgen Moltmann[116] is made to re-think the Trinity from the viewpoint of history. His acceptance of Joachim's circular methodology is here explicitly thematicized in dialog with the latest in modern thought. Refusing, on the one hand, to suffocate God within the narrow limits of subjectivity (Schleiermacher) and, on the other hand, to reduce God to an object (with its extreme consequences in modern pragmatism), he shows the journey to God One and Three to be a process of overcoming the idea of supreme substance or absolute subject so as to arrive at an *historical doctrine of the Trinity*.

In this history, "the starting point is the special Christian tradition of the history of the Son, Jesus. . . . The unity of God is no longer presupposed, either as homogeneous substance or as identical subject, but it is broached through this Trinitarian history and hence is elaborated on from a Trinitarian point of view. Western tradition began with the Unity of God and questioned itself about the Trinity; we begin with the Trinity of Persons and ask ourselves about their Unity. A more nuanced concept — and hence one more capable of considering divine Unity as union of the Tri-Unity — is thus delineated.''[117]

Consistent with this outline, Moltmann presents the theme of the "passion of God" and that of the "history of the Son" as events within the economy, from which starting points it is possible to confront the immanence of the mystery. Tied in, then, with this "Trinitarian economy" are creation, and the reconciliation and sanctification of the world, with the intention of studying in depth, in the *opera Trinitatis ad extra,* the relative *opera Trinitatis ad intra* (repectively, the external and internal works of the Trinity). One thus arrives at a reflection on the "mystery of the Trinity" in which criticism of "Christian monotheism" in its various forms is followed by an attempt at a theological characterization of Father, Son and Spirit, so as to speak finally of "person" as "being-in-relation" and of the "pericoresis" as the circuit of divine eternal life in the mutual relating and inhabiting of the Persons.

These general concepts, taken from the tradition of both East and West in an attempt at reciprocal appeasement, remain however insufficient to express the absolute originality and, at the same time, the absolute unity of the Three of which the economy speaks:

"In the doctrine of the Trinity, recourse should not be had to general concepts. . . . In the life of the immanent Trinity, everything is *singular.* . . . Definitively speaking, in the doctrine of the immanent Trinity one can only *narrate.* . . . We must stay on solid ground because, as history teaches, heresies are hidden in abstractions. The basis of orthodoxy, on the contrary, rests on narrative differentiation.''[118]

In this sense, the work of Moltmann appears as a *"narratio Trinitatis ad intra"* stemming from a *"narratio Trinitatis ad extra,"* by way of a doxological, more than an analogical, rapport; that is, one that is open to the depths of the transcendent mystery in awe and thanksgiving for the salvific experience:

"One knows oneself in *wonder* and in awe. Through awareness one participates in the life of the other. Knowing through one's own action does not transform the other into a possessor of the knower, but through sympathy the knower himself becomes a participant in the known. Knowledge establishes *communion*. . . . The new theological penetration of the Trinitarian history of God must free the reason in its operations, rendering it capable of perceiving the other, of participating in the other. Trinitarian thinking must pave the way for a freeing and healing reflection of the destroyed reality."[119]

If an objection is to be raised against Moltmann, it is that of not having always coherently pursued this point of view to its very end. The argumentation that he follows in his essay often manifests itself in an attempt at abbreviating, taking shortcuts which reduce the narrative density to a reasoned formula. One cannot avoid getting the impression that he sometimes wants to make the Trinity too "functional."

This is particularly evident in his elaboration of a "Trinitarian social doctrine." Under the influence of E. Peterson, whose theses have been debated and their motives criticized,[120] Moltmann affirms that "only when Trinitarian doctrine overcomes the monotheistic conception of the great universal Monarch who lives in heaven and of the divine patriarchs who live in this world, will any sovereign, dictator, or tyrant of this land be no longer able to find any religious archetype which justifies him."[121]

In reality, however, "even a monotheistic faith can guarantee a situation which does not make religion an instrument of power. To deny this would be the equivalent of ignoring the history of biblical prophetism."[122] Moreover, the sense of the transcendence of the Trinitarian mystery places one on guard against quick deductions concerning the life of men.

What remains valid about Moltmann's effort is the struggle to think through, by means of relations and by way of communion, starting from the doctrine of the Trinity, man's "rapport with God, with other men and the rest of the human race, as well as his communion with the whole of creation."[123]

The Trinity thus appears justly not as an abstract celestial theorem but as the divine history of love and freedom which stirs up and spreads freedom in love. In the liberated and liberating communion of love, a less unfaithful image of the Trinity is drawn, the dawn of the Kingdom of God:

"The Trinitarian doctrine of the Kingdom is the theological doctrine of freedom. The theological concept of freedom is the concept of the Trinitarian history of God. God wills incessantly the freedom of his creation. God is the inexhaustible freedom of his creatures."[124]

Historical thought about the Trinity reveals here its existential salvific fruitfulness. Recounting leads to further recounting. The Trinity, reflected on narratively, becomes the vitally narrated and lived experience of the liberating power of the mystery. The Trinity, from the viewpoint of history, relates history from the viewpoint of the Trinity, assisting the progress of a redeemed existence, of a reconciled community, of a wholesome and fulfilling relationship with the whole of creation.

"The *kingdom of glory* is to be looked upon as the fulfillment of creation by the Father, the universal affirmation of freedom by the Son, and the fulfillment of inhabitation by the Spirit. Creation is the real promise of glory: a creation full of intimations and signs of future glory. The kingdom of the Son is the historical promise of glory: a kingdom full of experience and hope, of fraternity and sorority; that is, of love. Finally, even though still under the conditions of history and death, the kingdom of the Spirit is itself the beginning of the kingdom of glory. The Trinitarian doctrine of the kingdom therefore sums up the 'work of the Trinity' (creation, liberation, glorification) and directs it toward the *fatherland of God One and Three*. The kingdom of glory is the end which traverses all the works that God accomplishes and the ways He follows in the course of history."[125]

3.

THE TRINITY
AS HISTORY

Why is it necessary to go from the "Trinity in *history*" to scrutinizing the "deep things of God" (1 Cor 2:10)? Why must one start from the economy of salvation in order to move toward the immanence of the mystery? It is a fact that, moving from the concrete account of the events of revelation, faith-reflection in time has always felt the need of attempting to give another account, that of the most profound life of the revealed God.

This need to go from "*Deus revelatus*" to "*Deus absconditus*," from the history of revelation to the unfathomable depths of God, is based on the structure of the "mystery" itself, narrated and celebrated by faith. In the biblical-Pauline sense, the mystery is the salvific design which the living God is carrying out in time, a plan "hidden for centuries," but manifested in Christ, our "hope of glory" (Col 1:26ff; Rm 16:25; Ep 1:9; 3:3; 6:19, etc.).[1]

Mystery is not so much a "path of human investigation interrupted" as it is the most great God's making himself present in a veiled way, the offering of Glory itself under the ever opaque signs of history. Mystery is not the silence of the human inability to speak, the inexpressible which gives weight to Wittgenstein's aphorism: "About that which one cannot speak, it is necessary to be silent."[2] Mystery is the divine Word itself who makes himself present to men in the words and in the events of salvation history.

Thus understood, the experience of the mystery of God entails the irreducible dialectic of hiddenness and revelation. God shows himself in his words but he does not allow himself to be imprisoned by them. He is "there," even though he is always "beyond," greater than the mediation of the event or of the word with which it is communicated to man. In revealing himself, God veils himself; in communicating, he hides himself; in drawing near, he withdraws. And, at the same time, when veiling himself, he opens himself up; in hiding himself, he shows himself; in distancing himself, he draws close. "Were not our hearts burning inside us as he talked to us on the road . . .?" (Lk 24:32).

The need for a nourishing and living awareness which the revelation of the mystery ignites in the one who experiences it is twofold: making God a companion on the way stirs up the desire, on the one hand, of knowing more intimately the Stranger who invites, and on the other, of knowing oneself better before him and in him: "Remain with us because it is evening and the day is practically over" (Lk 24:29). To the *theological* need of knowing him who first loved us is added the *anthropological* question of knowing ourselves and the meaning of life and history in God and in his love. This second knowing makes itself fully possible only on the condition of the first: man's depths, thanks to the revelation of the mystery, seem rooted in the depths of God!

By virtue of this twofold need, the recounting of the Trinitarian story of Easter needs to be reflected on precisely where the look of acknowledgment and love can be cast; and this can be only from the starting point of the actual living experience of the account, which is the mystery proclaimed, celebrated and lived in the uninterrupted tradition of the Church's faith. The Church as the community that narrates, celebrates, and spreads the Trinitarian event, offered in the story of Easter, is the place in which alone it is possible, in an attitude of adoration and attentive listening, to "scrutinize the deep things of God" (1 Cor 2:10).

In the ecclesial community that "theology" of the mystery becomes possible which is already "doxology," the glorification of God who is, at the same time, man's fullness of life in love. "In the tabernacle, which is the proper faith of the Catholic Church,"[3] we draw near in adoring humility and poverty to the threshold of the mystery, not so much to capture God as, rather, to let ourselves be made prisoners by him; not to mortify our humanity so much as to live to the happy end the risk of wanting to be truly human, truly alive.

Beginning with the Paschal event — the supreme revelation of the mystery — we shall try to recount the history of each of the Three, indissolubly united among themselves, so as to contemplate then, in the unity of the event itself, the Trinitarian unity of God who is in himself irreducibly distinct as Father, Son and Holy Spirit.

3.1   THE HISTORY OF THE FATHER

a) *The Easter Account*

The Easter event reveals the Father's story. It is he who *handed over* the Son out of love for the world (Jn 3:16; Rm 8:32; the formulae of the "divine passive voice" such as found in Mk 9:31 and parallels). It is the Father who raised Jesus from the dead, giving to him — and in him to sinners, separated and afar — the Spirit of reconciliation and of life (cf. the formulae of the Acts of the Apostles, e.g. 2:24; also see Rm 1:4; 5:8; Ep 2:4-6; Col 2:13).

Throughout the Nazarene's life, it is the Father who takes the initiative. It is he who sent him (cf. the theme of the Son's mission: Lk 4:17-21; Jn 7:28 ff; 8:29-42; Ac 3:2; Rm 8:3; Gal 4:4; 1 Jn 4:9-14). It is he to whom Jesus continually makes reference with the extremely telling and almost unheard of expression, *Abba* (Mk 14:36; Rm 8:15; Gal 4:6), probably underlying all the times (170 in the Synoptics) in which he turns to God, calling him Father. Even distinguishing "his" Father from "our" Father (Mt 6 and 7, where "my Father" occurs 5 times, "your Father," 7), the Nazarene shows that he shares with the Father an infinite and exclusive confidence: "No one knows the Son except the Father; and no one knows the Father except the Son and him to whom the Son wishes to reveal him" (Mt 11:27; Jn 10:15).

Between Jesus and the Father the relationship is one of reciprocal belonging ("What is mine is yours . . . ," Jn 17:10); reciprocal immanence ("The Father is in me and I am in the Father," Jn 10:38; 17:21); the deepest communion ("The Father is with me," Jn 16:32; "I do nothing of myself but as the Father has taught me, so I speak. He who sent me is with me and has not left me alone because I always do the things that please him," Jn 8:28-29); perfect unity ("The Father and I are one," Jn 10:30; "Whoever has seen me, has seen the Father," Jn 14:9).

This unfathomable unity shows through, appearances to the contrary, in Jesus' cry of infinite sorrow from the cross, "My God, my God, why have you abandoned me?" (Mk 15:34; Mt 27:46). The suffering of separation serves to reveal the intensity of communion! "The Father loves the Son . . ." (Jn 5:20). Jesus is the loved Son, "the well-beloved Son in whom the Father is well pleased" (Mk 1:11; Mt 3:17; Lk 3:22; also Mk 9:7 and parallels; Mt 12:18; Mk 12:6; Lk 20:13). He is the one Son (Jn 1:14-18; 3:16-18), loved by the Father (cf. Jn 15:9; 17:23), who remains in the Father's love (Jn 15:10), loves the Father and does what the Father has commanded him (Jn 14:31).

The Father is, therefore, he who loves the Son and loves us to the point of *handing over* to death his beloved Son in the exile of sinners: "God so loved the world as to give his only begotten Son, so that whoever believes in him may not die but may have eternal life" (Jn 3:16). "He did not spare his own Son, but handed him over for us all" (Rm 8:32). Such is the folly of divine love (cf. 1 Cor 1:18-25)!

Now, the Father is God. In the New Testament, God is designated by the word "Father" in almost every case.[4] "One never finds a text in which the evidence overwhelmingly persuades us that *ho theos* must be taken to refer to the triune God in the totality of the Trinity of persons. There are, on the other hand, many prevalent texts with which, by *ho theos*, the Father as a Trinitarian person is clearly intended."[5] He to whom Jesus prays is the God of Israel, his Father.

Inasmuch as God is the Father, and the Father is he who loves the Son and us, *God is love*. This is the conclusion that the first letter of John draws from contemplating the history of Trinitarian love, which is the story of Easter:

"The man without love has known nothing of God, for God is love. God's love was revealed in our midst in this way: he sent his only Son to the world that we might have life through him. Love, then, consists in this: not that we have loved God, but that he has loved us and has sent his Son as an offering for our sins. . . . We have come to know and believe in the love God has for us. God is love, and he who abides in love abides in God and God in him" (1 Jn 4:8-10, 16).

In the same attempt to plumb the mystery, the Apostle Paul can pray for the Christians of Corinth, probably echoing an early liturgical greeting in the Church, that "The grace of the Lord Jesus Christ, *the love of God* and the fellowship of the Holy Spirit be with you all" (2 Cor 13:13). The hope of Christians is based on the love of the Father: "And this hope will not leave us disappointed, because *the love of God* has been poured out in our hearts through the Holy Spirit who has been given to us" (Rm 5:5; cf. 1 Jn 3:1).

b) *The Father Is Love*

God the Father is love. This affirmation immediately projects us into "the deep things of God," the contemplation of the mystery. From the history of him who loved Jesus his Son and us in him, a transition to the eternal history of his love is made possible. The economy of history sends us back to the immanence of the mystery. The paschal event is the key, the impenetrable evocation of the life of God that is revealed, but not resolved, in the history of the cross and resurrection as the history of Trinitarian love.[6]

To begin with, since, in the economy, the initiation of love always pertains to the Father, we are given evidence that the

Father's love is the originating, fontal love: *the Father is the principle, the source, and the origin of divine life.*

"We confess that the Father was not generated, not created, but is ungenerated. He is the one, in fact, from whom the Son receives birth and the Holy Spirit, procession; he does not originate from someone else. He is, therefore, the font and origin of the whole of divinity."[7]

The Father is the "one not generated," the *Agenneton.*[8] For the Cappadocian Fathers, "not to be generated," "not to have any origin," is the distinguishing characteristic of the Father: "We know only one ungenerated and unique principle of all things: the Father of our Lord Jesus Christ."[9] Augustine calls the Father *"totius Trinitatis principium"* ("principle of the entire Trinity").[10] Thomas Aquinas sees in "innascibility" a notion proper to the Father,[11] and, "insofar as the Father is he from whom another proceeds," affirms that "the Father is the beginning."[12]

This rich language of the tradition of faith conveys the absolute freedom and gratuity of the love of the Father: "He alone can provoke, put in motion, the event of love, because he alone can *begin* to love without any motive to love. More. He has forever begun to love."[13]

God has always loved and will always love. Without being necessitated or caused or extrinsically motivated, he loves and will continue to love, always. He will never decrease in loving fidelity (cf. Ps 89:34 and also the theme of God's fidelity in Rm 3:3; 1 Cor 1:9; 10:13; 2 Cor 1:18; 1 Th 5:24; 2 Th 3:3, etc.). His love "has absolutely no need of anything to set it in motion from without."[14] Hence, one can speak of the absolute "spontaneity," the "originality," the "sovereignty," the inexhaustible "creativity" of divine love.[15] The Father is therefore the eternal provenance of love, he who loves in absolute freedom, always and forever free in love, *the eternal Lover* in the purest gratuity of love.

c) *The Father of the Son*

It is this pure originality, this gratuitous overflowing of loving love, this original diffusiveness of eternal love that makes of the *Father the Generator, the Father of the eternal Son*. His is not egotistical love of self, apprehended and imprisoned within the ego. His is a generating, original, fruitful love. In loving, God distinguished himself: He is lover and beloved, Father and Son according to the language of Christian faith, in the unfathomable essential unity of love, in the uncancellable distinction of him who loving generates and of him who in love is generated.

Paternity is the other property of the Father's love, together with his being the "beginning without beginning."

"By essence he is Father since, in an ineffable manner from an ineffable substance, he generated the Son" (or, according to a variant interpretation: "The Father, ineffable essence, has generated in an ineffable manner the Son of his substance"). "And nevertheless he has not generated other than what he himself is: God has generated God, the light has generated the light. From him, therefore, is 'every fatherhood in heaven and on earth' (Ep 3:15)."[16]

"That through which the person of the Father is distinguished from all others is paternity. Hence the proper name of the person of the Father is this name of Father, which signifies paternity."[17]

God is Father: God is original and originating love in the eternity of his life — ungenerated and generating love, infinite fecundity of gratuitous and eternal love.

In this distinction between Father and Son in the history of eternal love, one is permitted to contemplate the generosity of true love, its going out from itself to the other and its returning to itself in the communion of love. God alienates himself from himself in order to exist in the loved other and to return to himself: this eternal "alienation," this eternal "dispossession" of fontal love which eternally makes room for generated love, is the eternal "kenosis"

of love, of which the Trinitarian consignment of the cross is the
sign which makes this love visible to us, as it were, "through a
mirror, darkly" (1 Cor 13:12). It is the mystery of the origin,
sovereignly free and timeless, of the Son from the Father, the
eternal generation which manifests the overflowing generosity of
the First Love, that sovereign humility, consequent on the
superabundant richness of his love, which is "rooted in the deepest
part of divinity" (Master Eckhart).

d) *The Father and the Spirit*

It is this sovereign and humble generosity of the Origin which
is at the root of the movement of eternal love which overflows, so
to speak, "beyond" the Son. From the love that generates the
Beloved proceeds further love; to love is to transcend the other, nòt
to love the other less but more. It is thus that the love of the Father,
source of the Beloved, the Son, is also the font of a Third in love,
the Spirit. *The Father, who generates the Son, breathes forth
(spirates) the Holy Spirit.*[18]

This further distinction of love has been interpreted by faith-
reflection both in the sense of a real bond of love, received and
given, distinct from the Father inasmuch as received from the Son
and distinct from the Son, inasmuch as given by the Father,[19] and
in the sense of the "co-beloved" in love, of the friend of the Father
and the Son, who signifies the sovereign openness and fruitfulness
of their love.[20]

In the first case the unity of Lover and Beloved is made
evident; and the Spirit appears as the personal bond of their reciprocal communion, of the reconciliation greater than every distinction required even by the truth of love. In the second case, the
openness of the mutual love of Father and Son is elucidated; and the
Spirit emerges as the personal gift of their infinite generosity, the
personal locus where the Trinity makes itself both giver and
receiver.

"In Johannine terms we are speaking of 'God as spirit' when we interpret the separation between Lover and Beloved in such a way that the Lover and the Beloved 'cause each other to participate in' their mutual love. And we equally speak of 'God as spirit' when we interpret the separation which death itself brings about between Lover and Beloved in such a way that, in this most sorrowful separation, the 'one and living' God does not cease to be but rather is thus precisely and supremely God."[21]

The Father, eternal Lover, is the source of the Spirit both as unifying love and as open and receptive love. As unifying love, origin and goal of Trinitarian life, the Father breathes forth the Spirit of unity; as open and receptive love, source of every gift in love, the Father breathes forth the Spirit as gift.[22] *Active spiration* on the Father's part, then, means both the unifying force of original and eternal love and the infinite openness of the generosity of the Father's love.

It is to this aspect that God's "paternity" is bound in regard to all creatures (Ep 3:15), his dominion over heaven and earth, which is connected with the act of creation. It is what the words "I believe in God the Father Almighty, creator of heaven and earth," with which the professions of faith begin,[23] mean.

By means of the Son in the Spirit, the Father is the origin of all things "visible and invisible." From the one eternal source, beginning without beginning, flows not only the eternal life of the love of the Three, but also, by means of the creative act, the life of time, of the world and its history.[24]

In regard to creation, the Fathers' love appears with the same characteristic of pure originality, total freedom and gratuity, of superabundant generosity which characterizes it in divine life. Nothing necessitates God the creator; nothing moves him from without to create. In the perfect freedom of love, he is Father of everything and of all. His fontal love is free and therefore freeing in encounters with his creatures. Whoever creates in freedom, calls to freedom. Who freely gives cannot but will the gratuity of the gift.

One notices here the importance of this intratrinitarian rooted-ness for an exact understanding of the love of the Father toward his creatures. In the "adult world" of the modern era, the emancipa-tion of the father often takes on the character of a sociological liberation from every social authoritarianism, a psychological autonomy from every paralyzing dependency, and finally a metaphysical freedom from every reality which is not worldly.[25]

In the face of this "revolt against the father," the supposed prelude of a "society without fathers,"[26] the proclamation of a heavenly Father who loves in freedom and who is free in love, is the proclamation of a God who does not crush man, who is not in competition with him, who is truly "a God of men,"[27] whose glory is man living in the freedom of love.[28]

In this sense, whoever does not respect the freedom of the sons of God and who does not work with all his might for the liberation of the oppressed cannot acknowledge God as Father. He who is the unbegun beginning of every reality does not recognize enslaving possessiveness. His being "beginning without begin-ning" is at the same time the profound reason for his freedom and for the freedom of his creatures.

This is why only in a Trinitarian reading, where there stand out the initial originality and gratuity and free generosity of the love of the Father, in his distinction from and unity with the Son and the Spirit, does the Father's proclamation appear to man as "good news." Outside Trinitarian faith, a God who is an Omnipotent Father can remain an absolute monarch, a despot who refuses all appeals, the Other on whom the sad and invincible finitude of the human condition depends.

In our contemplation of the Trinitarian mystery, on the con-trary, the Father appears as the First Love, free and freeing, always first in love because he never tires of taking love's initiative, even in the face of the ingratitude and infidelity of his creature. Hence, "God is either understood as Father in the Trinitarian sense or cannot be understood as Father."[29] To him, source and goal of

every love in freedom, his people's act of thanksgiving rises.
Turning to the Father, through the Son in the Spirit, liturgical
prayer marvelously expresses faith in the pure originality of the
Father's love, from which comes every "perfect gift" (Jn 1:17)
and to which, therefore, the "praise of his glory" justly rises (Ep
1:12).

3.2   THE HISTORY OF THE SON

a) *The Easter Account*

The Easter event reveals the story of the Son. It is he who was *handed over* to death out of love for sinners in obedience to the Father (Gal 2:20; Ep 5:2). It is he who rose from the dead (Mk 16:6; Mt 27:64; 28:67; Lk 24:6, 34; 1 Th 4:14), who showed himself alive (Ac 1:3), and who poured out on all flesh the Spirit received from the Father (Ac 2:32ff; Jn 14:16; 15:26).

The active being of the Son, however, is always viewed in relation to the fontal primacy of the Father. His is a "received" existence, totally lived in doing God's will: "Behold, I come . . . O God, to do your will" (Heb 10:9; citation of Ps 40:9). "My food is to do the will of him who sent me and to fulfill his work" (Jn 4:34; cf. 8:29; 15:10). He does not exist for himself but for the Father and for those for whom the Father has sent him.

He does not lose time. He paves the way to the Kingdom of God for which he risks his life (one cannot help but think of the frequency with which the Kingdom of God is cited as an imperative in his life: 109 times in the Synoptics): "Jesus appeared in Galilee proclaiming the good news of God: 'This is the time of fulfillment. The reign of God is at hand! Reform your lives and believe the good news!' " (Mk 1:14).

The Kingdom is the fundamental option of the Nazarene, the

"cause" of his living and his dying.[30] His close, ongoing and irrepeatable relation with the Father, his unique and exclusive filial awareness revealed in a singular fashion by the mystery of his use of the word, *Abba,*[31] mark the whole of his existence right up to the supreme hour of the cross: "Abba, Father! You have the power to do all things. Take this cup away from me. But let it be as you would have it, not as I" (Mk 15:34 and Mt 27:46). "Father, into your hands I commend my spirit" (Lk 23:46).

Jesus lived for the Father, died in obedience to him on the cross for love of those afar, accursed and separated from God, and rose receiving the Father's gift, which he then poured out on all. His obedience to him who "is greater than I" (Jn 14:28) reveals the mystery of his life, to the extent that one of the oldest Christian theologies is "the Christology of the obedient Prophet."

This total relativity to the Father and this profound communion with him, however, did not prevent Jesus from being fully himself, of presenting himself even with an authority and a "claim" which startled and scandalized his contemporaries. Dependence on the Father made him free and freeing.[32]

It is on the basis of this unique and exclusive relationship of Jesus with God the Father that the early community reread the works and life of the Nazarene in the light of Easter and addressed him with the titles which he himself had used with caution or had completely avoided because of the ambiguity which they could have had before the events of Easter.[33]

While he loves to call himself *Son of Man* — the title which, in Daniel 7:13 and especially in the intertestamentary apocalyptic literature (see, for example, *Ethiopian Enoch* 37-41), indicates a being pre-existing in heaven, of divine condition and savior in the end times — he avoids the title of *Messiah* because it has so much political or apocalyptic or legalistic significance, as does that of *Son of God*, which in Judaism used to be the equivalent of the simple idea of "a just man." In the light of Easter, the nascent Church will be able to use these titles, charged now with new and even more profound significance, and will abandon those (like *Son of Man*) which were more restricted to the understanding of a Jewish circle only.

Thus, Jesus is addressed as *Lord*, the equivalent of *Adonai*, the Greek word which in the Septuagint referred to the God of Israel (think of the conclusion of the hymn in Ph 2:6-11:"And every tongue proclaim to the glory of God the Father: JESUS CHRIST IS LORD!" Paul adopts the title at least 85 times in his letters; Acts, 16 times; and 2 Peter, 8).

He is called *Christ*, a title which conveys at once the theological and soteriological quality of one raised up by God, that is, one whose very being is on a par with that of the Father, one who is our savior (Mk 1:1; Mt 1:1; Lk 2:11; Jn 20:31; Ac 2:36; 1 Th 1:1).

He is referred to as *Son*, or *Son of God*, an expression which seems to translate most faithfully the filial experience of the Nazarene as conveyed by his use of the word *Abba*, as well as his paschal condition of being the One living the life of the Father and the Giver of this same life (this title recalls 2 S 7:12-14; Ac 2:30ff; Rm 1:3; Heb 1:5; as well as Ps 2:6; Ac 4:25ff; 13:33; Heb 1:5; in the Synoptics, for example, see Mt 11:27; Lk 10:22; Mk 13:32; *the Son*: Mk 1:11; 9:7 and parallels; *the favorite, loved Son*: Mk 3:11; 5:7; Mt 14:33; 16:16; *Son of God*: Jn 1:14, 18; *the only-begotten Son*: Jn 1:34-49; 5:25; 10:36; 11:4-27; 20:31; the *Son of God* in Paul: Rm 1:3-9; 5:10; 8:29; 1 Cor 1:9; 15:28; 2 Cor 1:19; Gal 1:16; 2:20; 4:4-6; Ep 4:13; 1 Th 1:10; *the Son of God, his Son*: Col 1:13; Christ is *"the Son of his* (God the Father's) *love"*: and, finally, see the formula, *"the Father of our Lord Jesus Christ"* in Rm 15:6; 2 Cor 1:3; 11:31; Ep 1:3; 1 P 1:3; Rv 14:1).

Jesus is further addressed as *the Word*, a term which bespeaks the eschatological fullness of divine revelation and communication made present in the person and the saving work of the Risen One (thus the "word of God" in Col 1:25-27 is the "mystery," "Christ in you, the hope for glory"; in Rv 19:13, "the Word of God" is the eschatological judge; in the Prologue of the Fourth Gospel, the

Word of God, pre-existent and creative, takes on flesh as the Word of salvation, life and light for all people: see Jn 1:1-14; in 1 Jn 1:1-3 the pre-existing Word of life made himself visible to us and the object of our experience).

Jesus is then addressed as *image of the Father*, an expression which makes the pre-existence of the Living One and his being in the world the epiphany of the invisible God (cf. 2 Cor 4:4; Col 1:15 and also Heb 1:3, "the reflection of the Father's glory, the exact representation of the Father's being").

Jesus is *the power and the wisdom of God,* terms in which there re-echoes perhaps the Old Testament personification of divine Wisdom (1 Cor 1:24 and Wis 7:25ff to which Heb 1:3 refers).

Jesus is *God,* a word normally reserved to the Father in the New Testament because Christ is normally thought of in relation to the humble concreteness of the "days when he was in the flesh" (Heb 5:7), and yet sometimes attributed even to him whose divine condition is expressed by the many other titles cited: Jn 1:1, "The Word was God"; 1:18, "Only begotten God," according to a variant; 20:28, "My Lord and my God," Thomas's formula of adoration in which the echo of community worship can already be heard; 1 Jn 5:20, "He is the true God and eternal life"; Rm 9:5, "From them came the Messiah (I speak of his human origins). Blessed forever be God who is over all! Amen"; Tt 2:13 where it speaks of the "glory of our great God and Lord Jesus Christ."

The different titles converge, therefore, in attesting to a double dimension, theological and soteriological, in the Crucified-Risen One, present already in the name "Jesus," which means "God saves" (Lk 1:31-36, in relation to the mystery of God, and Mt 1:21 in relation to the salvation of sinners).

Jesus the Christ pertains, therefore, contemporaneously to the world of God and the world of men. He is their place of encounter and of reciprocal welcome. It is for this reason that with him, especially in Paul, is the theme of *grace* associated, the theme of divine favor in its absolute gratuity of love coming from above and tending to draw men upward in the celebration of divine glory:

"Praised be the God and Father of our Lord Jesus Christ, who has bestowed on us in Christ every spiritual blessing in the heavens! God chose us in him before the world began, to be holy and blameless in his sight, to be full of love. He likewise predestined us through Christ Jesus to be his adopted sons — such was his will and pleasure — that all might praise the glorious favor he has bestowed on us in his beloved" (Ep 1:3-6).

From the Word made flesh, "full of grace and truth . . . we have received grace upon grace" (Jn 1:14-16). Hence the early Church, in the lively experience of the celebration of the mystery, can wish: "*The grace of our Lord Jesus Christ,* the love of God and the communion of the Holy Spirit be with you all" (2 Cor 13:13).

b) *The Beloved Son*

Jesus is the Son of God, the Beloved Son, the Only Begotten. He is the Word, the Word of the Father. These titles, founded on the paschal account, propel the contemplation of faith from the eschatological fullness of the event toward the "deep things of God."

The theology of the pre-existence — developed very soon in the Christian community as the Christological titles and the formulas about the Son's mission attest — already opens a passage through the packed history of revelation in which the grace of divine love for us appeared, to the eternal history of this same love.

How does the Beloved Son of God allow us to delve into the depths of divine life? Which properties may be attributed to him in the eternal experience of Trinitarian love, starting out from his self-revelation in time?[34]

Commencing with the fact that, in the economy, the Son is always relative to the Father, there is evidence of how, in regard to him who is the beginning and the font, Love eternally loving, the

Son is the proceeder, the generated, the eternally loved: He is *the Son, the Word of the Father*.

"We acknowledge also the Son, born without beginning, before the centuries, of the substance of the Father; nevertheless not created, because the Father has never existed without the Son, nor the Son without the Father. And yet, not as the Son is from the Father is the Father from the Son, because the Father has not received generation from the Son but the Son from the Father. The Son is therefore God from the Father. The Father is God, but not from the Son. He is the Father of the Son, not God from the Son. The latter, instead, is Son of the Father and God from the Father."[35]

What characterizes the Son can therefore be gathered from his "birth from another," in *filiation*.[36] If the origin of love is the Father, the receptivity to love is placed in the Son. The Son is pure welcome, the eternal obedience of love. He is "the one loved before the creation of the world" (Jn 17:24), in whom, in time and in eternity, divine life flows, the source of the Father's fullness: "As the Father has life in himself, so too has he given it to the Son to have life in himself" (Jn 5:26).

The eternal Lover is distinguished from the eternal Beloved, proceeding from him through the overflowing fullness of his love. The Son is the other in love, the One on whom rests the movement of the infinite generosity of fontal Love. The Lover is the origin of the Beloved. Love at its source is the font of receiving Love, in the unfathomable unity of eternal love. This process by which the One living in fontal love posits the origin inasmuch as he is the beginning of the One living in receptive love, indissolubly joined to him, can be called *generation*.[37] The eternal act of this process is the eternal birth of the Son, his issue from "the womb of the Father. We must believe that the same Son was not generated or is born from nothing, nor from some substance, but from the womb of the Father (*de Patris utero*); that is, from his substance."[38]

By virtue of this process, this eternal history of Love, the Son is, in his pure receptivity, the divine "poverty" of his reception, he in whom the Father fully communicates and expresses himself, the full expression and communication of the Father, his eternal Word, the Word, the transparent and radiant image of him.[39]

This intratrinitarian history is the immanent root of the revelation that the Father provides of himself to men through the Son, and hence of the mission of the Son:

"The 'procession' of the Son as self-communication of the Father's divine reality is at the same time . . . the economic and free self-communication to Jesus as 'absolute Savior' and the necessary 'immanent' self-communication of the divine reality . . . , the expression of the Father, so that this exists from eternity and by necessity as the Word about such a possible and free self-manifestation to the world."[40]

As love fully received, that is, as Son loved by the Father, the Word, in the process of his eternal generation, is the immanent foundation of God's absolutely free and gratuitous communication of himself realized in creating the world and sending his own Son among men. Only the infinite receptivity of the Son, "by means of which and in view of which everything has been created" (Col 1:16) and who has been loyal to sinners right up to the exile of the curse and the death, approves the reception of the pure gift of being (creation of the world)[41] and of existing fully in love, which is the new life of grace. In the Word we are offered the "grace" of the Father!

c) *Love Is Distinction*

The eternal process of love, which is the generation of the Son, can be further characterized by two aspects, indissolubly joined: namely, distinction from and overcoming the distinction, of separateness and communion, of differentiation and unity.

Eternal love is *distinction*: the Lover is not the Beloved; the

Father is not the Son. Without this separateness, divine love would be the solitude of infinite egoism. This is the saddest thing about any modalistic reduction of the Trinity. Where the proper dignity and the originality of the Beloved are lost, also lost are the dignity and the originality proper to the Lover, and along with it the truth and the power of love. The Father is not a despot who annihilates the Son but is the Father in love! The Son is not a pure inconsistency, an empty form for the personal amusement of the divine Absolute, but is the Beloved, the eternal Son, the Favored One, the Only Begotten.

The receptivity of love has an infinite consistency in God. To accept love is not less personalizing than to give love. To let oneself love is love, and nothing less than to love . . . Even the receiving is divine! This self-limitation of love within itself, as loving Love and loved Love, is necessary for the truth of love. It is in this sense that the eternal generation of the Word responds to an essential requirement, which — as is the case in love, where freedom and necessity coincide by force of the gratuity — also does not involve in any way the free will of the Generating and the Generated.

It is in this separateness that the possibility of the separateness between God and his creatures is rooted, right up to the sad separation of a creatural freedom which may refuse the love of the Creator, with all the reflex of love's suffering which this refusal has in Trinitarian life. If the Son will always be the pure welcome of the Father; if, therefore, the eternal Beloved will always be the joy of him who loves him and the interplay of eternal love will always be a feast without beginning and end, it is not thus for the free creature, freely produced by the love of the Father for the Son.

In creating, Eternal Love has wanted, with infinite generosity, to run the risk of the freedom of the creature capable of refusing love. It is proper to the infinity of Divine Love to go so far as to accept the possibility of another's non-love. But this possible non-love, become a reality in the drama of sin, does not leave the one who loves indifferent. The Lover permits himself to be deeply marked by the other in the separateness of the Beloved, the in-tratrinitarian root of every other separateness.

Love becomes vulnerable. As Thomas a Kempis put it, *"Sine dolore non vivitur in amore"* ("Without sorrow there is no living in love"). Sorrow and love are part and parcel of one another in the interplay of freedom.

"Love signifies a unity which does not absorb the other but accepts the other precisely in his 'otherness,' confirms him thus as he is, and in this way actually establishes him in his true freedom. A love that does not give the other anything but itself means at the same time self-distinction and self-limitation. The lover must withdraw because what he is looking at is not himself but the other. Moreover, the love allows himself to get involved with the other and makes himself vulnerable in his own love. And thus *love and suffering emerge as strictly interconnected.* But the suffering of love is not only a passive involvement, but also actively allowing oneself to get involved. Precisely because he is Love, God can also suffer and thus reveal his own divinity."[42]

The sign of this free vulnerability of eternal love, of this divine sorrow for the non-love of the freely loved creature is the cross of the Son of God. The history of the passion, as history of the handing over which the Only Begotten does of himself and which the Father does of him, abandoning him to death for love of sinners, is the revelation of the mystery of God's suffering. God suffers! The Father suffers because of the "no" of the loved creature and throws a feast on his return (cf. Lk 15:11ff., the parable of the mercy of the Father of the two unfaithful sons). The Son suffers in solidarity with those who have exiled themselves from God (cf. Mk 12:1ff., the parable of the murderous vinedressers and of the Favorite Son sent for love of them).

This divine suffering is not in any way a limiting sign, passive suffering, which is undergone because of the finitude of being. It is, on the contrary, active suffering which reveals the fullness of being in love because it is freely accepted in the infinite generosity of creative and redemptive love. God suffers because he loves his creatures. The intra-divine condition of this possibility of suffering is the "distinction" between Father and Son, expression of infinite superabundance and of the radical fruitfulness of eternal love.

"The intra-divine eternal distinction of Father and Son is the theological-transcendental condition of the possibility of God's self-alienation in the incarnation and on the cross. And this is not speculation, however interesting, but serves to tell us that from all eternity there is in God a place for man."[43]

If God suffers, suffering no longer justifies any objection against him. He suffers with those who suffer because he loves them. And if sorrow is radically the fruit of a history of freedom which has refused love, it is redeemed (even if not divinized!) by the superabundant richness of God's compassionate love. Divine suffering is admissible, then, only in the light of the Trinity. It is not the suffering of one undifferentiated God, but suffering *in* God, the suffering of the Father who loves, and of his Only-Begotten Son, handed over to sorrow and to death out of love for sinners, the suffering of love in eternal history.[44]

In this history of suffering love — the expression of the infinite divine freedom in love — even the Spirit has a place, the Paraclete of the Trinitarian suffering of God and hence of the suffering of the world. The Spirit, proceeding from the Father, unites the Generated to the Generating, showing how the uncancelable distinction of love is not separation. He is the communion of Lover and Beloved which guarantees also the communion of the eternal Lover with his creatures and with their stories of suffering, not by prescinding from the Beloved but precisely in him and through him. The Spirit guarantees that the unity is stronger than the distinction and eternal joy is stronger than the sorrow provoked by the non-love of creatures.

Poured out on the Crucified on Easter, he reconciles the Father with the Abandoned One of Good Friday and in him with the passion of the world. He is the Spirit of unity, consolation, peace and joy. The "common spiration" of the Father and of the Son means that their distinction is assumed in the highest unity of the love which proceeds from the Father and, coming to rest and reflecting itself in the Son, returns to its Origin without origin. Therefore, the Father remains the beginning; the Son, the expression; the Spirit, their personal bond in the movement of eternal love.

d) *Love Is Unity*

If this love is distinction, it is no less *unity*. Divine history overcomes the distinct in the infinite depth of the Trinitarian communion. This unity is built above all on an essential level. By affirming that the Son is consubstantial with the Father, the Council of Nicea (325) defended the parity in divine being between one and the other against every subordinationistic reduction.[45]

"The Son is equal in everything to God the Father because he neither began ever to be born nor ceases to be. We also believe he is of the same substance as the Father for which he is even spoken of as *homoousios,* that is, of the same substance as the Father. . . . The Father is eternal and the Son is eternal. Because if the Father always was, so always was the Son of whom he was the Father. And for this reason we acknowledge that the Son is born of the Father without beginning. Not for the fact of being generated by the Father do we call this same Son particle of the divine nature; but we assert that the perfect Father has generated the perfect Son without diminution, division, because it is proper to divinity alone not to have an unequal Son. This Son of God, then, is Son by nature, not by adoption; and one needs to believe that God the Father did not generate him by will or necessity because in God there is no necessity, and will does not precede wisdom."[46]

The Son who is next to the Father from the beginning (cf. Jn 1:1), in the bosom of the Father (cf. Jn 1:18), is one with him: "The Father and I are one" (Jn 10:30).

It is this most profound unity which the Son makes accessible to men with his incarnation, passion, death and resurrection:

"That all may be one, as you, Father, are in me, and I in you; I pray that they may be one in us, that the world may believe that you sent me. I have given them the glory you gave me that they may be one, as we are one — I living in them, you living in me — that their unity may be complete. So shall the world know that you sent me, and that you loved them as you loved me . . . To them I have revealed your name, and I will continue to reveal it so that your love for me may live in them, and I may live in them" (Jn 17:21-26).

The eternal Lover and the eternal Beloved are one in the unity of eternal love! This, their unfathomable unity, is the beginning, the foundation and the end of every unity in the heavens and on earth. It is not dead, static, and undifferentiated unity but the living unity of the eternal movement of divine love which is distinguished from, and surpasses, the distinct in a dynamism without pause.

"Amor est in via": The unity of love is a perennial pilgrimage of love, a perennial going forth and coming back, ebb and flow (*exitus et reditus*), departure and arrival, distinction and communion. Without this unity the Son would not be God like the Father; and divine love could not issue from self into the other than the self while remaining infinitely one with itself. Without unity, the separateness of the Father and the Son would mark off the abyss between God who is love and the other, necessarily inferior and subordinate to him.

On the one hand, fontal Love would reach the point of distancing itself in an unreachable solitude. On the other, the Loved would no longer be one with the Father in divine life and could not give us access to the mystery of the beginning.

Here is where the poverty of every form of subordinationism lies, every Arian temptation which rends the unity of eternal love and our unity with God in the name of a presumed purity of the divinity and the "otherness" of God. In reality there is no other divinity of God than the eternal love of the Father and the Son in the Spirit. There is no other divine "otherness" than that of the distinction between Lover and Beloved in the unity of love, of which we have been made participants by pure grace. This perfect unity and co-eternity of the Son and the Father, by force precisely of its inexhaustible vitality is not exhausted in the interplay of love. It is open-ended unity, the generous love of two, a unity which, making room in itself for the distinction of the Beloved, makes room also for others in love.

We derive here the other role of the Spirit in the intratrinitarian and the economic rapport between the Father and the Son. Just as in regard to their distinction he is the personal bond of communion, distinct from one and the other because given by one and received by the other, other than the Father because received by the Son and other than the Son because given by the Father, so too, in reference to their communion, he is the "*condilectus*," the beloved of the Son and distinct from the Son because friend of the Father.

In this sense the "*communis spiratio*," like the eternal movement which reaches the Son from the Father and through the Son reaches the Spirit, in whom the Father loves the Son in the Spirit, and the Son receives from the Father the love with which to love him in the same Spirit, means the opening of Trinitarian love, its pure oblativity.

This is why in the economy God emerges from himself always in the Spirit, both in the origins of creation ("The Spirit of God swept over the waters . . . ," Gn 1:2) and in the beginnings of the redemption ("The Holy Spirit will descend upon you . . . ," Lk 1:35; Mt 1:20; "And, coming out of the water, he saw the heavens open up and the Spirit descend on him like a dove," Mk 1:10 and parallels) and in its completion (the Crucified is raised up by God "with power according to the Spirit of holiness," Rm 1:4).

"The Christian figure of God is Trinitarian. It breaks the circle of the Father-Son relationship with another image, that of the Breath or the Spirit."[47] In this sense the Spirit fulfills the truth of divine love, showing how true love is never a jealous shutting off or possessiveness, but openness, a gift, a breaking out of the circle of the two.

He "shatters the possible sufficiency of the 'face to face' of the first two figures. Christian tradition has identified with him a creative and dynamic role. He is the One who raises other differences. He is the opening up of divine communion to what is not divine. He is God's habitation where God, in a certain sense, is 'outside himself.' Because of this he was called 'love.' He is the ecstasy of God toward his 'other' — the creature."[48]

In the Spirit the Lover and the Beloved "open themselves up," in the immanence of the mystery and in the economy of salvation. Insofar as he is "beyond" the Son in the unfathomable unity of love, the Spirit is also the personal locus in which divine history passes over into human history, and vice versa.

3.3   THE HISTORY OF THE SPIRIT

a) *The Easter Account*

The Easter event reveals the history of the Spirit.[49] It is in him that the Son is offered to the Father in the hour of the cross (cf. Heb 9:14) when, as the supreme fulfillment of love, "he *delivered over his spirit*" (Jn 19:30). It is in him that the Father gave fullness of life to the Crucified, raising him up and reconciling the world to himself in the Risen One (cf., for example, Rm 1:4). These two functions of the Spirit — *making* the world of God *accessible* to the world of men to the point of enabling the Son's entry into the exile of sinners, and *bringing together into one* those who were cut off as took place in the hour of paschal reconciliation — are to be found over and over again throughout the history of salvation.

Even in the Old Testament, the Spirit (*ruah*), inasmuch as it proceeds from the living God (cf. Gn 1:2; Ps 33:6 and 104:29ff; Ws 1:7; 7:22 - 8:1), is the principle of life which opens up to the new and brings unity to the life process.

To the Spirit is connected the inspiration of the prophets who shape the future history of Israel and constantly recall the people to faithfulness to the Covenant (Nb 11:25; 24:2; 27:18; 1 S 10:6; 19:24; Is 61:1; Ezk 2:2; 3:24; Zc 7:12; 1 P 1:11 and 2 P 1:21). Messianic time is awaited as a time of the outpouring of the Spirit, the bearer of the eschatological future and of the new life with the living God (cf., for example, Is 11:2; 32:15ff; 42:1; Ezk 11:19; 18:31; 36:27; 37:1-14; Jl 3:1), just as the time of exile is by contrast marked by the absence of the Spirit, a time in which the future seems closed off and Israel is scattered (cf., for example, the meditation on the history of Israel in Is 63:7 - 64:11; and, in particular, 63:10).

The same Spirit is called the "Spirit of holiness" (Ps 51:13; Ws 9:17), an expression taken from the Septuagint with "*Holy Spirit*" (Dn 5:12; 6:3; Ws 1:5; 7:22), an adjective that refers to the most intimate characteristic of the living God (Ho 11:9; Ps 99:3).

According to the witness of the early Church, the Spirit of God acts in the whole life and work of Jesus of Nazareth. In this regard there is mention of a "Christology of the Spirit," not opposed to but integrating itself with the "Christology of the Word."[50]

Jesus *receives* the Spirit: in his virginal conception in Mary (Mt 1:18-20; Lk 1:35), in his baptism (Mk 1:10 and parallels), in the works and in the days of his life (Mk 1:12ff; Mt 12:28; Lk 4:14-18, etc.). Right up to his glorious resurrection, Jesus appears as the Anointed of the Spirit, the Messiah, the Christ.

In the Spirit "who proceeds from the Father" (Jn 15:26), the Son of God runs the course toward "otherness," from Trinitarian history to human history, even to imbibing the bitter chalice of deliverance for sinners. In the Spirit the estrangement of God out of love for the world — the most profound opening into human experience imaginable for the divine life, the salvific "*exitus*" of God into the history of the "godless" — is fulfilled. The same Spirit is then poured out by the Father in the paschal hour so that reconciliation may be effected, the "*reditus*," the return to the promised divine homeland which sinners — those with whom the Son had made himself one — will now be able to enter.

It is Christ himself who receives from the Father the handing over of the Spirit (see Jn 14:26). He then *pours it out* on every living person (Lk 24:49 and Ac 2:32; also see the Pauline texts on the

Spirit of Christ: Rm 8:9; Ph 1:19; and of the Lord: 2 Cor 3:17; of the Son: Gal 4:6; and, finally, the texts on the "Christology of the Word," in which the Spirit is seen in a functional relationship to the Christ whose work he accomplishes: e.g., Jn 14:26 - 15:26; 16:12-15, etc.).

Thus we participate in the life of the Trinitarian fellowship or communion through a communion proper to the present time (cf. the constant action of the Spirit in the Church according to the theology of Acts, the "gospel of the Spirit": Ac 2:1-13 and 16-21; 4:25-41; 8:14-17; 10:44-48; 11:15-17; 19:1-6). At the same time the whole of history is open in the Spirit to the future of God (Rm 8); and all of us are given access to the Father, to whom in the Spirit we can now turn as adoptive children, calling him "Abba" (Rm 8:15, 26ff; Gal 4:6), while there is offered to us the freedom of living in love, of journeying in the Spirit (Gal 5:13-25).

The down payment on future benefits (cf. Rm 8:23; 2 Cor 1:22; 5:5; Ep 1:14), the Spirit, in the richness and the variety of his gifts (cf. 1 Cor 12:4-30), of which the greatest of these is love (1 Cor 13:13), inspires and increases the unity of the Church Body in which Trinitarian unity is reflected: "There are different gifts but the same Spirit; different ministries but the same Lord; there are different works but the same God who accomplishes all of them in everyone" (1 Cor 12:4-6).

Even though the Spirit is never called "Love" in the witness of the New Testament — a term referred rather to God the Father (Jn 3:16; Rm 5:5; 2 Cor 13:13; 1 Jn 3:1; 4:8, 16), so much so that the "lack of a single word on the love of the Holy Spirit strikes one almost sadly"[51] — the Spirit is actually the one *who opens in freedom and unifies in love*. The Spirit is the spirit of liberty (2 Cor 3:17), of the truth that makes us free (Jn 14:17; 15:26; and 16:13 in relation to 8:32). It is the Holy Spirit through whom "the love of God has been poured out into our hearts" (Rm 5:5). And it is not by chance that in the liturgical greeting of the early Church, the *koinonia* is referred to the Spirit: "The grace of the Lord Jesus

Christ, the love of God the Father and the *fellowship* (or communion) *of the Holy Spirit* be with you all" (2 Cor 13:13).

b) *The "Filioque"*

The Spirit is, therefore, the one who *opens up* the world of
God to the world of men, human history to Trinitarian history. At
the same time, the Spirit is the one who *joins* the two worlds and
brings about unity among men in the love of the Father and the Son.
These facts allow the contemplation of faith to embark on the road
toward a deeper understanding of the mystery. How does the
history of the Spirit appear in the depths of God? Which properties
can be acknowledged as his in the immanence of the Trinitarian life
from the viewpoint of the economy of revelation?[52]

The answer to these questions is tied in with the discussion —
which has pitted the theological traditions of the East against those
of the West and which continues to be a lively topic today — in
regard to the formula added in the West to the Nicene-Constantinopolitan Symbol to affirm the procession of the Spirit from the
Father *and* the Son: the *Filioque* ("We believe . . . in the Holy
Spirit, the Lord and Giver of life, who proceeds from the Father
and from the Son").[53]

aa) *The Present Situation and Its History*

That the question is regarded as having great significance
even today is shown by the variety of positions taken on it among
the most significant representatives of current theology. From
denial to defense, from critical acceptance to critical tolerance,
nothing has been spared the *Filioque*.

Vladimir Lossky sees in it the root of all the debates between
Orthodoxy and Roman Catholicism, the dogmatic "diriment impediment" to communion between the two Churches. His rejection

is complete, severe: According to him the *Filioque,* affirming two principles in the Trinity, compromises the Father's monarchy and hence dissolves both the divine unity founded on it, and the Trinity of Persons which is related to it. His is the vigorous resumption of the thesis of Photius, who — against the arguments of the Latins — had wanted to demonstrate the necessity that "the Spirit proceeds from the Father alone."[54]

The consequences of the theology of the *Filioque* on Western Christianity would be enormous and dramatic. By affirming the dependence of the Spirit on the Son, Roman Catholicism would be able to subordinate charism to the institution, interior freedom to imposed authority, prophetism to juridicism, the mystical to the Scholastic, the laity to the clergy, the universal priesthood to the ministerial hierarchy and, finally, the episcopal college to the primacy of the pope![55]

Sergei Boulgakov admits that he does not share this radical thesis. "It was natural to expect," he writes in his work on the Paraclete,[56] "that the presence of so essential a heresy or of a primordial dogmatic divergence should have penetrated the life of the two Churches and all their doctrine. Over many long years, I myself have done my best to find the traces of this influence. I have sought to understand what was involved, what the *vital* importance of this divergence was, where and in what it showed itself *practically*. I confess that I have not succeeded and am not succeeding in finding it; moreover, I shall end up by simply denying it."

And, at the end of a close analysis of the question, he says decisively: "The *Filioque* does not constitute a 'diriment impediment' to the restoration of the unity of the divided Church."[57] The centuries of controversy appear to him rather as a true scandal: "In the history of dogma, there does not exist an example of analysis more foreign to the wish of the Holy Spirit than the controversy over the Spirit."[58]

Boulgakov's position duplicates that of the Russian Church historian, B. Bolotov. In his famous theses on the *Filioque,*[59] the latter distinguishes between "dogma" which concerns what is true and which requires an obligatory adherence of faith, *"theologoumenon"* which refers to the probable and does not have absolute authority, and "theological opinions," which are of concern mainly to theologians. He then qualifies the procession of the Spirit from the Father as "dogma" (thesis 1), Photius' addition "from the Father *alone*" as "theologoumenon" (thesis 7), and the addition of "and from the Son" as "theological opinion" (thesis 27). In this light the *Filioque* cannot be an insurmountable obstacle to the union among divided Christians.

This critically tolerant position, moreover, is tied in with that great theological edifice of the East: the synthesis of Gregory Palamas. This synthesis distinguishes in God the plane of existence from that of uncreated energies and affirms that the Holy Spirit proceeds "from the Father alone" as far as existence goes but his energies proceed from the Father through the Son or even from the Father and from the Son.[60]

In this way, even though excluding the *Filioque* on the plane of the Holy Trinity's existence, Palamas's interpretation allows it some reception on the level of the manifestation — both eternal and historical — of the divine Persons because at this level (that of Trinitarian activity or of "uncreated energies") the monarchy of the Father, from which everything flows through the Son in the Spirit, remains untouched.

That these positions cannot be shared — or perhaps really understood — in Western theological tradition appears to be demonstrated by the strenuous defense of the *Filioque* proposed by Karl Barth.[61] It is motivated by Barthian Christological radicalism in which everything that comes from the Father or goes to Him must pass through the Son:

"It is in the eternal mystery of God's being that one must seek the reason why no one can come to the Father except through the Son, because the Spirit by which the Father attracts men to himself is from all eternity also the Spirit of the Son and it is by means of the

Spirit that the Father enables us to participate in divine filiation in Christ. If Western Christianity has been right in acknowledging that the Holy Spirit attested to in revelation is none other than the Spirit of Christ, and if, acting thus, it has truly known how to proclaim the eternal God thus as it pleases him to meet us, we must without hesitation join the West in the struggle it has sustained to have the *Filioque* accepted."[62]

The formula, with all it signifies, becomes then a bulwark against every approach to the Father which does not pass through Jesus Christ. What this means, even politically, is shown by the First Thesis of the Theological Declaration of Barmen used by Barth against the Christian-Germans willed by Hitler:

"Jesus Christ, as he is witnessed to in Sacred Scripture on our behalf, is the one Word of God which we must heed and to whom we owe trust and obedience in life as in death. We reject as false the doctrine according to which the Church, as the fount of his message, can and must acknowledge, beyond and alongside this unique Word of God, still other events and powers, figures and truths as God's revelation."[63]

The *Filioque* thus becomes not only the sign of dogmatic truth but also of the Church's political freedom!

Not all Westerners, though, agree with this Barthian defense of the formula.[64] Apart from the disinterest of many in a question which seems foreign to the dramatic reality of the life of the Churches, there is a criticism which considers the *Filioque* an inadequate solution to a very real problem,[65] as there is the more radical one which — denouncing a kind of Western Christological monism to the detriment of pneumatology — views as deriving from the *Filioque* an ecclesiology and an anthropology which are completely iniquitous to the primacy of freedom and grace.[66] The *Filioque* would thus be a sign of a "Latin perversity" in theology consisting especially in a pneumatological loss from which it must be rescued.

The passion of denial, as that of defense, the enduring criticism, as well as the uneasiness among many in the West, show how the *Filioque* engenders questions which go well beyond simple word play and academic dispute with no practical application. It is into various and deeply complex levels that one must look in order to find, beyond possible solutions, the ultimate sense of the problem. At stake is not simply a formula but the need — noted by adversaries and advocates alike — of linking the doctrine of the Trinity more closely to the lived experience of the Church.[67]

The *Filioque* was not formally added to the Nicene-Constantinopolitan Symbol before 1014 when Pope Benedict VIII decided to condescend to the wishes of Emperor Henry II who was to be crowned by him, and inserted into the celebration of the Eucharist at Rome the Creed with the Latin interpolation.[68] The formula goes back much further, even to the fourth century. The doctrine in various modes is present in many of the Fathers, even the Greeks.[69]

Augustine took it up completely,[70] founding on the economy his theology of the eternal procession of the Spirit from the Father and the Son.[71] "Passionate by nature, Augustine always favored charity . . . Very soon he called the Spirit, *charitas*. The first indication of his interest in a theology of the Holy Spirit leaned toward this idea."[72] "The divine persons are three: the first who loves the person born of him, the second who loves the person from whom he is born, and the third who is love itself."[73]

However, even the God-Trinity is love; how can charity be proper to and characteristic of the Holy Spirit? The Spirit is the one who gives charity, as the economy attests, and hence — in God — is the love given and received, the "communion" of the Father and of the Son, proceeding from one and the other, even if *principally* from the Father because all that the Son has comes from the Father.

Following in Augustine's footsteps, the West accepted the *Filioque*. The formula was included in the recitation of the Creed in the liturgy in Spain (end of the sixth century; cf. the 3rd Council of Toledo, 589: DS 470), in England and then, through the efforts of Alcuin, at the court of Charlemagne and throughout the Empire.

Although he defended the doctrine in the controversy that arose in Jerusalem in 810 between Greek and Latin monks, Leo III firmly refused to add anything to the Symbol and even had the text in Greek and in Latin without interpolation inscribed on two silver tablets erected on the sides of the entrance to the confession of St. Peter.[74]

Thus, right up to the eleventh century it can be said that the Churches of the East and West remained in communion between themselves despite the two diversified traditions in Trinitarian theology and even though in the West there was acknowledgment of the procession of the Spirit from the Father and the Son.

The letter of St. Maximus the Confessor to the priest Marinus in 655 is a clear example of this communion in diversity and of the effort to achieve mutual understanding:

"Basing themselves on the testimony of the Fathers, (the Romans) have shown that they did not make of the Son the Cause of the Spirit. They know, in fact, that the Father is the one Cause of the Son and of the Holy Spirit, of the one by generation, of the other by procession (*ekporeusis*), but that the Father manifested this procession by means of him the Son thus showing the unity and identity of the essence."[75]

Communion in diversity was possible because the West has never wished to deny the monarchy of the Father! In the decrees of the Councils of union — Lyons (1274) and Florence (1439) — even though the Latins had persuaded the Orthodox to acknowledge the *Filioque* without making any concessions to them in return, the basic intent of affirming the monarchy of the Father, which constitutes the truth of Eastern monopatrism, was respected.[76]

While admitting the unilateral objective of its insertion into the Symbol on the part of the West, it cannot at the same time be said that its insertion goes against the disposition of the Council of Ephesus (431) which forbade the profession or the formulation of a faith different from that of Nicea,[77] not its eventual clarification.

From the historical point of view, three points stand out in all of this:
1. The insertion of the *Filioque* was certainly a unilateral gesture;
2. nonetheless this formula expresses a doctrine and a practice which were widespread in the West and which for centuries did not prevent communion with the East because,
3. faith in the monarchy of the Father has always remained common to both East and West.

The historical sense of the controversy over the *Filioque* is not to be sought in a split over dogma but rather in the progressive incapacity of two different worlds of life and thought, two different experiences of the living God, to dialogue with one another and reach an understanding through a reciprocal and beneficial receiving from one another which is the image of the mutual receiving of the three divine Persons. Paradoxically, the Trinitarian controversy between East and West mirrors the perennial struggle to reflect in concrete historical relationships the image of the Triune and One God, in whom Christians must always newly seek inspiration as source, model and goal.

bb) *The Theological Problem*

This brief run-down of the history of the insertion of the *Filioque* in the Symbol requires an explanation of the theological question underlying the process which led to the ultimate profession of the formula. Why did Augustine and the other Fathers of the Church, why did the "*lex orandi*" of the West (which is also the "*lex credendi*"), feel the need to affirm the *Filioque*? What was the urgency on the part of the faith, and hence the theological motivation, which guided them but which, at the same time, was so little comprehended by the Christians of the East?

The starting point of an elaboration of the theology of the *Filioque* lies in the silence of the Nicene-Constantinopolitan Symbol regarding the relationship between the Son and the Spirit.

The Son is related to the Father by way of eternal generation; the Spirit is likewise related to the Father by way of procession; the relationship between the Only Begotten and the Paraclete, however, remains shrouded in silence. The struggle against the Pneumatomachs, who tended to subordinate the Spirit to the Son, perhaps justifies this silence historically. But there remains the problem of the biblically attested and theologically decisive relationship between the Second and Third Persons of the Trinity.

In the New Testament reciprocity and complementarity between Christ and the Spirit is affirmed. The Easter Trinitarian rereading, bringing to light the presence of the Three by recalling the days of the Nazarene, shows the work of the Spirit in that time. Likewise, in the awareness of the early Church, it is in the Spirit that Christ is living and it is the Spirit that he pours out in fullness on every person, thus fulfilling the expectation of the eschatological time of God's new intervention for the sake of his people. Christ receives and gives the Spirit. His mission can, therefore, be described this way: "When you see the Spirit descend and rest on someone, it is he who is to baptize with the Holy Spirit" (Jn 1:33).

The Christology of the Word — which sees the Paraclete accomplishing the work of Christ, and that of the Spirit — which sees Christ as the Anointed of the Spirit, are (as has been said) both present and working in New Testament witness. By basing themselves on the texts of the former, the West elaborated the doctrine of the *Filioque*:

"The Spirit will give glory to me, because he will have received from me what he will announce to you. All that the Father has belongs to me. That is why I said that what he will announce to you he will have from me" (Jn 16:14ff). "Then he breathed on them and said: 'Receive the Holy Spirit. If you forgive men's sins, they are forgiven them; if you hold them bound, they are held bound' " (Jn 20:22).

These texts — together with expressions like "the Spirit of the Son" (Gal 4:6) and images such as that of the water issuing from the throne of God and the Lamb (Rv 22:1: the Spirit is seen in the water; see Jn 4:10ff; 7:37, 39; and Rv 21:6) — refer to the economy.

This view holds true also for the text which is the biblical reference for the procession of the Spirit from the Father: "When the Paraclete comes, the Spirit of truth who comes from the Father — and whom I myself will send from the Father — he will bear witness on my behalf" (Jn 15:26).[78]

The same passage from the economy to "theology" which the Symbol expressed through the procession of the Spirit from the Father, the Latins accomplished through the procession "even from the Son." It remains true, however, that apart from the biblical texts adopted to provide the basis for the *Filioque* — all of them drawn from the category of the Christology of the Word — there exists evidence proper to a Christology of the Spirit.

It is from this that the question is raised whether the relationship between the Son and the Spirit can only be expressed in one direction — from the Son to the Spirit, or whether the reciprocity and the interaction between them which is fully attested to in the New Testament, might not need further investigation.

In other words, does the *Filioque* not guarantee a kind of dominance to the Christology of the Word to the detriment of that of the Spirit? Or, more generally put, does it not lead to a kind of subordination of pneumatology to Christology?

It is a fact that the West, which affirmed the *Filioque*, has been characterized in its theological development by a kind of Christomonism.[79] The incarnational aspects of the Christian mystery, its visible dimensions, have been given privileged status in the conception and the practice of the Church, in its sacraments as well as its spiritual and moral life, to the detriment of the invisible depths of the experience of grace.

The value and the limits of the theology of the *Filioque* can be clearly seen from all of this. The theology answers a real need. It is biblically based and significant for the overall faith of the believer because it defines more precisely the relationship between the Son and the Spirit. All the same, this theology meets this need only part way because it does not sufficiently show the reciprocity existing between the two Persons. Nor is this reciprocity better expressed by the formula "*per Filium*" which is used in different theological contexts, from Byzantium to modern Western theology.

John Damascene writes: "The Spirit is the Spirit of the Father . . . but he is also the Spirit of the Son, not because he precedes him but because he proceeds *by means of him (dia)* from the Father since there is a single unique Cause, namely the Father."[80]

The Council of Florence, in relating the Western position to the theology of the *Filioque* and the Eastern one to the theology of the *per Filium,* wanted to affirm the compatibility and the equivalence of the two formulations, even their complementarity, based on the use the Fathers make of both one and the other.[81]

This is doubtless true if the intention of both formulas (clear in the *per Filium*) is to indicate a role of the Son, respectful of the Father's monarchy, in the procession of the Spirit. However, even the *per Filium* — apart from the criticisms which consider the role of the Son, a strictly instrumental one, as too weak[82] — does not reveal the interaction which, on the level of the economy is seen to exist between Christ and the Paraclete.

The problem, then, of the eternal relations, which are not relationships of origin (that is, between Son and Spirit), and the related question of the relationship between Christology and pneumatology have not found in the controversy over the *Filioque* explanations, either in the East or in the West, which are satisfactory. The meaning of the question concerning the procession of the Spirit is, therefore, still alive.

The silence of the Symbol on the relationship between the Son and the Spirit, compared with the New Testament witness regarding the interaction between Christ and the Paraclete, is still an open question which embraces many aspects of vital importance to the life of every Christian. Both the visible exaggerations of Christomonism and the Pentecostal and charismatic excesses call for a greater in-depth study of the relationship between Christology and pneumatology, as well as a fuller Trinitarian reading of the whole Christian mystery. The *Filioque* thus acquires an almost apophatic theological value. It makes sense not so much for what it says (and what it says has value), but for what it hints at and what it does not say.

The theological question remands us to the linguistic formulation it has received. Even on this level — one of great importance for the reciprocal understanding between culturally different worlds like the East and the West — the *Filioque* shows partiality. This can be gathered from a comparison between the Greek and the Latin texts of the Symbol of 381: *(pisteuomen) eis to pneuma to agion . . . to ek patros ekporeuomenon; (credo) in Spiritum Sanctum . . . qui ex Patre (Filioque) procedit.*[83]

The key word is *ekporeuomenon* in Greek, *procedit* in Latin. It must be said immediately that the two terms are perfectly equivalent.

Ekporeuomai, which the Symbol has taken from Jn 15:26, connotes issuing from the primary source, the absolute origin.[84] The verb's root is *poros*, meaning "passage," "ford," and *poreuo*, meaning "to allow passage," which is reenforced by the preposition of origin, *ek.* The middle form accentuates this value of source or origin of the express act of the verb.

The Latin word, *procedere*, has much less force. It indicates "to go forward," "to be developed" by an ongoing or continuous process. It derives from *cedere,* meaning "to move oneself," "to make room," "to retire," and the prefix, *pro,* which signifies "ahead." The form, *procedere* then, means to advance by opening a space between that from which we are distancing ourselves and to which we remain bound by the act of moving on. The idea is not one of issuing from the primary source of origin but of moving away from some starting point.

The Greek equivalent of *procedere* is *prochorein*, which has the same meaning as the Latin term. It is interesting to note in this regard how the Trinitarian term *circumcessio* corresponds to the Greek *perichoresis*, which does not indicate the relationship of origin but the reciprocal inhabitation of the divine Persons. *Ekporeuomai* and *procedere,* then, are not only not equivalent but they evoke different types of acts, the first original and absolute, the second acts proper to ongoing and continuous development.[85]

More than *processio,* the term *productio* might be better able to convey the relationship of origin connoted by the Greek *ekporeuomai.* The Latin does not succeed, in sum, in expressing the value the Greeks attribute correctly to the verb used in Jn 15:26. Therefore, while in Greek the formula "even from the Son" sounds like an attack on the monarchy of the Father, the unique origin and source of the Trinity, the same cannot be said of the Latin "*ex Patre Filioque procedit.*" It was St. Thomas himself who perceived the importance of this linguistic difference: "*Aliquid enim inconvenienter in lingua latina dicitur quod propter proprietatem idiomatis convenienter in lingua graeca dici potest.*" ("There are some things easier said in Greek than in Latin on account of the peculiar nature of the idiom.")[86]

Then, if account is taken of the correspondence in meaning between *procedere* and the Greek verbs *proiemi-procheomai,* used by the Fathers to indicate the mission in the world,[87] one could conclude that while the Greek version of the Symbol refers to the eternal relationship of origin between the Father and the Spirit, as shown also by the substitution of the preposition *para* of the Johannine text with *ek,* the Latin *procedere* has a greater sense of indeterminateness. Used with *Filioque,* the verb would express the mission of the Spirit apart from the Son, evoking only an intratrinitarian foundation for it, even though if joined to the Father, it recalls the idea of eternal generation conveyed by the Greek.

A similar "asymmetrical" reading of the Latin *procedere,* that is, different in relation to the Father and in relation to the Son, is not philologically without basis and could be acceptable even to the advocates of the Palamite distinction between existence and energy for whom the procession of the Spirit on the level of existence is from the Father alone while on the level of uncreated energies it can also be from the Father through the Son or from the Father and from the Son.

Benedict XIV, even because of this difference in meaning between the two languages, affirmed in his May 26, 1742 Bull, *"Etsi pastoralis,"* that the *Filioque* is not obligatory for Catholics of the Oriental Rite. Analogously, the liturgy in Greek of Roman Catholics does not include this formula. [88]

As one can easily guess, many of the equivocations which are in the controversy over the *Filioque* were owing to this linguistic difference. This fact reminds us of the relativity and provisional quality of every formulation dealing with the mystery of the Trinitarian God: *"Actus autem credentis non terminatur ad enuntiabile, sed ad rem."* ("The act of the believer does not terminate with the utterable, but with the object of the utterance.")[89]

In particular, the question of the *Filioque* puts us on our guard against the facile use of general terms in this area (such as *processio,* for example). In speaking of the immanent Trinity, we must not "concretize" but be concrete. It is necessary to narrate more than to deal in abstractions.

"Orthodoxy," says Moltmann writing of the *Filioque*, "has its foundation in narrative differentiation. At the heart of Christian theology, there is the eternal history which constitutes God one and triune in himself. Every narration needs *time*. To say that God is one and three, man must take his time. And this is more in keeping with the eternal presence of God than with the abstract concept which dissolves in time and does no more than suggest an intemporal eternity."[90]

Even in the linguistic sphere, the *Filioque*, then, is a sign of the process of investigation into that ulteriority of meaning which must always be sought in our speaking about God.

cc) *The Prospects*

At the root of the East-West controversy over the *Filioque*, there is not, however, only the more or less marked perception of a theological problem — that of the relationship between the Son and the Spirit — nor only a difference in language. One can affirm more radically that there is a difference in ways of thinking, a variety of approaches to the mystery. This diversity constitutes the hermeneutical level of the problem of the *Filioque* in which two worlds are compared, two forms of spiritual experience, two "paradigms" of theologizing. The terms of the difference are discoverable in the diverse way of understanding the relationship between the economic Trinity and the immanent Trinity, between the "*Deus revelatus*" and the "*Deus absconditus*."

"The diversity between East and West in what concerns the introduction of the *Filioque* into the Nicene-Constantinopolitan Symbol expresses the difference in relationship at the cognitive level between the economic Trinity and the immanent Trinity."[91]

The East tends to distinguish economy from theology. Heir to Greek thought, it certainly does not give up the resources of reason; it rather circumscribes them in the face of the transcendence of the Christian God, affirming the incomprehensibility and the unspeakability of the mystery. John Chrysostom wrote a tract on the incomprehensibility of God.[92] The pages of the *Life of Moses* by Gregory of Nyssa are a hymn to the inaccessibility of divinity.[93] The negative theology of Pseudo-Dionysius the Areopagite has influenced the Christian soul enormously.[94]

This strong sense of divine transcendence led, on the one hand, to the exaltation of the monarchy of the Father, from whom every gift comes and who is the source of Trinitarian unity, and, on the other, to the denial of the identification between the historical revelation of the triune God and his immanent and inaccessible mystery. The bridge is knowledge based on faith. Time's outermost edge is not eternity. The mystery in its totality is unfathomable. What we know about the sovereign and transcendent God is not exhausted by what revelation allows us to acknowledge. This is the root of the contemplative and adoring spirit proper to the great Eastern theological tradition.

The West moved in the opposite direction. The practical Latin spirit, which inclines toward the concrete, reasons from the historical place where the mystery itself is to be found — revelation. Theology cannot be separated from economy; access to the immanent Trinity cannot be other than through the economic Trinity. The mission of the Son from the Father establishes his eternal generation at the same time as the mission of the Spirit "*ex Patre Filioque*" is the basis of the procession from both. "The *Filioque* in Western theology was born of the refusal to distinguish between economic Trinity and immanent Trinity."[95]

We have seen how this thesis on the reciprocal identification of economy and theology in discussing the Trinity was thoroughly formulated in our day by Karl Rahner.[96] In the history of Western Christianity, such a way of thinking exercised no small influence.

Even without sharing Lossky's critical observations, one must acknowledge that the value attributed in the West to the visible and the historical in the experience of faith had its repercussions in ecclesiology with its "hierarchological" stress, in sacramental theology with the excesses of the doctrine of "*ex opere operato*," in moral theology with a kind of normative objectivism and hence an ethical heteronomy — all these consequences not only of the *Filioque* but also of the manner of thinking related to it.

It was by starting from such considerations that the criticism of Yves Congar moved toward the Rahnerian thesis and hence to the hermeneutical structure reflected there. Even though he admits that the economic Trinity is the immanent Trinity, Congar does not feel, in the name of divine unknowability and transcendence, that he can accept the "reciprocality" that Rahner adds to it apart from the eschatological self-communication of the Christian God of the "not yet," that is, of our believing hope.[97]

These observation help to temper the "Western" thesis and recover the value of Eastern apophatism and biblical eschatology. One could deduce from them the affirmation of a kind of dialectical rapport between economic Trinity and immanent Trinity — a rapport of identity because the economy finds its basis and its correspondence in divine immanence; a rapport of otherness because the transcendence of the Trinitarian God infinitely surpasses the limits of his self-revelation in history; a rapport of excellence because in the full eschatological revelation, when God "will be all in all" (1 Cor 15:28), the economic Trinity will be identified with the immanent Trinity.

This dialectic redirects us to the historic-dynamic mode of thought which surpasses the paradigm subject to the Western identification of economy and theology. This model derives from modern awareness of history in which the relationship between "*Deus revelatus*" and "*Deus absconditus*" is not resolved in the sense of simple identity (the Western approach) or in the sense of strong distinction or otherness (the Eastern approach), but in terms of identity in distinction.

If the identity between economy and theology leads to an acknowledgment of the *Filioque*, and the distinction between the two leads one to deny it, the dialectical approach accepts both the value and the partiality of the formula and directs us to a fuller plumbing of the historical reciprocity between Son and Spirit in its always unfathomable and yet undeniable immanent origin which will be fully revealed only in the promised glory.

The assumption of the historic-dialectic paradigm thus engages the whole gamut of Trinitarian theology. It requires us to make an "economic" or historical reading of the Trinitarian mystery (the Trinity "in history").

It prompts us to do humble and adoring in-depth study of the immanent correspondence of the history of the Father, Son and Holy Spirit (thinking historically about the Trinity, and deriving therefrom some idea of its dynamism starting from the reciprocity of the Persons attested to by the history of revelation: the Trinity "as history").

It forces us to do a Trinitarian reading of history and its meaning (to think "Trinitarily" about history), arriving at the consequences of intratrinitarian reciprocity in such a way as to get beyond every "Christomonism" and every "pneumatomonism" in Christian theory and practice (history "in the Trinity").

And it encourages us to be open to the eschatological hour of the Trinitarian fulfillment of history (history as Trinity?), which absolutely excludes every reduction of the transcendent mystery to the purely historical-worldly level.

The hermeneutical problem of the *Filioque* reveals, then, the hermeneutical problem of Trinitarian theology as a whole which needs rethinking based on new forms of thought so as more faithfully to take up the complexity of the biblical witness and the spiritual experience of believers, overcoming the ancient counter-positions of East and West through the use of a different model of reflection and life.

In this sense, it can be said that "the true problem, the only one which from the ecumenical point of view is full of promise, is located at the level of approaching — once again and after so much travail — the relationship between economic Trinity and immanent Trinity: that is a new Trinitarian articulation."[98]

The ecumenical problem thus sends us back to the hermeneutical problem: Diversity of content reveals diversity of spheres of thought. Overcoming this diversity through dialogue is the ecumenical "metanoia," the change of mind and heart, needed in order to rethink the Mystery in a new way.

What prospects emerge both for ecumenical dialogue and for theological research from these various levels of meaning attached to the question of the *Filioque*?

From the viewpoint of ecumenical dialogue, it is necessary to acknowledge the historical fact of the unilaterality of the insertion of the *Filioque* on the part of Western tradition. The original form of the Symbol of 381 — which is professed by Eastern Christians — is the only normative one for all.

It must at the same time be understood that the insertion did not come about to the detriment of orthodoxy but as an attempt to explain, albeit partially, the text's silence about the relationship between the Spirit and the Son. The monarchy of the Father has never been placed in doubt by the Latin Church just as the Eastern Church never wanted to deny a special relationship between the Spirit and the Son. "In the faith, East and West concur."[99] The *Filioque*, in this sense, is the Latin expression of the same and only faith which the Greeks have expressed differently, speaking of the procession of the Spirit from the Father, absolute source, by means of the Son.

"What is to be looked for, what is possible to attain is the acknowledgment at the same time of the unity of faith of the two parts of catholicism and the legitimate difference between the two dogmatic expressions of the mystery."[100]

Over and above the signs of intolerance which were not lacking, this was the intention of the Council of Florence! It is therefore not a case of admitting inadmissible dogmatic pluralism but of accepting a theological pluralism which in the end is more respectful of the elusiveness of the Mystery. Consequently, the Latins could seek to make the *Filioque* optional in the Symbol[101] and the Greeks could acknowledge fully, even thanks to this gesture, the uninterrupted communion of dogmatic faith with the West which was not damaged by the insertion of the formula.

The problem generated by the silence of the Symbol remains an open one from the viewpoint of theological research. The reciprocity of the Son and Spirit, of Christology and pneumatology, needs deeper study. Possible reductionisms need to be overcome both in the "Christomonistic" sense, with exaggerated accentuation of the visible mediations of the experience of grace, and the "pneumatomonistic" sense, with spiritualistic or charismatic excesses. A pneumatological Christology within a complete and consequently Trinitarian theology needs development.

The latter task redirects us in turn to the assumption of an ecumenical model capable of negotiating the straits of the East-West contrasts. From this effort the following reflections will not shirk, offered as they are for the development of a theology of the Holy Spirit within a Trinitarian theology which "speaks of God, telling Love's story."

c) *The Spirit as Personal Love*

How is the history of the Spirit to be considered in the Trinitarian history of God? Proceeding from the economy of salvation, in which the Spirit manifests itself as the one who opens out in freedom and unites in love, as the one who is the Spirit behind the separation of the Cross and the communion of Easter, it is possible to have a single vision of the twofold message of East and West.

In the awareness of being always on the threshold of mystery, one will then say that, *in respect to the distinction between Father and Son*, eternal Lover and eternal Beloved, the Spirit receives principally from the Father and from the Son, inasmuch as the Spirit was given by the Father to the Son to be *the personal bond of their unity,* he himself essentially one with them.

In respect to the unity of the Father and the Son, the Spirit represents the Third in love, the one whom the Father loves through the Son, beyond and by means of the Beloved, and hence the Spirit is *the gift of love* in person, the ecstasy of the Lover and his Beloved, the beginning and the end of their pure self-offering, another in respect to the two.

The Spirit is *the personal bond of unity* between the Father and the Son, the love given by the Lover and accepted by the Beloved, other than the Father because received by the Son, other than the Son because given by the Father, one with them because the Spirit is love given and received in the unity of the process of eternal love.

In this sense, the Spirit proceeds from the Father, principle and source of divine love and, inasmuch as the Father communicates love to the Beloved and the latter, in love received, is one with the Father, the Spirit also proceeds from the Son.

"We also believe that the Holy Spirit, who is the third person of the Trinity, is God one and equal with God the Father and God the Son, of one and the same substance and also of one and the same nature; not generated, however, or created but proceeding from both, Spirit of one and of the other. We also believe that this Holy Spirit is neither ungenerated or generated, so as not to affirm two Fathers by calling the Spirit ungenerated, or not to seem to be predicating two Sons by calling the Spirit generated. However, we do say that it is not the Spirit of the Father only or of the Son only, but of Father and Son together. In fact it does not proceed from the Father in the Son, nor does it proceed from the Son to sanctify the creature, but it is shown that the Spirit proceeds together from one and the other because it is acknowledged that charity and holiness are of one and the other."[103]

Adored and glorified with the Father and with the Son, called like them by the title of Lord,[104] the Spirit is God like them, one with them on the plane of divine being in the eternal history of love. From them he is distinguished inasmuch as he proceeds from them as a communion of one and of the other, nexus or bond of their loving themselves, reciprocal love of one and the other, the *we* of Father and Son in person.[105] "The Spirit is therefore a certain ineffable communion (*ineffabilis quaedam communio*) of the Father and the Son."[106]

"This Holy Spirit, according to the Sacred Scriptures, is not the Spirit only of the Father, or only of the Son, but of both; and hence he makes us think about the common love (*caritas*) with which the Father and the Son mutually love one another."[107]

"If the Spirit be in fact the unity of the one and the other, or their sanctity, or their love because the Spirit is their holiness, it is clear that the Spirit is not one of the two; it is the one in whom the other two are joined and in whom the generated is loved by the one generating and the one in whom the one generated loves the one who generates him . . . The Holy Spirit is therefore what is common to the Father and the Son . . . their consubstantial and co-eternal communion itself.''[108]

For this reason, when speaking of the Father and the Son, one cannot speak of the Spirit because, just like their unity and peace, the Spirit's presence is presupposed:

''Why does the Apostle not speak of the Holy Spirit (in passages like 1 Cor 3:22ff or 1 Cor 11:3)? Perhaps because wherever one names a reality united with another with such a profound peace that it makes these two one, need one think about this peace even though it is not mentioned?''[109]

As far as the communion of one and the other is concerned, their unity and peace, the Spirit proceeds from one and the other, even if primarily from the Father, because everything that the Son has he receives from the Father:

''If in fact all the Son has he has from the Father, he receives also from the Father that the Spirit should proceed also from him . . . The Son is born of the Father. The Holy Spirit proceeds principally (*principaliter*) from the Father and — through the gift that the Father makes of the Spirit to the Son without any interval of time — the Spirit proceeds from both the one and the other together (*communiter*).''[110]

In the eternal history of love, the Spirit is therefore the love pouring forth from the Father and flowing into the Son who, receiving it, is one with the Father and, hence such that love proceeds even from him. Other in respect to the Father because given by him, the Spirit is love that is distinguished from Love loving; other in respect to the Son, because received by him and proceeding from him united with the Father, the Spirit is love that distinguishes itself from Love loved. Distinct therefore from the Father and the Son, as mutual love is distinct from Lover and

Beloved, in what is the Spirit differentiated from the love common to the Three?

Augustine called attention to the importance of this question: If the Spirit should be identified with the substantial love of the Father and the Son, there would be no more Trinity, but only two, Lover and Beloved, in the one reality of love. Hence love as given and received must be distinguished in the relationship between the Father and the Son from the love that is common to all Three.[111]

In the first case there is *personal Love*, the Spirit insofar as it is distinct from Lover and Beloved, even if one with both in love. In the second, there is *substantial Love* which is the divine nature itself, the very essence of divinity.[112]

It is relationship that distinguishes persons in divine Love: the relationship between Generator and Generated, Lover and Beloved (the "paternity" of the Father); the relationship between the Generated and the Generator, Beloved and Lover (the "filiation" of the Son); and the relationship of the Spirit to the other two as their love received and given (passive "spiration"; that is, being given by the Father and received by the Son, which is distinct from active "spiration," which, inasmuch as it is the act of giving and receiving, is immediately identified with the Father who gives and the Son who receives respectively).

"The Holy Spirit is, next to the Father and the Son, a third divine relationship, the relation of the relations . . . Only in the *unity* of the sacrificing Father and of the sacrificed Son is God the *event* of the sacrifice which, in the relationship between Love and Loved, *is* Love itself. Only the *Spirit*, who comes from the Father and the Son, constitutes, preserving the distinction, the unity of divine being as that event which is Love itself . . . Only the Spirit of God as relation of relations constitutes the Being of Love as event."[113]

It is this characterization of the Spirit as personal love, bond of unity between Father and Son in his distinction from them, and as unifying love, which provides the intratrinitarian root of the work of unity which the same Spirit fulfills in the history of salvation.

The Spirit effects the unity of believers in space and time, in the image of Trinitarian unity.

In time, the Spirit unites past and present, making salvific events real again in the efficacious memory of the mystery celebrated and lived: "These things I said to you when I was still with you. But the Consoler, the Holy Spirit whom the Father will send in my name, will teach you everything and will *remind* you of all that I told you" (Jn 14:25ff).

Analogously, the Spirit joins present to future, "pulling" the future of God into the present of men. He is the first fruits, the pledge (cf. Rm 8:23; 2 Cor 1:22; 5:5; Ep 1:14), the token of that hope which does not delude (cf. Rm 5:5).

In space, the Spirit unites believers among themselves as the principle of unity in the Church: the Spirit of communion (cf. 2 Cor 13:13) who brings about the unity of the Body of Christ (cf. 1 Cor 12:3; Ep 4:3; Ph 2:1, etc.).

Thus, thanks to the action of the Holy Spirit, ecclesial communion is the icon of the Trinity, nourishing the experience of the unity of love of Father and Son!

d) *The Spirit as Gift*

If, in relation to the distinction between Father and Son, the Spirit is the personal bond of their unity, unifying Love between Love the Lover and Love the Beloved, in regard to the unity of Father and Son the Spirit is *the Gift of Love* in person, their overture to one another and to this Other itself, the third in love, Beloved by the Father through the Son in the movement of divine love's infinite self-offering.

In this sense, the Spirit proceeds from the Father, source of divinity, through the Son, by means of and beyond him according to the order indicated by the economy of salvation. God the Father pours out his Spirit on the Son who, in turn, hands it over to the Father at the hour of the cross and, having received it in full in the new hour of Easter from the Father, pours it out in abundance on every person.

The Spirit is the "giver of life,"[114] "sent from one and the other, as the Son from the Father, but is not regarded as less than the Father and the Son, as the Son claims to be less than the Father and the Spirit by virtue of his assumed flesh."[115]

The Spirit is the gift of God (cf. Ac 2:38; 8:20; 10:45; 11:17; Heb 6:4; 1 Jn 4:13; and Jn 4:10: "If you but knew the *gift* of God," read in relation to Jn 4:14: "The water I will give" and 7:37: "If anyone thirsts, let him come to me; let him drink who believes in me. Scripture has it: 'From within him rivers of living water shall flow' Here he was referring to the Spirit, whom those who came to believe in him were to receive." This is Augustine's exegesis to show that the Spirit is God's gift).[116]

The idea of the Spirit as gift, ecstasy of God given to others, is taken from the Greek Fathers through the most frequent formula: "From the Father, through the Son, in the Spirit."

"It is the enunciation of a dynamic in which the Spirit is the one in whom the process ends . . . Discussion is of an economic order which translates, however, that of the immanent Trinity. According to this order, the Spirit is the one by means of whom God's communication *is brought to completion*. Economically it is to him that holiness and perfection are attributed. In the Tri-unity of God, the Spirit is the fulfillment . . ."[117]

In this sense, the Spirit is the superabundance of divine love, the overflowing fullness, the ecstasy of God, "God as pure excess, God as emanation of love and grace."[118] And, precisely on this account, he is Spirit-Creator who calms the hearts of the faithful, the Paraclete who succors and comforts, the gift of God most high, the loving font, the fire of love, the spiritual anointing from above (cf. the hymn *Veni, Creator Spiritus*).

The dynamism of the immanent overture of divine love —

through which, from the Father through the Son, love overflows in the Spirit — is thus reflected in the dynamism of creation and salvation in which everything is given existence and salvation by the Father through the Son in the Spirit. This is the object of the contemplation of the East,[119] its living message, which does not contrast but is integrated with that of the West in a stronger soldering together of economy and immanence in the adoring and reflected experience of the mystery.[120] The Spirit is the personal irradiation of divine love: "In God (love) does not exist only as Lover and Beloved but goes beyond itself as Holy Spirit and thus determines also the relationship between me as Lover and you as Beloved."[121]

Precisely as the free superabundance of love, the Spirit reaches the other in absolute gratuity. That is, the Spirit does not have to rest above all on what is already but calls all things from nothing. The Spirit does not reach out to the one who is good and beautiful but makes good and beautiful the one to whom he reaches out. In the Spirit, God loves the stray sheep (cf. Mt 15:24 and Lk 15:4-7), sinners and the ill (Lk 5:31ff), the lost (Lk 19:10) — in a word, the least, those whom no one else loves.

"God chose those whom the world considers absurd to shame the wise. He singled out the weak of this world to shame the strong. He chose the world's lowborn and despised, those who count for nothing, to reduce to nothing those who were something" (1 Cor 1:27ff).

As the radical and gratuitous overture of divine love, free and freeing, the Spirit offers himself as the one who overturns history, who disturbs the status quo, stirring up the future, shaking up the comfortable and stimulating inquiry. "The function of the Spirit . . . is to exile from one's original and imaginary homeland so as to set out on the road of an unsuspected future."[122]

His very name — wind, breath — bespeaks the freedom of the new, unmasking the insufficiency of the now. That is why it is the Spirit who acts in the prophets (1 P 1:11 and 2 P 1:21). It is the

Spirit who is the ''father of the poor'' (cf. the *Veni Sancte Spiritus*), who have no other hope but the Lord. It is the Spirit who is God as the future of the world.

And as the eternal going forth of love from Lover and Beloved, infinite and perennial self-giving of divine love, it is to the Spirit that can be given, in the poverty of language, the name ''future'' of God, of the eternal immanent future of the history of Trinitarian love.[123]

But this thought requires that the account of the eternal history of Father, Son and Spirit be now put together in a unified way, in a synthesis which reflects the density of the paschal event in which this history has been told to us. ''This is the way of speaking about the Holy Trinity as it has been handed down.''[124] The narration of the history of each of the Three, given at the beginning of revelation and by its living transmission in the history of the Church's faith, ends here. It is time now to pass on to the contemplation of the mystery of the Trinity's living unity as history.

3.4 THE TRINITY AS HISTORY

a) *The Eternal History of Love*

The Easter event reveals the Trinitarian history *of God* — that is, not only the history of the Father, Son and Spirit who reveal themselves in it in the fruitfulness of their reciprocal relationships and in the marvelous gratuity of their love for the world. It also reveals the unfathomable unity of the Three who make history in the unfolding of the events of the paschal mystery, united in the indelible differentiation from one another (cross) and in the deepest possible communion (Easter).

They are united in the history of Love which hands Love over (the Father), which allows itself to be handed over in absolute freedom (the Son), which, handed over to make the divine entry into the exile of sinners possible, is poured out in fullness in the paschal hour so as to bring about the entry of sinners into the unifying and living homeland of divine love (the Spirit). The unity of the paschal event is the unity of the event of love which loves (the Father), which is loved (the Son), and which unites in freedom (the Spirit: cf. 1 Jn 4:7-16).

At Easter it becomes manifest how love not only produces and creates unity but rather presupposes it, since it is not so much a question of union between strangers as it is of a reunion among themselves of persons who have estranged themselves for love of the world and, from the exile of estrangement, have returned to their original, and simultaneously new, oneness of their heavenly homeland.[125]

All the mission and the work of Jesus of Nazareth are accomplished in the sign of his pre-existing and eternal unity with the Father and the Spirit: He who receives and gives the Spirit (Jn 1:33) is the Son of God (Jn 1:34), one with the Father (Jn 10:30), who calls for and establishes by his Paschal sacrifice the unity of men in the Trinitarian unity of God:

"On that day when the Spirit will be poured out (Jn 16:17) you will know that I am in my Father, and you in me and I in you . . . He who loves me will be loved by my Father. I too will love him and reveal myself to him . . . anyone who loves me will be true to my word, and my Father will love him; we will come to him and make our dwelling place with him" (Jn 14:20, 23).

". . . that they may be one as we are one — I living in them, you living in me — that their unity may be complete. So shall the world know that you sent me, and that you loved them as you loved me" (Jn 17:21-23).

It is to this living unity of the Triune God that all people have access by means of baptism. Taking into account the Semitic sense of "name," which means the living essence of what is referred to, to be baptized "in the name of the Father, and of the Son, and of the Holy Spirit" (Mt 28:19) means to begin to take part in the unique mystery of their being, of their unfathomable unity.

How is this Trinitarian unity, revealed and communicated in the Easter event, to be understood? Where and how are we to direct our contemplation of the mystery so that from the economy of history we might, as far as possible, delve into the immanence of divine unity? Church faith has defended God's unity against whoever sought to deny or water it down.

The affirmation of the Council of Nicea (325) regarding the "consubstantiality" of the Son with the Father holds, against

Arian subordinationism, that Father and Son are on the same plane of divine being; that is, they are one in divinity, of the very same "essence."[126]

The Council of Constantinople in 381, against the Pneumatomachs who tended to subordinate the Spirit to Christ, affirms the same parity in divine being of the Spirit with the Father and with the Son, with whom the Spirit "is adored and glorified" as "Lord and giver of life."[127] The Symbol *Quicumque* clearly professes: "The Catholic faith is that we venerate only one God in the Trinity and the Trinity in unity, without confounding the persons and without separating the substance. Other in fact is the person of the Father, other that of the Son, other that of the Spirit, but one is the divinity of the Father, of the Son, and of the Spirit, equal the glory, co-eternal the majesty."[128]

"In acknowledging the three persons, we do not acknowledge three substances but only one substance and three persons."[129]

This divine unity, against the background of the world of thought in which it was primarily defended and conceptually formulated in an effort to put into words the experience of the unity of the salvific event, was therefore conceived as the unity of the divine "essence" or of the divine "substance" or of the divine "nature."

These terms mean "what the thing is," "what it comes under." To say that the Three have only one "essence," "substance" or "nature" means, then, to affirm the unity of their divine essence, their perfect parity on the plane of divinity, and therefore their being one God only. Their unity is expressed thus in the most radical fashion, as unity of being, ontological unity.[130] Within this unity the three Persons are distinguished for their reciprocal relations, for that (relative) distinction from one another in their (essential) identity which is the "subsisting relation," the "person" in God.[131]

This interpretation, while strongly safeguarding divine unity, risks ceding a certain predominance of attention to the dimension of divine essence at the expense of the personal life of the divinity, giving rise to that Christian essentialism in speaking of God which is biblically deficient and one of the principal causes of ignoring the Trinity in Christian thought and practice.

The Christian God is not "just any" God but properly and specifically the Trinitarian God. Christian monotheism is not one among many but is Trinitarian monotheism! It is this aspect that the development of thought, especially in the West, has left in the shadows even if, on the level of the expression of the faith, there is no doubt that the formula of the unique divine essence or substance or nature of the Three precisely corresponds with the facts of revelation though in categories different from the historical ones narrated in the paschal proclamation.

To overcome the essentialism of classical thought, the modern era has proposed, even in Trinitarian theology, a new evaluation of subjectivity. This is why the unity of the Trinitarian God has been interpreted, starting with Hegel, as the unity of the unique divine subject in the eternal history of the Spirit, God the Father who differentiates himself in the Son and identifies himself in the Holy Spirit.

This conception has the merit of including the movement of life and history in the idea of God, and hence of appearing closer to revelation's image of the living God. In reality, however, it completely depletes the personal Trinity, reducing it to the future of the unique divine Subject, assimilated moreover in the ultimate future of the history of the world. Hegelian monism of the Spirit is no closer to Christian monotheism than is any other indeterminate monotheism!

In order to overcome the risks of an "exaggerated" essentialism and the falling into subjectivity, we are offered the route of historical thought in interpreting the unity of the Christian God. Divine unity in this approach is considered not as static essence but as dynamism, process, life, as the history of Trinitarian love.

Beginning with the revelation of love Loving, Loved and Unifying in freedom, which is the Easter story, it goes on to affirm that unity, or, if you will, the one and unique divine essence (dynamically understood) is love, that the only God is Love, in the indelible Trinitarian differentiation of Loving, Loved and Love personified.

It is the route already glimpsed by Augustine, even though it was not pursued by him to the end,[132] perhaps under the influence of the predominant essentialism in the thought of his time:

"In truth you see the Trinity if you see love."[133] "Behold, there are three: Lover, Beloved and Love."[134] "And no more than three: one who loves him who comes from him, one who loves him from whom he comes, and love itself . . . And if this is not some thing, how *is God love?* And if this is not substance, how is God substance?"[135] "To speak of the being of God cannot nor must it mean anything other than recounting the love of God."[136]

"God is love. God is not only *in* love, as those who love each other are *in* love. God is not only I the lover and you the beloved. God is rather the radiating event of love itself. He is that . . . loving not only himself but — always forgetful of self even in so grand a love of self — loving you apart from himself, and *thus* he is and remains himself. God possesses himself in giving himself and only in giving himself. But thus giving himself, he possesses himself. Thus, *he is.* His self possessing is the event; it is the history of a giving of self and in this sense he is the term of every mere self possession. As there is *history* so there is God; indeed, this history of love is 'God himself.' "[137]

The essence of the living God is, therefore, his love in eternal movement issuing from self, as loving Love, welcoming self, as loved Love, and returning to self in infinite openness to the other in freedom, as Spirit of Trinitarian love. The essence of the Christian God is love in eternal process. It is the Trinitarian history of love. It is the Trinity as the eternal history of love which sets in motion, assumes and pervades the history of the world, the object of his pure love. The paschal event reveals naught but the divine essence as the eternal event of the love among the Three and of their love for us.

"Only this love which is taking place constitutes the essence of the divinity, so that only in the three divine relations — the Father who of himself loves, the Son who is loved and has always loved, and the ever new event of the love between Father and Son, which is the Spirit — does it become possible now to think about the full identity between divine essence and divine existence. The concept of the Trinitarian God who is love implies, therefore, an eternal newness according to which the eternal God is his own future. God and love never grow old. Their being is, and remains, in the future."[138]

God's unity is then the unity of being and love, of his essential love, which exists eternally as Love loving, Love loved, and Love personified or, if you will, as the coming, the arrival and the eternal future of love,[139] the source, the acceptance and the gift of self, paternity, filiation and overture in freedom, Father, Son and Holy Spirit.

This concept of the divine essence as the eternal history of love is tied in with the idea of the Trinitarian *pericoresis*. Starting with such texts as Jn 10:38 — "The Father is in me and I am in the Father" (cf. Jn 14:9ff; 17:22, etc.) — the expression intends to convey mutual compenetration (whence the Latin term *circumincessio*) and inhabitation (whence the Latin *circuminsessio*) of the divine persons, the inexhaustible movement of Trinitarian life, its pouring out of itself and gathering together of itself in love. This is how St. John Damascene, the first, it seems, to uses the term, illustrates it:

"The remaining and residing of one in the other of the three Persons means that they are inseparable and cannot be parted but have among themselves a compenetration without confusion, not in such a way that they themselves are dissolved in one another or mixed together but in such a way that they are joined . . . One and identical is the movement because the impetus and the dynamism of the three persons is one, something which is not found in created nature."[140]

The grandeur of this vision, proper to the East but not restricted thereto,[141] lies in the fact that, denying every conception of the Trinity which goes against either unity (modalism) or personal distinction (tritheism), it shows how in God unity and singularity of persons not only do not contradict but reciprocally affirm one another.

The divine essence as love does not exclude but rather includes personal differentiations. And this holds both for the immanence of the divine life (Trinitarian pericoresis) and in the mystery of this life participated in by men (the God-man relationship and Church communion). True love never annuls differences, even if it takes them up into a unity more profound than they.

In this light, even the principle of "*opus Dei ad extra indivisum*" ("the works of God outside the divinity are indivisible," and therefore must be attributed to the Triune God as a whole rather than to the individual persons), the undivided work of God vis a vis creatures, the consequence of the fact that "in God everything is one where there is no opposition of relations,"[142] must be reread.

The principle cannot mean that divine activity "ad extra" is undifferentiated, almost as if in God's turning to his creatures in the creative act, the personal properties of Father, Son and Spirit disappear. This would contradict the concrete account of the history of salvation, so much so that even in the most rigorously essentialist perspective there is felt the need to elaborate a theology of "appropriations,"[143] which would allow associating essential attributes with individual divine persons, attributes through which the properties the persons have in the immanence of the mystery are better manifested in the economy.

Even activity "ad extra" must then be understood in the "*pericoretic*" sense; that is, from the viewpoint of the living dynamism of divine unity. This means that the Father does nothing without a corresponding activity of the Son and of the Spirit; and the Word does nothing without the Father and the Spirit; and the Spirit does nothing without the Son and the Father. Every act of Trinitarian love toward creatures implies, that is, the differentiation of Lover, Beloved and Love personified in their unfathomable unity. The *"opus ad extra"* is always an *"opus amoris"* ("a work of love") in which the Three are present and involved, each according to his own attributes.

Love is never indifference! Consequently, there is no salvific experience of a divine person which does not entail the encounter with the whole Trinity. No "Christomonism" or "pneumatomatism" is admissible, no unilateral absolutization of one divine person only. And no abstract undifferentiated monotheism either. Only that monotheism which respects the movement of otherness and communion in the unfathomable unity of love which is the eternal history of God.

Only such a conception of the one God, which is true Trinitarian monotheism, shows men the face of the Christian God who is always Father, Son and Spirit in the unity of divine love, in himself and for us. Only Trinitarian monotheism speaks of God, *telling Love's story.*

b) *The Attributes of the God of Love*

In the light of divine unity as the eternal history of love, how are we to consider the doctrine of the *divine attributes*; that is, the essential characteristics of the one God? How should one speak of the unique God of love and at the same time describe in some way the various aspects of his free activity?[144]

A twofold approach is needed in our contemplation of the mystery, one that must begin with us who are speaking of him. On the one hand, the mystery of the one God will be scrutinized "from below," that is, from our condition as creatures who adore the otherness of the Creator and Lord of heaven and earth. On the other, we will try to speak of it "from within," that is, starting from the experience of divine love operating in creation and redemption.

A first glance will be given, as far as possible, to the attributes of divinity as such, in their pure transcendence (attributes traditionally called "absolute" or "uncommunicable" or "quiescent"). The second will look at God's free ways of acting, his operating in the freedom of love for the sake of creatures (attributes called "relative" or "communicable" or "operative").[145] The two viewpoints will continually crisscross because God, the Other, is always also at the same time the God who is near to us in love, the God who comes.

"God's coming is the concrete historical expression apt for designating the experience of a divine nearness which, nevertheless, is not yet perfect union, and of a distance which does not entail an effective separation. God as 'He who comes' is the unity, conformable to the experience of distance and closeness, of the mystery and of the revealing act, of the future and the present, a unity proper to divine Being in his relationships with man."[146]

As an event of eternal love, God manifests himself at the same time as the transcendent origin and future of love, as well as his present for us.

The one God is *absolutely transcendent, totally Other* in regard to the finitude of the worldly:

"One is the living and true God, Creator and Lord of heaven and earth, omnipotent, eternal, immense, incomprehensible, infinite in intelligence, will and all other perfections. And because his is a singular spiritual substance, completely simple and immutable, it is necessary to proclaim that he is really and essentially distinct from the world, fully blessed in himself and by himself, and ineffably above everything which exists and can be thought of outside himself."[147]

The transcendent and other God does not allow himself to be caught in the network of like and penultimate. He is the dissimilar, the first and the last: "Between Creator and creature it is impossible to note likeness without having to note between them an even greater unlikeness."[148] "God is God and man is not God!" (K. Barth).

The total otherness and transcendence of the one God are rooted in the inexhaustible fullness of his immanent life, in his being purely from himself and not from another (divine *aseity*), love at its most absolute source and gratuity which make him unconditionally free in regard to his creatures.

With this total fullness of life, God presents himself as the absolutely simple, as that which does not know composition because in him everything is, simply, God. Essence and existence are one in him. And since it is said that God's essence is love, it can also be said that God's being, which subsists in the infinity of what God is, the "subsistent" being of his eternal future, is love.

In this light, the one true God is the eternal event of love, love which is perfectly simple. God is the *simplicity* of love! In the simple fullness of this divine life of love, every perfection of being thus comes to rest: all goodness, truth, and beauty is in God. God is the *goodness*, the *truth*, and the *beauty* of love! Hence his joy is perfect: He is the eternal *beatitude* of love!

Before this extraordinary fullness, hardly evoked by the finitude of the word, before that which is perceived as the completely transcendent origin and future of love, there cannot but arise adoring wonder, a sense of the abyss which separates us from him and also attracts us to him: "Come no nearer! Remove the sandals from your feet, for the place where you stand is holy ground!" (Ex 3:5).

By virtue of this same fullness of life and love, the one God can be considered beyond our finitude, the negation of all negations. He is the *eternal* history of love precisely because in him history is not marked by the limits of space and time as in our case.

He is beyond space, not because he is spatially beyond but because he embraces everything in himself, infinitely excelling everything else and remaining in everything else. It is the mystery of his *omnipresence*, as the omnipresence of divine love.

"God is in everything through his power insofar as all things are subject to his sovereignty. He is in all things through his presence, insofar as everything is bare and open before his eyes. He is in all things by his essence, insofar as he is present to them as the cause of their being."[149]

"If on a dark night on a black rock there is a black ant, God sees it and loves it!" (Arab proverb)

In the area of love, God is immense! This omnipresence of divine love cannot be ordered to the supreme divine presence in history, which is the personal presence of the incarnate Son of God. In the Beloved, made man for us, there is rooted that receptivity of love on the part of every creature which makes it open to loving divine omnipresence.[150]

The one God is also beyond time, not because he is temporally outside time but because he embraces within himself — as the eternal identity of the beginning and the end of all things, "alpha" and "omega" of the created (cf. Is 41:4; 44:6; 48:12 and also Rv 1:17) — all that is to be. It is part of the mystery of his *eternity*, of the perennial "being present" of his divine life and, in biblical categories, as the fidelity of his love to every "today" of love.

Even divine *immutability* is to be understood in this sense. It is not the indifference of a "lazy God" nor the inactivity of a "dead God" but the perennial dynamism of the love of the living God, always the same as far as he himself is concerned and always new, in absolute fidelity to his promises.[151] God does not change because he has always loved, forever, and in this "today." God is immutable in the fidelity of his love! But in this same free fidelity, he is always new in love!

"A man was walking along the seashore. Turning, he saw on the sand, next to his own, the footprints of another wayfarer. He thought: 'They are God's.' Looking further on, however, he saw just one set of footprints. He thought that God had abandoned him on the journey. But God said to him: 'No, that is the time I carried you in my arms' '' (The Parable of the Footprints, a popular tale).

The omnipresence of divine love in earthly time is ordered to the supreme presence of eternity in time and of time in eternity, which is the paschal event. "There is nothing to fear. I am the first and the Last and the One who lives. Once I was dead but now I live — forever and forever. I hold the keys of death and the nether world" (Rv 1:17).

The mystery of the future *in* God, as entrance into otherness and as a "new" communion with the Father and the Son in the Spirit, is manifested in the future of the cross and resurrection. What is thus expressed in relation to Trinitarian life can be acknowledged in relation to the one God, unfathomable and living unity of the Three, as the mystery of the future of the immutable God. Divine immutability is the permanent fullness of the life of God as the eternal process of his love.

Beginning with his work on our behalf in creation and redemption, the one God can be contemplated in all the depth of his being as he who loves in freedom, as God-for-us (one thinks of the revelation of the divine name in Ex 3:14 as the guarantee and promise of this fact in the face of his people's imminent march for freedom: "I am he who is for you"[152]).

"If we need to summarize in *one* word what has been definitively manifested in Christ regarding God's treatment of us, then we would have to say with John that in Christ it is definitively revealed that *God is love* (1 Jn 4:8). Any and all other assertions of the doctrine about God must ultimately be understood in the light of this assertion."[153]

Inasmuch as God is he who loves, God is also he who knows (sees) all things: "*Ubi amor, ibi oculus*" (Richard of St. Victor). Nothing is hidden from love! This is the mystery of divine *omniscience*, which is not neutral, detached knowing, but knowing in the biblical sense, a loving, and hence attentive and engaging knowledge such as that which is revealed in all its fullness in the relationship between the Son of God in the flesh and his own: "I am the good shepherd. As the Father knows me and I know the Father, so I know my sheep and mine know me. And I offer my life for my sheep" (Jn 10:14ff).

Divine omniscience, viewed in this way, is not in conflict with the freedom of the creature, since truly loving knowledge never takes away the freedom of the beloved. And it is in this light that divine *omnipotence* even must be viewed. Certainly he who is absolute fullness of life can do everything in love! In love he orders everything to the good. It is the mystery of his providence.

Precisely because his infinite power is such in love, and love is such in freedom, God never exercises his provident power against the creature's freedom. Rather, he accepts appearing powerless and deaf to the cries of the dying. He who wills that "all be saved and come to a knowledge of the truth" (1 Tm 2:4) will save no one against his will: "He who created us without us will not save us without us" (St. Augustine).

It is here that light is shed also on his apparently intolerable tolerance of evil: "If God is just, why is there evil?" The answer, of course, is precisely because he is a just God who loves in freedom. He has accepted the risk of love, the possibility of denial and betrayal with all the consequences which derive from it in the whole of creation (see Rm 8:20-22: "Subject to futility, not of its own accord but by him who once subjected it . . . , all creation groans and is in agony even until now"). The evil of the world is, paradoxically, the sign that divine omnipotence is love in freedom, capable of infinite respect and at the same time of active "compassion."

"Divine compassion does not exempt the creature from sorrow. But neither does it abandon him. Rather it assists him to the end, even without revealing itself" (I. Silone).

Faced with these various dimensions of the love of God — the attributes and the free modes of his acting — the believer's response cannot but be that of celebrating the glory of such a great love. This is the profound meaning of the confession of the *unity* and the *oneness* of God in biblical tradition. This profession — which unites Christians with Israel and Islam — is much more than the profession of an abstract idea. It is an act of adoration and at the same time a task, a doxology and a life challenge:

"Hear, O Israel! The LORD is our God, the LORD alone! Therefore, you shall love the LORD, your God, with all your heart, and with all your soul, and with all your strength" (Dt 6:4, the great confession of Hebrew monotheism!).

"For the Hebrew to confess the unity of God means to unify God. In fact, this unity is present in him who works: it is to become unity. And this becoming one has been entrusted into the hearts and hands of man."[154]

"The unity of God, which we can qualify without hesitation as the one 'dogma' of Israel, is neither a mathematical nor a quantitative unity, to be understood with rigid uniformity, but rather a live and dynamic unity which, by its very essence, looks to the unification of the human race in the reconciliation of a universal *shalom*."[155]

He who confesses one God enters the mystery of God's unity and tries to draw others into it in justice and peace. And this becomes concretely possible to the Christian faith since it is this same divine unity which opens up to us, offering itself as unity of Love, loving Love, loved Love, Love unifying God and the world in freedom.

It is here that the monotheistic confession — the confession of the one God as love, which includes distinction and is open to otherness — to be consistent, needs to become Trinitarian, so as to provide for the circulation of eternal love. Whoever enters the unity of God confesses the unity of God. But to allow oneself to be part of the eternal history of love is to enter into divine unity. And it is here that the radicalization of Hebrew monotheism begins to coincide with the Christian Trinitarian confession.

c) *The Three Persons in the History of Love*

Against the background of this divine unity as history of eternal love, how are we to consider the Three who take part in the paschal event? In the linguistic elaboration and arduously arrived at concept of the dogmatic faith of the first centuries, they are commonly designated by the name *persons*. In the unique divine substance or essence, three persons are confessed, or the one divine substance is said to subsist in three persons.[156]

Because the Latin term "*persona*" corresponds conceptually, even if not terminologically, to the Greek "*hypostasis*," the Trinitarian formula "one essence (or nature, or substance) — three persons (or hypostases)" can be said to unite East and West. What is to be said about this very ancient and common terminology and conceptualization?

What needs to be looked at, before all else, is that the use of one term to indicate Father, Son and Spirit as agents in the divine life is not without ambiguities.[157] This use generalizes and adds what properly can neither be generalized nor added because what is truly common to the Three is only the unique and single divinity. The use in this sense serves only to avoid a modalistic misunderstanding which would oppose the originality proper to each of the Three.

On the other hand, in the light of the modern concept of person which exalts subjectivity in conscience and freedom, to say that there are three persons in God could give way to a tritheistic equivocation, almost as if three separate spiritual centers were being treated. Augustine in his day already saw the difficulty:

"If you want to know what these Three are, it is necessary to acknowledge the extreme insufficiency of human language. Certainly, we answer 'three persons' but more for not remaining without saying anything than for expressing this reality."[158]

This is why Barth and Rahner have suggested some alternative formulas to the term "person," such as "mode of being,"[159] "mode of subsistence,"[160] feeling that these would better render the idea of substantial identity in the relative distinction of the Three.

While acknowledging the weightiness of these expressions, one cannot hide the disadvantage connected with the impression of a kind of modalism (openly denied, however, by them) and especially the ponderousness of so technical a language little familiar to believers. This is why the task that needs doing seems to be to keep the term "person" and to try, rather, to understand it in the light of historical thinking on the Trinity.

It is a task, moreover, which — in the categorical outlook of his time — Thomas Aquinas sought to perform.[161] Working from Augustine's genial intuition, which saw in the relationships between Father, Son and Holy Spirit the element of distinction in the bosom of divine unity, Thomas brought to the fore its profound ontological insights, rooting the relationships — which give rise to the persons (procession) — in the unique divine essence (*subsistentia*), which is the being with which God is what he is (*substantis*: what God is, the divine *nature*).

Person, in the concept of the Trinity, is presented as "subsisting relationship"[162] where the term "*relatio*" means that which distinguishes the Father from the Son (the relationship of paternity), the Son from the Father (the relationship of filiation) and the Spirit from both (passive spiration), while the adjective "*subsistens*" refers to the ontological reality of the person itself, founded on the unique divine subsistence.

"Father, Son, and Spirit are distinguished only 'relatively,' exactly insofar as, in their diversity, they cannot be thought of as constituted by anything that could signify a differentiation which existed prior to their reciprocal relationship, and hence which established it as its ulterior consequence."[163]

The grandeur of Thomas's interpretation lies in his having known how to reunite in a concept dense with meaning the diverse aspects which characterize the divine persons in their salvific self-revelation, as in the adorable immanence of the mystery. The person is understood in its real consistency, the expression of the one divine reality, in its self-projection toward the other and in the reciprocity of this communication of knowledge and of love.[164]

If the real consistency of each of the divine persons is their *esse in* through which they identify themselves with the unique essence, going out from self toward the other and welcoming the other in the self are their *esse ad*, their reciprocal relationship. In this sense the originality of the persons does not conflict with their unity. The person is more person the more he communicates himself in his absolute originality. He becomes another person in the other and receives the other to himself in the fruitful reciprocity of their relationship. A divine person thus becomes eternally what he eternally is: unity.

Thus the conception of the person as subsistent relationship can be fully assumed into a vision of the divine essence as the eternal history of love. In the unity of divine love, the Father is the Lover who relates to the Beloved, generating him as Son; the Son is the Beloved who is related to the Lover, accepting divine life totally from him as Father; the Spirit is Love personified which, insofar as it unites Lover and Beloved and opens up their love in freedom, is related to one and the other as the Spirit given by the Father and received by the Son, accepted by the Son and by him given in freedom.

In this perspective the divine persons appear as the Three who, in their eternal relationship in love, provide the process of eternal love, "subjects" of the eternal history of love: He who loves in the welling up of love; He who is loved in the receptivity of love; He who unites Lover and Beloved in the reciprocity and the free fruitfulness of love.

Certainly this does not mean that the three subjects of the eternal history of love are three subjectivities and therefore three autonomous spiritual centers in consciousness and in freedom. If divine love is one as the common essence of the Three, then all

Three share one divine consciousness and one divine freedom, even if each according to his own personality or subsistent relationship. [165]

Even for the sake of consciousness and freedom in God, it is worthwhile, in the most profound unity and singularity, that the distinction come from relationship. The one divine consciousness is paternal, filial, relational; so is divine freedom. For this reason, if it is true that it is the one God who is love, aware and free, it is no less true that this is brought about insofar as God is he who loves in awareness and freedom: Father, Son and Holy Spirit.

In love, God derives in truest form the strength of the principle approved by the Council of Florence: "In God everything is one when there is no opposition of relationships." [166] Love is truly "distinction and the overcoming of the distinct" (Hegel)!

One also understands, in the light of what has been said, the profound difference between divine persons and human persons or, if you will, between the eternal history of love and worldly love. While the divine person is unity (of essential love), which is distinguished (in its relationships of love) and united (in relationship and in essential love), the human person is distinction (subsistent individuality) which tends toward unity (by means of love relationships). God is unity which eternally becomes itself in love; man is solitude which profoundly tends toward communion.

This is why only in participation in Trinitarian life, made possible by the mission of the Son and the Spirit, can man truly realize himself and the human family. His thirst for unity appears justly, in this time of exile, as a "nostalgia for the Totally Other" (M. Horkheimer); only in the Trinitarian homeland will this be fully satisfied.

Meanwhile, perennially on a march, man must grow toward this unity in love revealed and offered to him in the history of the paschal event. He is not, nor will he ever be, Love, as, on the contrary, the God of Jesus Christ is. But, believing, he will be able to be *in* love and, as a pilgrim of unity, thus always more profoundly become a human person in the full dignity of his calling.

"We have come to know and to believe in the love God has for us. God is love, and he who abides in love abides in God, and God in him" (1 Jn 4:16). "As the eternal history of love, the Trinity truly unveils man to man and lets him know his most sublime vocation" (cf. *Gaudium et Spes*, 22)!

4.

HISTORY IN THE TRINITY

The paschal event as a Trinitarian event, narrated in the witness of the early Church and thought out with effort in the concept of faith, reveals not only the Trinitarian face of the God who is Love but, in it and through it, the face of man and the meaning of history.

The experience of believers, their work and their very life, attests to this twofold and very meaningful Trinitarian confession: On the one hand, it affirms in the Trinity the origin and site of all existence — *In the name of the Father and of the Son and of the Holy Spirit*; on the other, it adores in the Holy Trinity the mystery of the future homeland, glimpsed from afar but not yet possessed: *Glory to the Father and to the Son and to the Holy Spirit.*

In the light of these two confessions, history appears to the believer as a parable of the Trinitarian life in which the action of the personal love of the Three is expressed.[1] Everything comes from the Father through the Son in the Spirit; and everything, in the same Spirit, returns through the Son to the Father.[2]

In this vital process, Trinitarily articulated, the Easter rereading of the faith, transmitted by the continuity of the proclaimed, celebrated and lived mystery, derives its basic structure and its historic sense. The "*exitus a Deo*," the world's and man's coming from God, is read in the light of the missions of the Son and the Spirit. The "*editus ad Deum*," man's return and that of the world to the divine wellspring, is reflected on from the viewpoint of the ultimate reason for these missions — the glory of the Father.

Between mission *from* the Father and glorification *of* the Father, the arc of time is seen to distend itself within the infinitely greater bosom of the Trinity.[3] The beginning, the present and the future of worldly events are read in the context of Trinitarian history which thus provides a basis for and gives a value to the historic future. The unity of the Three in their action is such that all

Three, present in the various seasons of time, are acknowledged and adored, each one personally.

The unity of the Three in their being, which occasions in them the confession of the one unique God of love, gives rise to the expectation on the part of man of an ultimate unity within the very mystery of divine unity, an expectation such as to make sense of the multiple and fragmentary future of man.

The revelation of Easter thus illuminates the hope and the burden of history. It is necessary, therefore, to examine this now under the intense light of our in-depth study directed toward the immanence of the mystery and to investigate, after our account of the Trinity in history and of the Trinity as history — an account which was necessarily more cautious and tentative — the entry of history itself into the Trinity, the meaning and task, that is, which derive from the recounting so as to continue to narrate — in words and works, in time and through eternity — the history of Love in the life of men.

4.1   THE TRINITARIAN ORIGIN OF HISTORY

a) *Creation as Trinitarian History*

The Easter recollection of the early Church recognized the presence of the Trinity in the very act of creation. Various Christological hymns (e.g., Col 1:15-17; Jn 1:1-3) and different professions of faith (e.g., 1 Cor 8:6; Heb 1:1-4) attest to the profound conviction that the God operating in the salvific events of Easter is also the God who in the beginning gave and gives existence to all things.

Like Israel, the Church went from its knowledge of God as savior to its understanding of God as creator. And, as the people of the Old Covenant projected onto the God of the universe characteristics of the God of history,[4] so the new Israel could not help but project onto this God of creation their Trinitarian experience of the God of the new and final fulfillment.

In the light of the Easter event — and of the reflection done from this point regarding the immanence of the mystery — it is therefore possible to acknowledge the proper presence of the three divine Persons in the unity of the history of the beginnings.[5]

Creation is attributed above all to the *Father,* as the one who is the origin and principle of every life. Just as, in the eternal history of love which is Trinitarian life, the source of love itself is attributed to him, so from this same inexhaustible font, all that exists is said to have its origin.

This is the reason why the confessions of faith attach to the first divine person omnipotence, creation, and sovereignty over creation: "I believe in one God, the Father almighty, Creator and Lord of heaven and earth, of all things visible and invisible . . ."[6] "From him is 'every fatherhood in heaven and on earth' " (Ep 3:15).[7]

Eternal wellspring of the divinity, the Father is also the source of all created life. It is the superabundance of his love, its absolute gratuity, which makes him the eternal Generator of the eternal Generated, eternal Lover of the eternal Beloved. It is the same pure gratuity which, in absolute total freedom, brings him to give being, to create objects of love, his creatures.

"Love is, *par excellence,* that which causes things to be" (Maurice Blondel). Love is radiant, self-diffusing. Love creates. These expressions, which can be uttered properly only of God, give evidence of the absolute transcendence of the Creator in regard to the creature. Nothing else motivates God to create except his love. The creature is called from nothing into being. It is not loved because it exists, but it exists because it is loved. "*Ipso amore creatur*": whatever is created, is created by virtue of the same love which loves it!

The world's contingency thus reveals the absolute gratuity and freedom of God's love. The abyss which separates creature from Creator is the depth of eternal love, the possibility of the freedom of God and hence of human liberty, the certainty of the pure generosity which is at the source of all history. Where this abyss is removed, where creation is seen as the necessary expression or emanation of divinity, love, too, is removed. Hence, whoever denies the infinite otherness of creature and Creator denies in the end the very dignity of the creature, the object of pure love, called from freedom into freedom out of love.

The creative act, carried back into that wellspring of love which loves eternally, by that very fact becomes linked with the eternal generation of the Son. Granted unchanged the distance which separates eternity from time and heaven from earth, the source is the same, the Father, in an analogous vital movement, which in eternity is the procession of the Beloved, and in time the creation of the creature. *"Sicut trames a fluvio derivatur, ita processus creaturarum ab aeterno processu personarum"*[8] ("as streams derive from a river, the procession of creatures derives from the eternal procession of the persons [of the Trinity]"). The eternal process of love is welded to, without becoming confused with, the temporal process of history.

In the distinction between Father and Son, the communion in infinite otherness between Creator and creature finds its place: "The rapport between the divine persons themselves is so vast that the entire world finds space there" (Adrienne von Speyr). The procession of the Beloved from the Lover is the eternal foundation and model of the communication of life and being to the creature.[9]

While the first, however, takes place eternally *"ad intra,"* that is, in the bosom of divine life, the second is realized *"ad extra,"* where this expression is not to be taken in a spatial sense (in God time and space do not exist) but in a qualitative sense to indicate the infinite difference which exists between Creator and creature.

The fact that creation is a work of the Trinity *"ad extra"* does not mean to say that it is not embraced by the divine being which gives it a share in existence and life. Neither, in any way, does it exclude that, *"ad intra,"* in the bosom of Trinitarian life there is an eternal process which corresponds to it as its eternal foundation and model. The created is surrounded and permeated by divine love which raises it up and maintains it in being. It rests, so to speak, in the eternal procession of the love of the Generated by the Generator, of the Son by the Father.

This correspondence between intradivine procession and creation casts light on the being of the creature itself. Just as the Son is characterized in the eternal history of love by receptivity, by his being purely love which receives, so the creature, which in the procession of the Son has the eternal model and foundation of his creation, is also structurally marked in a way which is original and indelible by the receptivity of love. Everything has been given to the creature, starting with his very being. All he is he is by pure reception.

In this pure and original letting himself be loved by the eternal Lover in the eternal Beloved is based the radical and pristine goodness of the being of the creature, every creature. "Everything is grace" (Georges Bernanos). Everything — existence, life, the possibilities of matter and spirit, in time and in space — is a gift. It is everything that mankind, prior to original sin, lived and experienced according to the traditional doctrine of the "pristine state." It is therefore a faithful reflection of this rooting of the act of creation in the mystery of divine immanence. Everything that comes into being and is surrounded by the mystery of divine Goodness is originally good!

The verification and full revelation characterizing all things created as receivers of love are provided by the Incarnation of the Son. The Incarnation explains not only how Trinitarian being can communicate itself but also how creaturely being can present itself as pure acceptance. "*Ipsa assumptione creatur.*" It is the very act of assuming our human nature which concretely places the man Jesus in being!

Thus, in the mystery of the Incarnation, the very constitution of the creature is revealed. It is "received existence," the receptivity of love which, loving it, causes it to be. One then understands in what sense everything has been created "through Christ and in view of him" who is "the first fruits of all things" and in whom "all things subsist" (cf. Col 1:16). In the eternal receptivity of the Beloved, "the firstborn of every creature" (Col 1:15), is rooted the vocation to be of every created thing as a vocation to love.

The original goodness of the creature is illuminated also by the correspondence between creation and the other intradivine procession — that of the *Holy Spirit*. It is in the Spirit that everything is created (cf. Gn 1:2) and it is in the Spirit that everything is maintained in being (cf., e.g., Ps 104:29). Just as in the divine life the Spirit unites the Father to the Son, as unifying Love of the Lover and the Beloved, so too he unites creature to Creator, guaranteeing the original and constitutive unity of the created with God and hence the original goodness of everything that is, its being rooted and founded in love: "And God saw that it was good" (Gn 1:4, 10, 18-31).

As unity of the Father and the Son, the Spirit is therefore the guarantee that everything which is created by the Lover in the receptivity of the Beloved is also constitutively united to them in the bond of love. Thanks to the Spirit it can be said that where there is being, there is love, and that everything has been eternally loved by the eternal bond of divine charity.

In the life of the Trinity, however, the Spirit is also the one who sets love free. The Spirit is the friend, beyond the Beloved, in the superabundant fruitfulness and gratuity of love. In an analogous way, in dealing with creatures he is the guarantee of their autonomy, of their being "other" and hence of their freedom in love. In the Spirit, the creature, in the very depth of his being, is brought into unity with the Creator, but also into the full dignity of his own being. Hence, in the creature which embraces the whole of creation, man, the Spirit safeguards the possibility of accepting or refusing love.

The tragedy of sin, which invests the whole of creation and makes the Spirit moan in it (Rm 8:19ff), is precisely this refusal of pristine and originating love, this "wanting to be like God" on the part of man which ends up in a profound alienation of the creature. Man, who was made to love, finds love fearful and fatiguing. He who could be like God in love, in denying love, denies himself.

In the freedom given him by the Spirit, man chose to make of his constitutive receptivity a jealous possessiveness. This deep disturbance of his being, this original and free reversal from being receptive into being acquisitive, which from now on will influence the tendency of all of creation, is what has come to be called "original sin." This demonstrates just how far divine love goes on behalf of freedom. Man's freedom is shown in this refusal to love, which affirms not only the greatness of the possibilities open to the creature, the exalted and simultaneously tragic dignity of the free being, but also the depth of divine freedom in love, the Trinitarian humility of God who in the Spirit is freedom: "Where there is the Spirit of the Lord, there is freedom" (2 Cor 3:17).

And inasmuch as this risk of freedom is given the creature in him who is at once the Spirit of freedom and the Spirit of love who unites, it is possible to affirm that even when man separates himself from God, God does not separate himself from man. If the creature uses freedom badly, refusing love, the Spirit, in whom freedom has been given him, does not cease to be the bond of communion and hence does not cease to assure him of the Father's closeness.

This closeness is the closeness of the "suffering" God, of him who, infinitely loving in freedom and accepting the risk of love, opens himself up to the possibility of active suffering, freely accepted out of love. In the Spirit the Father is "com-passionate, because he is not without heart."[10] In love "not even the Father is impassible . . . He suffers the passion of love . . ."[11] Does not he who calls a feast for the son who is found again, suffer because of that same son who was lost, whose freedom, however, he respected to the bitter end (Lk 15:11ff)?

The evil which devastates the earth is permitted by him who, in the Spirit, calls into being and calls to freedom. But it is certainly not willed by him who, in the same Spirit, never abandons his creatures though he must suffer for their love. Before the Son dies on the cross in solidarity with sinners, the suffering of love already dwells in the Trinitarian heart of God. Suffering is nothing other than the face of that love which creates in freedom, and hence accepts to the bitter end the risk of the creature's otherness.

"There was a cross in the heart of God before there was one planted on the green hillside outside Jerusalem. And now that the wooden cross has been carried away, the one in God's heart remains and will remain as long as there will also be one sinner for whom to suffer'' (C.A. Dinsmore).

It is the mission of the incarnate Son to give to creation the possibility of returning to its pristine state of receptivity, in a way and at a level, however, which surpasses the creature's highest possible expectation.

b) *The Creator and the Creature*

If creation is the history of the Father, and of the Son, and of the Holy Spirit — the unfolding of the story of the beginning which is based, according to an analogy constructed on the basis of the Easter event, in the eternal processions of Love — then creation is the Trinitarian history *of God*. Hence it is legitimate to say that the one God is the creator of the world. [12]

With this powerful affirmation, founded not only on the "pericoretic" unity of the Three who act in creating but also on their essential unity, our intention is to stress divine transcendence and freedom in regard to creatures. The Creator is infinitely other and more in regard to what is created by him. The world of God does not allow itself to be captured and explained by the world of man. In no way is the Creator determined by the creature; rather it is the Creator who gives life and being to the creature.

This divine otherness and sovereignty is not to be conceived, however, as foreignness and separation. Precisely insofar as God is the Absolute, nothing can exist "outside" him. "Is it not perhaps true that God has created the world '*in se*:' time *in* his eternity, finitude *in* his infinity, space *in* his own omnipresence, and freedom *in* his own disinterested love?" [13] Existing "outside God," as other and limited in respect to him, the world exists "in God" insofar as it shares in the being given it by the Creator and is surrounded by the mystery of his Love, which is, after all, the mystery of the divine essence itself.

God, in this sense, is in everything more profoundly than that which is most profound in everything: "Insofar as anything has being, so far is it necessary that God be present in it, according to the mode in which it has its being."[14] Supreme transcendence thus coincides with supreme immanence: *"Superior summo meo, interior intimo meo"* (St. Augustine). He who infinitely transcends the world is also the heart and bosom of the world, the one in whom "we live and move and have our being" (Ac 17:28).

This being in God of the world, which is also other than God, this paradoxical identity of the transcendence and immanence of God the Creator in regard to the creature, justifies a twofold inquiry. The first concerns the possibility of knowing the Totally Other as the Totally Within: Is it possible to know God from the starting point of creatures? The second concerns the relationship between the original communication of being to creatures and the new gift of divine life made possible by the redemption. Being treated here, respectively, are the problems of the natural awareness of God and that of the relationship between nature and grace.

The question of the awareness of God moving from his creatures does not refer to a simple conceptual abstraction but touches more in general on the vital process by which a person opens up to God: It is the problem of the access to divine reality starting from resources over which the creature has control.[15]

Taking into account this existential complexity, it is possible to give only one dialectically articulated answer to the question. In the first place *the possibility of a natural awareness of God* should be acknowledged. This is what is affirmed against fideism and traditionalism, which would reduce access to God to the ambit of faith alone, and it would contradict the living transmission of revealed truth as expressed by Vatican I:

"God, the beginning and the end of all things, can be known with certainty from the things that were created through the natural light of human reason, for 'ever since the creation of the world His invisible nature has been clearly perceived in the things that have been made' (Rm 1:20)."[16]

This awareness (not demonstration) of God is therefore affirmed with certain possibility (not as "fact"). It is the same profound presence of the Creator to all things which explains why it is possible through them to approach his mystery in some way. As Totally Within, the Totally Other is not far away from those who seek him (cf. Ac 17:27); insofar as the world is in God, it is possible to investigate in it the signs of him who, immanently, is also sovereignly transcendent and other. As God is in the world, present in the deepest part of all things, it is possible to discern in them the degree of his transcendence.

These signs and these degrees have been variously singled out in the history of research about God. Against the backdrop of the primacy of being, Thomas Aquinas has reduced them organically to his five ways:[17] from the starting point of different aspects of the reality of experience — movement, efficient causality, contingency, the grades of being and the finalism which governs all things — his ways point to an ultimate cause which does not form part of the chain of penultimate causes because this one, inasmuch as it is infinite, remains marked by the finitude of not giving itself being but receiving it. This ultimate cause, which gives being to everything but receives it from none because it is being in all its fullness, is the Prime Mover, the First Cause, the one Necessary Being, endowed with every perfection and with supreme intelligence that gives order to the universe.

The force of the five ways lies in their rigorous conformity with the mode of thought in which they were expressed, a mode of thought marked by a lively sense of the objectivity and the primacy of being. Confronted by the radical contingency of all things worldly, what is and what *can* not be, these indicate the only possible foundation of reality in that being which is and cannot not be. God's being thus becomes the guarantee of the world's consistency, otherwise enveloped by nothing, the only response possible to the radical metaphysical question: Why does something and not nothing exist? The necessary God who gives being to everything and receives it from none is the ontological bulwark against all nihilism, the objective force on which the world's and man's destiny rests, the foundation and ultimate meaning of all things.

The ontological argument of Anselm of Aosta[18] tends to the same conclusion. He begins, however, not from below, from the known world of creatures but from the idea itself of God who shines forth in the mind of man, created in his image. This idea is that of "the being of whom nothing greater can be thought."[19] As such, God, rich in every perfection and greatness, must exist because if he did not, one could think of a still greater being endowed with existence, which in reality would be God himself.

Anselm takes the primacy of being to the very heart of the subject and of his thought. It is at this level that the divine being manifests itself breaking with the self-evidence of its idea and, in turn, of its reality. Anselm thus works a reversal of the research on God. One no longer starts from the world in trying to establish a proof of the existence of God but, in a certain sense, it is by starting with God that one must verify the world.

It is this turnabout that, against the background of the primacy of subjectivity emerging in the modern era, will be made its own (and misrepresented) by Hegelian thought. In the latter, the history of the world becomes the history of the spirit which, in its highest form, is Absolute Spirit, the divine Subject which distinguishes itself and identifies itself in the dialectic process, of which the subjective spirit is the initial phenomenology. Man's becoming aware thus becomes in reality a level of God's becoming aware. And in the history of the world, the "curriculum vitae" of God, the very history of the Absolute, begins to make itself explicit.

Coming to an awareness of the idea, the self-possession of it in the distinction from self, is then the "given" of divine existence. In the process of the spirit, it is God who presents himself, from now on a God so completely settled in the world which, for its part, is taken up completely into the eternal and necessary experience of the Absolute. God, as idea, is not proved He is there; and in the process of the awareness of the truth, he is self-evident.[20]

The reflection of faith reacts against this idealistic way of capturing God, made prisoner by a kind of "monism of the spirit." While the Neo-Scholastics ask for a return to objectivity,[21] the school of Tubingen seeks a balance between objectivism and idealistic reductionism in a fruitful rediscovery of history.[22] It is in line with this historical sense that the proof of the existence of God is more and more regarded as a concept born of the experience of an encounter. If, on the one hand, there is evidence that it is God who lets himself be known, offering himself as the meaning and the foundation of life and history, on the other, the radical problematic (Marcel) is also invoked as is man's self-transcendence as opening to the divine infinite (Rahner).

While the crisis of modern reason has done away with any presumption about emancipating the world from God through a pure and simple elimination of the divine "partner" (the theological about face of so-called "dialectical illuminism," the critical overthrow of the absolutizing pretensions of reason), existentialism and personalism have rediscovered the value of the individual in their radical questions and the force of love which is capable of giving meaning to life. Wonder, the thirst for freedom and justice, the need for personal and collective meaning all reveal a "nostalgia for the Totally Other" (Horkheimer) which is not filled by a purely this-world "hope principle" (Bloch).

It is in this direction that man's paths offer themselves as "interrupted paths" (Heidegger); and the appeal to getting to the bottom of things can be understood as the search for an encounter with God, the absolute future capable of offering himself as the goal of the adventure of mankind, otherwise prisoner of evils past and present and of a future which is obscure.

Speaking about God by telling of these encounter experiences with him is offered as one, if not the last, way to realize such an encounter. It is to revive the story of love in the many human stories of suffering.[23] Experience, as direct knowledge characterized by the risk of freedom,[24] becomes the fruitful demonstration of one's encounter with God, and the way toward an ever new realization of it. To the "argued" God of the philosophers and the wise men is thus preferred the "narrated" God of Abraham, Isaac and Jacob.

If these different approaches to the mystery of divinity indicate different ways in which man can open himself up to a natural awareness of God, they also reveal certain *limits*. However probative an argument or an account may be, the proof of God always remains an appeal to free choice which requires a personal decision to assent before it translates itself into an effective encounter with the divine reality. God remains a risk.[25]

Vatican I affirms this in opposition to every kind of rationalism which would presume to imprison the divine in the web of human reason, acknowledging that it is due to *revelation* that "such truths among things divine as of themselves are not beyond human reason can, even in the present condition of mankind, be known by everyone with facility, with firm certitude and with no admixture of error."[26]

Negative theology has constantly emphasized these limits and weaknesses in man's natural knowledge of God, connecting it not only with the effective limits of our human capacity to know (man's darkness) but also and especially with the limitless richness of the transcendence of the mystery (God's obscurity).[27]

It is here that the affirmative and the negative ways both become an appeal to the one "*via eminentiae*," to a *higher route to God*, which is connected with his own coming to us. He who is sought beyond our finitude and who remains hidden as the Greater and the Beyond of our journey is invoked and presents himself as the God who comes. God is he who is other, because in coming he is not yet reached by man; God is he who is near, because in coming he determines, by that very fact, the existence of man; God is he who is alive because, already present though not yet fully given, he gives rise to that permanent passage from the present to the future by which life is properly understood.[28] To live, then, is to seek God; but to live fully is to find him.

These last reflections are wedded to another question placed as a result of the identity between immanence and transcendence in God the Creator — that of the relationship between his original self-communication in the gift of being and the supreme divine self-communication, established by the mission of the Son and that of the Spirit. It is the problem of the relationship between nature and grace, and hence of the legitimacy or less of the natural presuppositions of grace, and hence of the rational presuppositions of the faith which permit a reasonable homage to God who reveals himself.

Karl Barth,[29] in our century, has taken a position in opposition to all so-called "natural theology." He sees in such a theology a residue of liberal thought intent on measuring God by human reason and not vice versa — an idolatrous temptation. Such a complete refusal, motivated by the urgency to say "No" to any attempt to put something human in place of the one true God (the tragedy of Nazism comes to mind), has since been somewhat tempered in Barth and in those who have followed him (Pannenberg, Ebeling, Jungel).

The rediscovery of the *humanity of God*, following that of his *divinity*,[30] has carried with it the need to join to the great and necessary divine noes regarding the world the many, often humble, daily yeses which man needs to live and, yes, to die. These affirmations would seem to include a "Yes" to the human possibility of faith. The rationality of belief sacrifices nothing of God's transcendence but rather affirms the profoundly humanizing effect which accompanies any encounter with the living God.

Natural theology is presented, then, as a way of giving witness to the free and gratuitous initiative of the grace which is within us: "Sanctify Christ as Lord in your hearts. Always be ready to give an explanation to anyone who asks you for a reason for your hope'' (1 P 3:15). This ''giving a reason for your hope'' takes place by showing how the divine offering in revelation does not contradict the original gift of creation and, positively, by showing how it surpasses it, exposing the deeper sense of things and their exalted participation in divine life.

A threefold relationship can be derived between nature and grace. In the first place, *grace affirms nature*. If Creator and Redeemer are the same God, there can be no opposition between the communication of his life and his being in the beginning and the participation in his nature granted in the ''fullness of time.''

In this light, if the history of revelation reveals God as love, faith in creation as an act of the Trinitarian God affirms for us that *love is divine*. *''Ubi caritas et amor, ibi Deus est.''* ''Where charity and love exist, God is there.'' The presence of love is the presence of God. And the way that leads in the most perfect way to an encounter with him who is in all things is the way of love which opens up the mystery of being. This love, impressed as a vocation in the very depths of the creature, is the wellspring of freedom: ''Love, and do what you will'' (St. Augustine).

The tragedy of sin, though, and the infinite sorrow of the cross, cast light on the second aspect of the process which is established between nature and grace: *grace denies nature* insofar as it judges in nature everything which opposes grace as a closing off of oneself from the living God. The original refusal of love on the part of the free creature has resulted in a deep disturbance in being itself. What is constitutively receptive has become the slave of possessiveness.

It is here that the pure gift of grace, the absolute receptivity of the incarnate Word, cannot but be opposed to fallen nature because of sin. Pure love judges the world's non-love. And since, on the basis of his capabilities alone, corrupted by original sin, man of himself is not capable of loving purely, it must be said that *simple natural love is not God*. *''Ubi caritas est vera, ibi Deus est.''* ''Where true love is, there is God.'' It is in the truth of love that

God is present. Where love is defiled, radically corrupted by the spirit of possession, there the divine presence is obscured to the point of becoming unrecognizable (one need only think of the many ways in which love is vulgarized, dehumanized).

Therefore, it is necessary that *grace overcome nature*. Not in the sense of annihilating it but in the sense of bringing it not only to its primitive state of receptivity to love but also and especially to a new and indispensable level of welcome and spread of the gift which is realized in the supreme handing over of the Son of God on the cross and in the paschal communication of the Holy Spirit.

In the light of this salvific event, unprogrammable and un-claimable by nature alone, because founded on the absolute free-dom and gratuity of saving divine love, it is possible to affirm that *God is love* and that "he who abides in love abides in God and God in him" (1 Jn 4:16). According to this triple relationship — of affirmation, negation and eminence — it is therefore possible to say that "Grace does not destroy nature but presupposes and perfects it."[31] According to this same relationship, it is possible to affirm that divine love does not destroy human love, but presup-poses it and brings it to perfection.[32]

The human need to love and be loved — in which, by virtue of the fact that God is love, it is possible to acknowledge what the Medievalists called the natural desire to see God — finds in the gratuitous and perfect Easter communication of love its highest, unprogrammable and subversive fulfillment.

c) *Man, Image of the Trinitarian God*

In the ambit of creation, man is the apex, the handiwork of God completed by him on the day before his rest: "God looked at everything he had made, and he found it very good. Evening came, and morning followed — the sixth day" (Gn 1:31). Among all the creatures, man alone was made in the image and likeness of the

Creator: "And God said: Let us make man in our own image and after our own likeness" (Gn 1:26).

The reason for his being created in the image of God will be reread by the Easter community in a Christological and Trinitarian sense: Christ is *par excellence* the image of the invisible God (cf. Col 1:15; 2 Cor 4:4; Jn 1:18; 14:9 and Heb 1:3). In him, "the last Adam" (cf. Rm 5:12-21; 1 Cor 15:20-22, 45-49), man, created in God's image (1 Cor 11:7), is recreated as the "new man" in the image of the Creator (Col 3:10; Rm 8:29; 1 Cor 15:49 and 2 Cor 3:18).

In the light of this paschal rereading, patristic tradition has seen in the plural of Gn 1:26 ("Let *us* make man in *our* image") an evocation of the Trinity.[33] The vision that Christian faith has of man is therefore properly Trinitarian. Just as creation is the Trinitarian history of God, so too its highest expression is profoundly marked by the constitutive and essential rapport with the Trinity.[34] Man is the image of the Trinitarian God.

The divine image in man shows itself especially in the fact that, in his origin and in the new creation of Easter (Col 3:10), he reflects the Creator, the *Father*. As the Father, in eternal love, is the pure wellspring, so he bestows on the human creature the ability to be in time *a source of love*. This means that man is constitutively capable of loving, is called to give love. Loved from eternity, he is made to love. "Man," says the Lord, "consider that I was the very first to love you. You were not yet in the world, the world was not yet, and I already loved you. As long as I have been God, I love you."[35]

Certainly without this eternal initiative of love, any temporal wellspring of love would be unthinkable. It is because he is "first" loved that man can love. Moreover, in this, his power to love, is reflected, albeit with an infinite difference, the eternal principle of love, the wellspring without beginning and without source of the eternal Lover.

Man is, in time, a subject of love. Incapable of giving being and life to the beloved, man is nonetheless capable of helping his beloved discover being and life and love in a new way through those signs which in every age characterize love, spoken to the other in word and example: "Thank you just for being! I'm glad that you exist!"

Loving in this sense, man reproduces somehow the original creative assent: "Every expression of human love ('It's good that you are here') is a reproduction of the creative love of God in virtue of whose approval every being, including this person loved by me, actually exists."[36] Love makes life bloom.

Man, then, is the image of the Trinitarian God insofar as — in his origins and in the fullness of Easter — he has been created by means of the *Son*, in view of him and in him (Col 1:15-17). Just as the Son, in virtue of his pure acceptance, is the perfect image of the Father, so too man is the image of God, receptivity capable of accepting the love of the eternal Lover to the highest and most transparent degree possible in creation.

In the eternal Beloved, man is constitutively the *object of love*, radically open, the "hearer of the Word" (Rahner), called to let himself be loved in the joy of gratitude. Whoever does not know how to receive love will never truly exist. The poverty of acceptance is the prerequisite of love and hence of being. Whoever does not know how to say thanks will never be truly and fully human. Where there is no gratitude, the gift is lost.

Whereas in the Son receptivity is absolutely pure, in the creature it can turn into possessiveness and egoism which enslaves love. Here one discovers the original need and blessedness of losing oneself, of not wanting to hold on to love, of knowing how to let oneself love in poverty, without having to be the "protagonist" of love: "Whoever wants to save his life will lose it, but whoever loses his life for my sake will save it" (Lk 9:24).

And it is here that the continual discovery of the need of others' love is also made. Insofar as we are marked constitutively by receptivity, we need others. Our being is not the incommunicable solitude of individual substance (being *in se*) nor the solitary self-possession of the subject (being *per se*) but is — in the relational sense of Trinitarian history — personal being, being with others in the communion of love. Others are not, therefore, the limit of our own existence but exactly the opposite. Insofar as man is receptivity, others are the threshold where one truly begins to exist: "No man is an island" (John Donne). From the beginning, in the depth of his being as a creature marked with the stamp of the eternal Beloved, man needs the other!

In the realization of this constitutive call to companionship in life, man reveals in himself the presence of the *Holy Spirit*. Present at the act of creation (Gn 1:2), the power behind the new creation (Mk 1:10 and parallels), the Spirit impresses on the human creature a certain reflection of what he is in the mystery of God. Just as he is, between Lover and Beloved, the eternal bond of unity and at the same time the one who provides the infinite opening out of their love to others, so too in man he is the Spirit of unity and egress from the self.

Subject and object of love, man is *the living unity* of this twofold movement of love. Loving, he makes himself love; letting himself love, he loves. There is no contradiction between initiating and receiving love. Rather, one cannot truly subsist without the other. "*Amor a null' amato amar perdona*" "Love does not forgive those who do not love" (Dante).

This unity of source and receptacle is the foundation of that reciprocity of knowledge in which the human person is fully realized. This reciprocity, however must never become an egotistical confrontation. The Spirit, present in man, continually pushes him to break the circle of lover and beloved, to flee the captivity of exclusivity and to move toward the need to love others, all others. "To love is not to stand and look into each other's eyes, but to look toward the same goal together" (Antoine de Saint-Exupery).

Man, then, is constitutively called to *freedom in love*. He loves truly and hence truly *is* if he loves in freedom. And he is free if the action of love's initiative and acceptance brings him to flee each and every asphyxiating relationship which would prevent his growth in love. This doesn't mean that the person cannot live in love relationships of varying degrees of exclusivity; but even the most authentically exclusive relationship, such as that between spouses, must always be inclusive of others, too, such as their children who are the sign of the fecundity and the freedom of their love.

By virtue of this constitutive relationship with the Holy Trinity, man is therefore the image of God the Father, through the Son, in the Spirit. In him is reflected loving Love insofar as man is loved originally in the unity and freedom of love. In other words, the Trinitarian God, communicating being to the creature, also impresses on him something of the eternal movement of his life and thus makes that creature an image of the eternal history of love. It is therefore possible to say that man reflects the one and triune God inasmuch as he reflects the unity in communion and essence of the dynamism of divine life.

Herein lies the real value of all the analogies or "traces" of the Trinity which faith reflection in time has come to discover in the human spirit. Certainly these traces were never meant to explain the Trinity by man. Rather, these analogies have sought to understand man by starting out from Trinitarian revelation so as then to more fully enter into that mystery of which the human creature is the image.[37]

"The Trinity is one thing in its very own reality; the image of the Trinity in a different reality is another. It is precisely because of this image that that in which these three powers are found (memory, intelligence and love) is also called image."[38]

This analogy takes into account the infinite distance between the single human subject, in whom the three powers are present, and the three divine Persons in the oneness of their nature.[39] Nevertheless, the reason for the image assures us that in the reality of man one can find a reflection of the reality of God.

Insofar as this divine reality is the eternal history of love, the image makes itself apparent especially in the dynamism of the wellspring, the receptivity and the open reciprocity of human love. The earthly history of love reflects the eternal history of love. *Man is the image of God in his historicity*, in his proposing himself to the other and in welcoming the other, thanks to the unifying and freeing relationship of love.

Man is, therefore, the person-image of God not in the closure of a spirit sated with itself (modern subjectivism) or in the static solitude of an incommunicable substance (ancient objectivism) but in the openness and reciprocity of the communication of love, in being with others so as to build up the future with them and narrate in time a history of love which is the least unfaithful reflection possible of the history of eternal love.

And, since the communication takes place historically among men in the sign of *corporeity*, that is, of the perceptible mediation to the other in time and space, it is here that the value of corporeal being as the image of God is rediscovered, for the initiating and the welcoming of love require a concrete reciprocity made up of words and deeds, flesh and blood.

Every disembodied spiritualism is alienation. Man reflects his God not by fleeing from matter and the world but by fully living in love his corporeity with others and at the service of others. The body, inasmuch as it expresses the wellspring, the receptivity and the communicative and freeing force of love, is the image of the living God! The dualism which tends to view the divine presence in a soul made captive of the body has nothing to do with the Christian concept of creation as Trinitarian history, which impresses on the totality of the human being that dynamism which is the image of the divine life in love.

This idea of man as the image of the Trinitarian God clarifies, finally, how there is no competition between God and man. If the divine Trinity has made of the human creature an icon of his eternal movement of love, this means that in the design of creation, man has a most high dignity and is constitutively called to grow and extend himself in love, that is, always to be more himself in freedom, living in time the imprint of the timeless future of divine love.

The image, which can be disfigured and obscured by the denial of love, can also be developed and perfected by the acceptance of love. "This is what happens in those who progress day by day in good."[40] They become transparent like the saints, capable of transmitting the light of Trinitarian love to the highest possible degree. The effective difficulty in this growth lies in the increasingly stronger existential call to an even higher divine communication which not only restores but makes new in the Son, the eternal image, the temporal image of the living God.

This "non-competition" between God and man takes away from *atheistic humanism* every pretense of consistency. It makes no sense to be an atheist for love of man if the first one to love man and to will his full realization is his very Creator!

This form of atheism has in fact become possible only by making the human subject absolute, raising the creature to the level of absolute source, antithetical to every possible divine origin.[41] Modern atheism preaches a kind of emancipation from the heavenly Father so as to put the world in the hands of man: "God is dead, and we have killed him! . . . Is the magnitude of this deed too much for us? Must we not become gods ourselves so as to appear worthy of it?"[42]

The history of the emancipatory process begun during the Enlightenment has shown the limits of this attempt. The "dialectic of illuminism" is the proclamation of a human world which is its own prisoner, that is, the prisoner of an organizing and manipulating reason, often organized and manipulated itself.[43]

In contrast to this, the living God is presented as the Totally Other, of whom modern man feels such nostalgia and need.[44] Not a God, who crushes man but a Creator who has willed the human creature to be his image and who delights in seeing this fully accomplished: "The glory of God is living man; the life of man is the vision of God."[45]

This human and humanizing God has also deprived the *atheism of protest* of consistency. If he is not the obscure counterpart to the world but the God who is near, who in the Son made himself totally one in human suffering, to attack him because of the evil that exists in the world is to begin again the trial of the Innocent.

It is true that protest is often connected with many who have acted in his name: "The problem of Job, of Ivan Karamazov, of Albert Camus has come down upon us. Auschwitz was the work of Christians. And when they finished, their God became an absurdity."[46]

All the same, the atheism of protest hides a subversion of the original receptivity of love which is constitutive of man. It places the creature at the center of things and "pretends" love without sufficiently analyzing the historical human responsibility for its denial which stands as the ultimate cause of every suffering in the world. The God who handed his own Son over to death out of love for man cannot will human suffering! On the contrary, in the infinite receptivity of the Word Incarnate, he does not cease to give love to a world without love so that every story of suffering may find freedom and be transformed by it.

The living God also drains any semblance of consistency from that kind of *practicing atheism* which sees in him a useless evasion of the duty to free the individual who is oppressed and to construct for all a more just and human society. Hidden here is a subversion of the stamp of unity in freedom which, thanks to the Spirit, has been impressed on man.

The God in whose image man was made wants a relationship of reciprocity in freedom among men, which is therefore a relationship of justice for all. Every oppression of man by man mars the divine image and offends the Creator. Every authentically freeing practice expresses the deep calling of the creature to freedom and renders glory to the Lord of heaven and earth. To work for the humanization of the world is to work for God. It is to develop the whole man in every man, that is, in all men. It is to restore to all the divine image imprinted in man from the very beginning. Far from being "the opium of the people," and "the seduction of souls," the God who created man in the Spirit of love and freedom is the God of liberation who loves in freedom and frees in love, sustaining the efforts of all who work for freedom, doing so with love.

d) *The Trinity and the Human Community*

These last reflections justify the question about the relationship between the Trinity, the origin of history, and the human community.[47] If God the Creator desires the full realization of the human creature, and this cannot be accomplished apart from the sociality of love, there cannot but be a relationship between the eternal history of the Trinitarian communion and the historical process of building up the human family. It is possible to find this link in the relationships of the divine Persons as each relates to the others in love.

As the communion of Persons in the Trinity is related to the *Father*, the eternal source of love, so the communion of people on earth is related constitutively to God the Father, Lord of heaven and earth. This means that the community is a *communion of different springs of love*, which must be related among themselves in order to become together a single *wellspring of life and love*. A community in which the dignity of each, his or her autonomous creativity in the initiative of love, his or her originality and unrepeatability, are not respected will not reflect the Father. But neither will the Father be reflected in a community in which these different personalities don't know how to converge in communion so as to become a common, higher wellspring for all.

That this cannot be accomplished under the standard of man's dominion and absolute power over man (and hence by authoritarian and oppressive means) is certain given the fact that such a way of building community would contradict the original plan of the Creator written in the very depths of every human heart. Far from being the "universal monarch" who justifies despotic earthly authorities, God the Father of the Trinity calls each to be himself, and to be so while respecting the dignity and source of love proper to all others.

"The affirmation of the one God, and in particular of his attributes of absoluteness and omnipotence," it must be admitted, "while not figuring into the confession of the Trinity, can lend itself — and in the history of Christianity has lent itself more than once — as a theological pretext for supporting political and ecclesiastical structures bearing the standard of dominion and power of man over man."[48]

In this sense the conclusion, "One God, one Lord, one people, one reign" — if it corresponds to the Greek nostalgia for the One by whom that which exists "does not want to be badly ruled; therefore, it is not good that there be several lords; let there be one Lord only"[49] — then it absolutely contradicts the Christian image of God the Father and his reflection in history. This conclusion, moreover, contradicts the Old Testament monotheistic God of the prophets in whom the Easter Church recognized the face of the Trinitarian Father.

God is not cold omnipotence which might be used to justify man's exercise of absolute power on earth. "What is omnipotent is only his passionate and passible love." Therefore, "the monarchy of a sovereign does not correspond to that of the One and Triune God. The One and Triune God rather resembles a communion among men in which privilege and submission are not acknowledged."[50]

The community which reflects the face of the eternal Lover is the product of the greatest possible development of the riches of originality possessed by each member, in a communion which is greater than the sum of the gifts of each one, a productive source of love and life for all, and that which empowers each one's capacity to love.

Just as the individual person is related to the *Son* in the welcoming and the accepting of love which render him, in the Son, the image of the Father, so, too, the human community is called to be the place of welcome in which one receives the other and all receive everyone else. *A communion of different receptivities in love*, the community is *reception*, deeper than the simple sum of the receptivity of each one. And just as the receptivity of the Son found its highest expression in obedience to the Father up to the cross where he allowed himself to be handed over for love of sinners, so, too, the receptivity of the community must express itself in its willingness to welcome the other, the one different from itself, to the point of the sacrificial gift of self.

An authentically human community must know how to welcome everyone not because of the individual's merits but because of his or her simple existence, out of respect for what the individual is, in the acceptance of his or her diversity and, finally, of his or her "nothingness." In this sense the community is truly human and reflects in itself the face of the Son of God which accepts the least and courageously denies every discrimination of power, wealth, race, sex, or culture.

"In the cross of Christ, understood in the light of his life as obedience to the Father and to him alone, in the full manifestation of his divine love and in the sharing of our defeated and sinful condition, the mystery of God is revealed as the victorious challenge of every dominion of man over man and of every legalism, and as the foundation of the overture to political action at the service of the least."[51]

The radical receptivity of the human community signifies its permanent openness to the future and the new. Nothing of the present can be idolized, no peaceful possession is allowed, were it even the security of the political (or ecclesiastical) order ideologically absolutized. One's welcome needs to be lived out in the permanent dynamic of the provisional:

"The confession that Jesus is the Truth of God and the judgment of history, and that only in the Spirit must we approach him not only in memory but also in expectation, prevents us from absolutizing any ecclesiastical mediation and any political arrangement. In fact, neither one nor the other can identify itself with the reign of God; neither can any social or political order present itself (in the abstract or the concrete) as the best possible on earth. The totalizing exigency of all our projects is thus constrained in Trinitarian faith by the humility of the provisional."[52]

Finally, since in the bosom of the Trinity the Spirit is the bond of unity and openness in love and, insofar as man, in the *Spirit*, is the image of God through his capacity to join others and to give himself in freedom, the human community will reflect the Spirit's action to the extent that it learns how to be a *communion in the reciprocity and in the permanent tension of freedom*. The richness of the originality of each individual does not build up the community if it does not overcome the solitude and the isolation of each in the reciprocity which fosters communion. And this is not the work of ideologies which ideally strive to reconcile differences but of love, contracted and contagious.

"The gift of the Spirit situates us not outside the Trinity but within the otherness and the reciprocity of the three persons. Thanks to this, Trinitarian faith sets itself apart from ideological interpretations which make its historical and political meaning ambiguous."[53]

The communion thus realized must express itself in an ongoing and unending "freedom march" through the initiation of social projects which take up the different needs which are pointed out by the human community in the light of the Trinity and which are continually verified and renewed in the school of history and in fidelity to God, Creator and Savior, living the decisive effort of "mediation" without facile ideological entrapments or false flights from the fray.

"The revelation of the mystery of God as gift and as communion requires social projects under the banner of acceptance and appreciation of the originality of persons and their call to reciprocity. The Trinitarian mystery does not however present itself before such projects as the generic or finished model of unity and diversity, even because it is not such; but it rather enjoins risk-taking in fidelity to the unmistakable identity of the Father, the Son and the Holy Spirit and of their work in the history of salvation."[54]

The Trinity is not a formula which allows itself to be transposed through simple analogous deduction.[55] It is much more a horizon which transcends us, a place in which to put oneself ever anew, a history of love in which to include oneself and to narrate by choices of justice and freedom in man's life and works.

Thus God's image in man is extended to the whole human family. Not just the nucleus of the family with its relationships of reciprocity and communion,[56] but the entire human community and its history become the reflection of the divine process of love.

And if all that is violence, dependent and oppressive systems, despoilment and injustice, obscures the original relationship of Love the creator, then all that is peace, liberation and justice offers itself as the image of and participation in the Trinitarian history of love. Thus the eternal comes to tell of itself in time through the poor gestures of solidarity, reconciliation, freedom given and received, and of the passion for justice, stronger than any defeat.

4.2   THE TRINITARIAN PRESENT
OF HISTORY

a) *The Trinity and the Present Time*

Between the Trinitarian origin of history and the promised
land in the glory of the Trinity stands the present time, the
"meantime." It is not the first time or the last; it is the "penultimate" time. How is it characterized in relation to the eternal
process of Love? How does it open up to the mystery of the Trinity,
making it a part of itself to the point of becoming the "today" of
God (cf., for example, Lk 19:9)?[57]
Inasmuch as time has its origin in the Trinitarian act of
creation, and inasmuch as the eternal event of love was manifested
in the temporal event of Easter which the Spirit does not cease to
make present in history, it can be said that the intermediate time,
that is, the present hour, is *the time of God for man*. Creating man
and then assuming him into the hour of Easter, the Trinitarian God
has fashioned time precisely to give all time to man as a time of
salvation, an hour of grace (2 Cor 6:2). This profound affirmation
must be understood in a Trinitarian sense. Time without time
(eternity) reaches into the time of men as *provenance*, as *coming*,
and as *future*.
In his eternal future "God is provenance, coming, and future.
God is provenance from himself insofar as he is the origin of
himself. The provenance of God is his past which does not pass.
God is the coming of himself to the extent that he is his own end.

The coming of God is his present which does not pass. God is his own future inasmuch as he is the mediation of himself. The future of God is not the passing of his past and present. It is, all the same, the going ahead of God."[58]

As provenance or origin in the divine life, God is Father. As its coming or end, he is Son. As the future or eternal unity of the origin and the end, in their free opening up of the self in love, God is the Holy Spirit. It is thus that at Easter the Trinitarian God presents himself as the origin of the event, or the Father who sends; as its end, or the Son who is sent; as the Easter opening up of divine life, or the Spirit, handed over by the Son to the Father in the hour of the cross, as the hour of supreme separation, and given by the Father to the Son in the resurrection, as the hour of supreme communion. In the paschal event, the Trinity makes history and definitively marks the future of time as pertaining to the eternal future of God.

Thus, the origin of every present, the progress from the past of every today, reveals the rooting of the actual hour in the mystery of the Father who is the unique origin of everything that exists. The positing of the present instant, the coming or the occurrence of every now, reveals the rooting of the actual moment in the mystery of the Son; the opening up to the future in every present, in permanent continuity with today and with the past, and the coming of the hour reveals the rooting of the instant which is lived in the mystery of the Spirit.

In every actual event, God is provenance, coming and future! The temporal event thus evokes the eternal event in which it is rooted. The flow of past into present, which is the permanent advent of the future, is given us as a kind of branch from the eternal flow in love of the Lover in the Beloved, in the unity and freedom of the Spirit of one and the other. Every instant comes from the Father through the Son in the Spirit, and in the same Spirit goes through the Son to the Father.

Every time is constitutively marked by a wellspring, a reception, and the unity in an open-ended future of one and the other. Insofar as it is rooted in the past, the present is the locus of the source; insofar as lived in the moment, the present is the locus of reception; insofar as it is the unity of both moments in an opening out to the future, the present is the locus of freedom and of love. The unity of the origin, moreover, in the unity of the present time, reflects both the end and the future, which in God is the unity of the eternal movement of the love of all Three.

This profound and pristine Trinitarian structure of time, however, remains unfruitful if it is not assumed in freedom by the conscious act of man who is the lord of time. God's time for man remains an invitation without a response if there is not a *time of man for God*. This means a mindful acceptance through which the human person goes from being the object to constituting the subject of his history, living fully his present in the creativity, the reception, and the freedom of love.

It is a passage from purely *quantified* time, which is the simple flow of life in its natural succession of seasons and days, to *qualified* time where the present instant acquires a new coherence by virtue of man's choices. In the language of the New Testament, it is the passage from *chronos* (cf., for example, Mt 25:19; Mk 2:19; 9:21; Lk 8:27, 29, etc.) to *kairos* (cf., for example, Mk 1:15; Mt 8:29; 26:18; Lk 19:44; Rm 3:26; 5:6, etc.).[59]

According to paschal faith, this passage takes place precisely at the moment in which the person decides for Christ, in freedom and in love. In this act, man lives the source of the initiative, the reception of the gift, and the unity open to the future of one and the other. Opening himself to the coming reign of God, the human creature makes efficacious for himself the original act of creation on the part of the Father and the sending he does of the Son, and thus re-presents in himself beginning and time as provenance.

He appropriates, in the reception of the Son handed over to death, the gift of divine life given at Easter, and thus realizes in himself the coming of Love and time as an event of grace. He opens

himself up in his welcoming yes, the unity of initiative and receptivity, to the future of God in his life, and thus, in the Spirit of
freedom and love, moves toward the future and makes of time the
present terrain of what is to come.

In man's hands, therefore, there is the possibility of making
penultimate time an original reflection of eternity, and the history
of the world an image of the Trinitarian history of God, the history
of love. Time can be pure and simple duration or fully-lived
existence, a cycle which repeats itself in the monotony of a happening closed in on itself, or open-ended history, oriented toward the
future in freedom.

Authentic life is that of the one who chooses and risks the
present in love, in order to take hold of an uncertain future.
Unauthentic existence is that of the one who, for lack of freedom,
goes around in circles, repetitiously, without "going out to him
(Christ) outside the camp" (Heb 13:13). Whoever hopes for a
permanent city here on earth is wasting his time. Whoever seeks
the future in God has already found it, and has made of the present
the time of the Trinitarian love of God (Heb 13:14).

Time is always, in the Trinity, a creature of that divine love
which has left its imprint on it. But the Trinity only explicitly
enters time when man decides to live in freedom and in love: "If
anyone loves me, he will keep my word and my Father will love
him, and we will come to him and make our home with him" (Jn
14:23).

b) *The Trinity in Man*

Man's decision for Christ, therefore, opens up existence in
time to the reception of eternal life. In present history, the eternal
history of love comes to be told. How does this passage properly
take place? How does man — in whom the image of the Holy
Trinity is impressed — enter Trinitarian life itself? And how does

the Trinity enter, in a new and full way, into the most exalted of its creatures?

From the beginnings of Christian faith, the decisive act of this passage was performed and celebrated by baptism in the name of the Trinity: "Go, therefore, and teach all nations, baptizing them in the name of the Father, and of the Son, and of the Holy Spirit" (Mt 28:19). Christian existence is a baptismal existence and, since in baptism Easter is represented and hence the Trinity is told about and given, it is an Easter, a Trinitarian existence.

The liturgy expresses this mystery by linking baptism in a special way with Easter night and with the articulation of the profession of faith required at baptism by the triple question, relative to Father, Son and Spirit respectively and to their role in the history of salvation.[60] In the life of him who gets baptized the divine life of the Three, their "nature," thus comes to be communicated (2 P 1:4) and thus the eternal history of their love gets to be told.

"Baptism is participation in the death and resurrection of Christ (Rm 6:3-5; Col 2:12); purification from sin (1 Cor 6:11); a new birth (Jn 3:5); illumination through Christ (Ep 5:14); a clothing of oneself in Christ (Gal 3:27); renewal through the Spirit (Tt 3:5); the experience of salvation from the waters of the flood (1 P 3:20); exodus from slavery (1 Cor 10:1ff) and freedom in view of a new humanity in which the barriers of sex, race and social position are overcome (Gal 3:27; 1 Cor 12:13)."[61]

Through baptism people become the adoptive sons and daughters of *God*, in the one eternally beloved Son (Gal 3:26ff; 4:4ff). They are buried together with *Christ* in death so that just as he was raised from the dead, they too might walk in a new life (cf. Rm 6:3-11; Col 2:12; 3:1; Ep 2:5ff). And, in the gift of the *Holy Spirit*, "anointing, seal, pledge" (2 Cor 1:2; Ep 1:13), they are regenerated and renewed (Tt 3:5) and from now on can turn to God, calling him Father (Rm 8:15, 26; Gal 4:6).

The new life of baptism comes from the Father by means of

assimilation to the dead and risen Christ, in the grace of the Holy Spirit. It is life which reflects Trinitarian unity, in the incorporation in the ecclesial body of Christ (Ep 4:4) and in the anticipation of the future unity of the reign of God.[62] Baptismal existence is, therefore, rooted and founded in the Trinity and unfolds with a dynamism which carries with it the analogy of the life of God himself.

From the beginning this explanation of the paschal existence, inserted in the Trinitarian mystery thanks to baptism, has been cultivated in the theological life of faith, hope and charity (cf. 1 Th 1:3; 5:8; 1 Cor 13:7, 13; Gal 5:5; Rm 5:1-5; 12:6-12; Col 1:4; Ep 1:15-18; 4:2-5, etc.). In the Trinity, the Christian is a believer, a hope-filled person, someone in love![63]

Insofar as man is brought back to God the Father in baptism, as his adoptive child and restored image (cf. Col 3:10; Rm 8:29; 1 Cor 15:49; 2 Cor 3:18), he reflects in himself what is proper to the Father, the wellspring of love, Loving love.

This reflection of him and of his history is *charity*, the greatest gift because it brings one into relationship with the origin and the principle of all things and all love (1 Cor 13:13); it inspires and makes valid every effort for good (1 Cor 13:1-6); it is at the basis of faith and hope since "it believes all things, hopes all things" (1 Cor 13:7).

Thanks to charity, man can love with the welling up, the gratuity, the creativity that he would not have alone but which are communicated to him by the Father. "*Ubi caritas et amor*, Deus *ibi est*" ("Where there is charity and love, *God* is there"). In the love of charity, baptismal existence makes God himself present and "visible"! Inasmuch as with baptism man is incorporated into the incarnate Son, in his paschal existence man reflects in himself what is proper to the Son: the receptivity of love, being love Loved.

This reflection in him and in his history is *faith*. It is the reception of the gift of God, loving obedience, the faithful listening to the Word (cf., for example, Rm 1:5; 6:17; 10:7; 2 Cor 10:4; 1 Tm

1:6; 2 Tm 1:8, etc.). Believing, man participates in a certain manner in the eternal movement of love through which the Son accepts without measure the love of the Father and becomes its eternal image. To believe is, in this sense, to allow oneself to be loved by God, "to let oneself become the prisoner of the Invisible" (Luther).

Faith does not seek guarantees, does not bargain, does not calculate. It accepts, trusts, obeys. Thus it is that Christ, the object of faith, is also the model of our faith, he who has preceded us in the battle of the faith (cf. Heb 12:2).[64] In the life of the believer, the mystery of the obedience of the Son is re-presented. Even theological existence is a totally received existence!

Finally, inasmuch as man is filled at baptism with the gift of the Holy Spirit, he reflects in his theological life what is proper to the Spirit — to be the bond of unity and openness of freedom in love.

This reflection in baptismal existence is *hope*; it unites the present to God's future, opening the heart of the believer perennially to what is coming and what is new. Far from ending in passive expectation or in sterile evasion, theological hope is the militant anticipation of the promised future. It is a "passion for the possible" (Kierkegaard), which causes God's tomorrow to be drawn into men's present.

Hope gives imagination to the source of love and courage to the obedience of faith: "They who hope in the Lord will renew their strength, they will soar with eagles' wings; they will run and not grow weary, walk and not grow faint" (Is 40:31). This hope, which unites the boldness of love to the patience of faith, will not be disappointed (Rm 5:5).

The industriousness of charity and the reception of faith united in the freedom of hope, therefore, characterize redeemed existence as Trinitarian, Easter existence. They consequently do not exist separately but support one another in a vital dynamism which reflects the inseparable dynamism of the wellspring, the receptivity, and the free openness of eternal love which is the life of the Trinity. Baptismal existence, then, will be so much the more fulfilled the more one learns how to receive into himself the vivifying presence of the Trinitarian mystery and express it in gestures of love and faith, in the hope that does not disappoint.

The space for this ever new and ever deeper reception of the Trinity into the life of the baptized person and through it into human history is *Christian prayer*. The latter is not "dialogue at a distance" with an unreachable and obscure divine counterpart. Nor is it a flight from the world to attain a separate and celestial beyond. The Christian does not pray to *a* God! He prays to the God and Father of his Lord, Jesus Christ, to whom he is united by virtue of the Holy Spirit. He prays *in* God: "Through Christ, with Christ, and in Christ, in the unity of the Holy Spirit, all glory and honor is yours, almighty Father, for ever and ever. Amen."

As the liturgy teaches,[65] Christian prayer is always constitutively Trinitarian.

It addresses itself to the *Father*, acknowledging in him the source of every gift, to whom, consequently, thanks and the prayer of petition and intercession are raised.

This prayer is accomplished *by means of the incarnate Son*, with him and in him, because it is in his infinite welcome of God's gift that every reception of his gift is possible for us. And it is in his uninterrupted dialogue of love with the Father that we are received by virtue of the grace of baptism. Christ is the mediator (1 Tm 2:5), the model, and the locus of Christian prayer, the one who "always lives to make intercession for us" (Heb 7:25).

It is, finally, in the *Holy Spirit*, bond of unity and point of permanent access to eternity in time and to time in eternity, that the Christian prays: "In him we cry, 'Abba, Father!' " (Rm 8:15), while he "comes to help us in our weakness because we do not know how we ought to pray but the Spirit himself intercedes for us with groans that words cannot express" (Rm 8:26).

Christian prayer, therefore, is filial prayer, made possible in Christ thanks to the Holy Spirit. It is to say with one's life, in obedience to the Lord's word, "Our Father" (Mt 6:5-13). The vital movement of prayer, consequently, comes from the Father, origin of the Son and of the Spirit and Creator of all things, and returns to the Father by way of the Son in the Spirit, in the heart of him who prays.

In such a sense, prayer places man in the Trinity and causes the Trinity to enter into human existence. It is a being "hidden with Christ in God" (Col 3:3) and an inhabitation of the living God in the heart of the believer (Jn 14:23). It is, in the language of the Greek Fathers especially, a "divinization" of man.[66] To pray is to let ourselves be loved by the Father in his Son and our Lord, Jesus, so that the Spirit himself may come to us and, in him, we may be able to present ourselves to the Father through Christ (Ep 2:18).

Prayer, therefore, is where an alliance between the Trinity and history takes place. In it the human condition is always newly brought to the living God in the form of praise and invocation. And the living God offers himself ever anew to vivify and sustain the history of love of his creatures.

In praying, the Christian experiences how his God is truly his Emmanuel, his "God with us," on our side, and for us. And he has no fear of bringing to this God the truth of his life, made up of acts of thanksgiving but also of requests for pardon and petitions for concrete needs.

Christian contemplation, precisely because it is founded in Christ and in the Spirit, is always then filled with history. Far from being evasion and flight, it is the contagious and liberating experience of the love of the God of the covenant who reaches down into our daily life with all its humble burdens and makes of it the story of God with men and, hence, also of man with man in the journey of love. In the mystery of Christian prayer, the Trinity enters into history and history into the Trinity![67]

c) *The Church, Icon of the Trinity*

Inasmuch as it communicates itself to man, the Trinity, essential unity and most profound communion of the Three in love, cannot but bring about communion. This community of people gathered together into the unity of Father, Son, and Holy Spirit, this "icon" of the Holy Trinity[68] (not a simple deferment to it, that is, but its efficacious expression), is the *Church*, a people gathered together by God the Father through the missions of the Son and the Holy Spirit, the *Church of the Trinity*.

The Church does not arise "from below," from the convergence of purely worldly interests or out of the inspiration of some generous hearts. It is not simply a fruit of this earth. Like its Lord, the Church is from above, "*oriens ex alto*," close to God, placed in time through the marvelous initiative of Trinitarian love.

It is the *Church of the Father*, who with "the most liberal though hidden designs of wisdom and goodness" has called it together in Christ, prefiguring it from the beginning of the world and preparing for it in the history of the covenant with Israel.

It is the *Church of the Son*, who with his incarnation and Pasch has inaugurated on earth the kingdom of heaven, albeit under the opaque and often sorrowful signs of human experience, making the Church his Body, mystically (that is, "*in mysterio*") crucified in time.

It is the *Church of the Holy Spirit* who, dwelling in it and in the hearts of believers as in a temple, vivifies it ever anew, guides it toward the whole truth, unifies it in communion and in service, providing it with his gifts and making it beautiful with his fruits (cf. *Lumen Gentium*, 2-4).

The Church proceeds from the Father through the Son in the Spirit. Work of the divine missions, it is the place of the encounter between heaven and earth in which the history of the Trinity through the free initiative of love passes into the history of men and assumes and transforms it in the movement of divine life. Arc of the new covenant, *the Church comes from the Trinity* and springs up from it ever anew, presence among all the presences of history, the sign even of another Presence.

It is what Vatican II wanted to affirm by prefacing its entire reflection on the Church with the chapter, *"De Ecclesiae mysterio,"* "On the Mystery of the Church." Recalling the Pauline biblical concept of mystery as the plan of God being realized in time, the Glory hidden under the signs of history, the Council wished to present the Church in its deeply Trinitarian aspects, in its origins which make it hard to pin down in purely worldly terms, a gift to welcome with awe and to live with concrete availability.

Coming from above, springing forth from the Trinity, the Church is also structured after *the image of the Trinity* — one in diversity, communion of different charisms and ministries brought about by the one Spirit, the Church lives by that circulation of love of which Trinitarian life is, besides its source, the incomparable model. As *"in God"* love is the distinction of the Persons and the overcoming of these distinctions in the unity of the mystery, so too in the Church, except as regards the infinite distance which separates earth from heaven but also by virtue of the infinite communion established by the missions of the Son and of the Spirit, love is "the distinction and the overcoming (*Aufheben*, abolition) of the distinct" (Hegel).

The variety of gifts and services must converge in unity, just as the variety of local churches, each the full realization of the *Catholic* Church in concrete and different space-time coordinates, is called to live and express itself in their reciprocal communion. Structured on the Trinitarian model, the Church will have to keep away from both a uniformity which mollifies and mortifies the originality and the richness of the gifts of the Spirit as well as from every rending counterposition which does not resolve, in a communion with the Crucified, the tension between different charisms and ministries, in a fruitful and reciprocal reception of persons and communities in the unity of faith, hope and love (cf. chapter two of *Lumen Gentium*, *"De populo Dei"*).

The Trinity, source and image of the Church, is finally its goal. Born of the Father, through the Son, in the Spirit, the ecclesial communion must return in the Spirit through the Son to the Father until that day when everything will be subject to the Son and the latter will consign all things to the Father, so that "God may be all in all" (1 Cor 15:28).

The *Trinity* is the origin and the promised land toward which the pilgrim people travel. It is the "now" and the "not yet" of the Church, the fontal past and promised future, the beginning and the end. This final destination to Glory into which the communion of people will be inserted in the fullness of the eternal in the divine life is the basis of the eschatological character of the pilgrim Church. The Church does not have its fulfillment in this present time but awaits it and prepares for it right up to the day when its Lord will come anew and everything will be perfectly recapitulated in him.

The Church is, therefore, on its way, never arriving. And for this reason it is *"semper reformanda,"* always in the process of reformation, in need of continual purification and perennial renewal with the help of the Spirit which operates in it so that God's promises may reach fulfillment.

Disturbed and critical of itself in the incessant task of its own reform, the Church is likewise critical and disturbed with regard to happenings in the world whose shortsightedness it must report, proclaiming at the same time the higher goal open to the world by the hope of the Kingdom of God.

Thus, in this season of the "meantime," which runs from the first coming of Christ to his glorious return, the Church lives faithful to the present world and faithful to the world to come, nourished by what has *already* been given it so as to grow toward what *has not yet* been accomplished in it. The Church in the meantime moves toward the Trinity in invocation, praise and service under the weight of the cross of the present and enriched by the joy of the promise (cf. chapter seven of *Lumen Gentium* on the eschatological character of the pilgrim Church and on its union with the heavenly Church).

The Church comes from the Trinity, goes toward it, and is modeled after its image: *"De unitate Patris et Filii et Spiritus Sancti plebs adunata"* "The people are made one from the unity of the Father, Son and Holy Spirit" (St. Cyprian). The Church is brought together by divine unity in the mystery of its unity in time (apostolicity) and in space (catholicity).

Unity in time, which is the bond between the actual faith and the fontal past of the apostolic witness by way of living Church tradition, is then read in the light of Trinitarian life and hence of the reciprocity and complementarity of the Son and the Spirit which originate in their being from the Father.

"A Christological reading (of tradition) alone shows the care taken of the datum, of the objective deposit of faith. A pneumatological reading alone gives evidence of the discontinuity between fontal past and present, filled with the always surprising newness of the Spirit. A reading based on both the reciprocity and the complementarity of Christology and pneumatology shows *tradition as the history of the Spirit* (with all the newness inherent in it) *in the history of the faith and the practice of the Church* (the Christological-incarnational element). The Spirit is the living memory of Christ in us and through our creativity."[69]

Likewise, the unity in space of the ecclesial community, bound up with its full self-realization (catholicity as "fullness") in each local church, by virtue of the one Word, one baptism, one Eucharist and one Spirit, is to be read in the light of the divine communion, and hence of the immanent rapport reflected in the relationship between the Son's mission and that of the Paraclete:

"The present of believing, personal and ecclesial existence can be interpreted in a Christological sense only — and then evidence will be had of visibility, institution, authority, hierarchy, law, letter, primacy — or in a pneumatological sense alone — and then emphasis would fall on invisible depth, charism, freedom, universal priesthood, grace, the spirit, collegiality. A reading historically attentive to the reciprocity and the complementarity of Christology and pneumatology, though, will show the reciprocal and dialectic inclusivity of the visible and the invisible, institution and charism, authority and freedom, community and ministries, law and grace, letter and spirit, primacy and collegiality. The task of believers seems to be not only to execute a project already in place (the merely Christological perspective) nor only to fashion it as one goes along (the merely pneumatological perspective) but to be creatively co-responsible in its acceptance and realization."[70]

Finally, in the mystery of the unity of the Trinity there is to be found the unity of the Church with its fully revealed future, the Kingdom of God, and hence the eschatological character of the entire ecclesial community which is the other face of its apostolicity, its bond with the celestial Jerusalem founded on the twelve Apostles of the Lamb (cf. Rv 21:14).

"In relation to the future, a Christological reading brings one to affirm only the identity of Church and Kingdom; a pneumatological one, only absolute otherness in the millennial expectation of a Kingdom totally different from history. The historical reading of the reciprocity and the complementarity between these two poles will bring one to see in the Church the 'Kingdom of Christ present in mystery' (*Lumen Gentium*, 3). In the present we will discover the eschatology which is being realized through our effort, open to the newness of the Spirit."[71]

d) *The Eucharist, The Trinity, and Ecclesial Communion*

The place where Trinitarian origin is re-presented ever anew, thus raising up and nourishing the Church as one communion in diversity tending toward the final unity of the Kingdom, is the Eucharist.[72] It can be said that the Eucharistic celebration is the point of concrete encounter between the Trinity and the Church, where the origin and the promised land of the ecclesial community meet to generate the Church ever anew in the present.

The profound reason for the Eucharistic character of the covenant, which unites heaven and earth, lies in the fact that the Eucharist is the *memorial of the passover of the Lord*. The biblical idea of memorial (*zikkaron, azkarah; anamnesis, mnemosunon*), rediscovered by the theological research of our century, conveys exactly the opposite of what is expressed by the Greco-Western category of memory.

While memory is a movement of the spirit from the present to the past, by a kind of dilation of the mind which remains purely ideal ("*extensio animi ad praeterita*"), the biblical memory is the movement which goes from the past to the present, by virtue of which the one, definitive or unrepeatable event of salvation, in the power of the Spirit of God, is made present, contemporaneous with the celebrating community.

The memorial is a representation, an actualization of the "wonders of God," the "*mirabilia Dei*," which, in the act of being celebrated in the holy narration, touch, "infect," and transform the present. In Israel, the memorial of the Pasch, tied in with the vigil banquet, reactualizes the covenant of the exodus out of which the people of God were born and with new vitality generates the community in time.

Selecting the Paschal banquet as the context for the institution of the Eucharist, Jesus intends to substitute for the old a new memorial, that of his reconciling Pasch, out of which are born the people of the redeemed, reconciled with the Father and among themselves. Every time, then, that in obedience to the command of the Lord, the Church celebrates his memorial, the death and resurrection of Christ — unique and unrepeatable salvific events — are made present in the celebrating community. And, in the Spirit, they present the Church to the Father so that from the Father there may come in abundance — through the sacrifice of the Son — the creative and reconciling outpouring of the Paraclete.

In the Eucharistic memorial the Trinity passes through the Church and the Church passes through the Trinity. The movement of Trinitarian love begins to give rise to and assume the dynamism of ecclesial love. The Trinity enters time — ''God has time for men'' (Barth) — and time enters the Trinity.

This strict rapport between Trinity-Eucharist and Church results from the very structure that the Church's liturgy has given to the Eucharistic prayer in fidelity to the Lord's command.[73] Joined to the act of thanksgiving to the Father, the font of all holiness, is the invocation of the Spirit (the *epiklesis*) by virtue of which is fulfilled the memorial of the Pasch of the Son. In these three moments, ascribed to the same economy of the divine initiative which embraces the merciful design of the Father, the mission of the Word and that of the sanctifying Spirit, it is possible to put together the origin, form and destination of the Church's communion and mission. In the Church that confects the Eucharist there appears the living and nourishing mystery of the Eucharist which confects the Church.

The Eucharist is, in a special way, the great *act of thanksgiving to the Father*, Lord of heaven and earth, for all his benefits. In line with the Hebrew prayers of blessing, the people of the new covenant celebrate the marvels of their God and of the universal design of creation and redemption willed by his love.

In this ''sacrifice of praise'' the Church gives voice to all that is created. The bread and the wine, fruits of the earth and of man's work, ''are presented to the Father in faith and thanksgiving. The Eucharist thus signifies what the world must become — an offering and a hymn of praise to the Creator, a universal communion in the body of Christ, a kingdom of justice, love and peace in the Holy Spirit.''[74]

The Church born of the Eucharist, the sacrifice of praise, is then especially communion in the praise of God, a people who give thanks, who adore the mystery of the Father and allow themselves to be formed by it, placing themselves in continuity with ancient Israel in the blessing of its God and in solidarity with the whole universe, whose ultimate vocation is the glory of the Creator. A people "contemplative" by vocation, the Eucharistic Church perceives itself in the very act of praise as the gift of the free and gratuitous initiative of divine love, and in the reception of the celebration disposes itself for the ever new work of its Lord.

Like Mary, the Eucharistic community magnifies the God of the Fathers and exults in him, allowing itself to be covered by his mystery so that the universal plan of salvation may be realized in human history.

Memorial of the Pasch of the Son, the Eucharist is the sacrament of his sacrifice. It re-presents, that is, the event of his death and resurrection which took place once for all on behalf of all humanity. The reconciling power of the Trinitarian history of Easter unites those who participate in the sacred banquet and makes them the ecclesial Body of Christ.

The Eucharistic Body of the Lord, sacrament of his historical body, generates his Body in time, which is the ecclesial community. This is why the first Christian millennium designated the Church and the Eucharist, without distinction, by the same expression: "*Corpus Christi.*"

It will be only after the rationalizing interpretations of the "new" logic of dialectics, aimed at denying the truth of the Eucharistic Body of the Lord, that — between the ninth and the eleventh centuries — the need will be felt to add the adjective "mystical" to the expression to designate the Church.[75] To the "*corpus Christi verum,*" which is the Eucharist, will be opposed the "*corpus Christi mysticum,*" which is the Church. And the separation thus introduced in the mystery will be reflected in the ecclesiological conceptions which, from then on, will always tend to favor more the visible and juridical aspects of the ecclesial reality than the profound Trinitarian aspects of the Church.

Thus there spread in the West that vision which Congar has characterized as "Christomonism."[76] The term refers to the privileged attention paid to the incarnational aspects of the Church and therefore to the visible and organic dimension of the universal unity of all the baptized.

If one rediscovers the origin and the Trinitarian form of the Church from the starting point of the Eucharist, he will arrive anew at the unity of the mystery. Christ is not separated from the Father and the Spirit. And his ecclesial Body is seen as his real and profound presence in history rooted in and nourished by his Eucharistic Body.

A basis is thus provided for that "sacramental" vision of the Church by which in it the visible and the invisible stand in a relationship to one another which has a "not weak analogy" with the relationship between the Person of the Word and his assumed humanity (cf. *Lumen Gentium*, 9). Nothing in the Eucharistic Church is reducible to the pure coordinates of this world. Everything is run through by mystery because in everything the presence of the Risen Lord is realized.

The conflict between institution and charism, visibility and invisibility, between Law and Spirit is overcome in a higher conciliation. The ministeriality of the whole Church, that is, the variety of services which all the baptized are called upon to exercise so as to render Christ the reconciler present in the face of the various needs of the people of God and the human family, shows how the community, born of the memorial of the Lord who makes himself the Servant, is his presence in history, the fullness (always yet to come) of his Eucharistic Body. Participation in the Body of Christ makes us the Body of Christ. The Eucharistic memorial of Easter extends itself to the whole existence of the Church which thus celebrates in life and in history the memorial of the Lord.

The Eucharist, finally, is the invocation of the Spirit (*epiklesis*). The Spirit is especially invoked so that he may come to sanctify the presented gifts, and next because through those gifts sanctified by him and made the sign of Christ's real presence, believers may be reunited in the one Body of the Lord. That is, the Spirit carries out the promise contained in the words of institution, makes present him who is dead and risen in the Eucharistic signs and in the Church, and thus unites the baptized to the Father through Christ and among themselves in him.

"The bond between the Eucharistic celebration and the mystery of the Trinitarian God reveals the Spirit's role as that of him who makes present and alive the historical Word of Jesus."[77]

It is not possible to separate Christ from the Spirit either in the Eucharist or in the Church. The memorial of Easter is realized through the Spirit, and the community thus generated is not just the historical institution ("Christomonism") nor is it solely a spiritual event ("congregationalism") but it is at once the Body of Christ and the Temple of the Holy Spirit. Indeed it is the Body of Christ even precisely because it is raised up and enlivened by the Spirit.

The Eucharistic Church is the community of the Spirit of Christ. This is what an old and very profound formula of the faith conveys, namely, the expression contained in the Apostles' Creed, "the communion of saints."[78] This phrase refers especially to the holy realities of the Word and of the Eucharistic Bread which generate communion among those who participate in them. More in depth, however, this participation in the holy gifts shows itself rich in unity because in these gifts the gift of the Spirit is communicated to believers.

The "communion" is truly a "communion of saints," a communion in the power of the Spirit, which makes the Bread and the Word living. It is from this "contagion" of the Spirit in the holy gifts that the "communion of saints" arises in the sense of the unity of all believers who, partaking of the table of life, have been incorporated into Christ by the Paraclete. The *epiklesis*, from the moment the mystery is celebrated, extends itself to the point of becoming a dimension of the entire ecclesial mystery, lived in life and in history.

e) The Eucharist, the Trinity, and Mission

Its Trinitarian origin creates for the Church a missionary need. The Church of the Trinity is the Church in a state of mission.[79] Inasmuch as it springs from the divine missions, the Church is "originally" missionary. It is the place where, by virtue of the Spirit, Christ is made present to fulfill his salvific mission.

The Church receives the Spirit ever anew so as to give him ever anew and to leaven history for the time of Glory when God will be all in all. The pure grace of the Trinitarian initiative, which establishes the Church in its communion, is not privilege but task, not possession but mission.

The ecclesial communion is strictly linked to the sending. The event in which this sending of the Church takes place and is given life by the divine missions is the Eucharist. In it the dynamic activity of the Trinity flows into the activity of the Church, and vice versa. Sacrifice of praise of the Father, memorial of the Son, invocation of the Spirit, the Eucharist models the Church's mission after that of the Trinity, as a "mission of love."

As *an act of thanksgiving* to him who is the origin and the end, the Eucharist begets the Church as a community whose task in history is the glory of the Trinitarian God. The whole universe is recapitulated in Christ and in him led back to the Father. Man's work, joy and sorrow, life and death, hope and love, peace and war are to find an echo in the praise and the invocation of the pilgrim people.

The Eucharistic Church must make itself the voice of him who has no voice, turning back to the living God, offering him the sacrifice of praise, and receiving in return the gift of God. And, at the same time, it must give witness to people of their supreme vocation, without fearing to point out the shortsightedness of presumptuously absolute horizons. It must make itself the critical conscience of human situations, in the name of the whole universe's profound destiny to Glory which is signified by the bread and the wine of the Eucharist that become the Body and the Blood of the Risen One.

"The Lord left behind a pledge of this hope and strength for life's journey in that sacrament of faith where natural elements refined by man are changed into his glorified Body and Blood, providing a meal of brotherly solidarity and a foretaste of the heavenly banquet" (*Gaudium et Spes*, 38).

In the rendering of thanks to the Father, which is the Eucharistic sacrifice of praise, the contemplative and the political vocations of the Church — its being the adoring presence of history before the God of Glory and, at the same time, a prophetic, because disturbed and critical, sign of the hope of Glory in living history — are both contemporaneously established.

As *memorial of the Son's Pasch*, the Eucharist generates the Church as the community sent to celebrate his living and powerful memory in all human situations. This establishes the Christological, communal and ministerial character of the Eucharistic Church. Repeating the action Christ performed on the evening of the Last Supper, the community breaks the bread of fraternity and drinks the chalice of sharing in his destiny. Not just any bread, not just any chalice, but the bread and chalice included in an action which in the Hebrew world was loaded with a communitarian and social significance.

The memorial is a banquet which establishes a deep community of life and destiny between him who presides and the invited and of the invited among themselves. To obey the Lord's command, "Do this in memory of me," that is, to celebrate his memorial in life and in history, which is then the mission of the Church, requires communion with Christ and communion with the brethren.

And as Jesus presented himself on the evening of the Last Supper in the form of a Servant, indeed of the Suffering Servant, so too the Eucharistic Church, born and sent in communion with him, must present itself to the world as a community of service which freely shares what it has freely received from its Lord. From the Eucharist, memorial of the Crucified and Risen One, the mission of the Church is born as a mission under the cross, to spend itself in sharing and offering life.

Finally, as *epiklesis of the Spirit,* the Eucharist begets the Church as the community sent "in the Holy Spirit." This means above all that the first agent of the Church's mission is the Spirit. It is the Spirit who makes the proclamation of the Good News efficacious. It is the Spirit who, in those who hear the Word of salvation, "moves the heart and turns it to God, opens the eyes of the mind, and gives to all a certain sweetness in consenting to and believing in the truth" (*Dei Verbum,* 5).

The Eucharistic Church, then, will live its mission faithfully if it is a community open to the Spirit, capable of giving thanks and of receiving the gift of God. Through praise, invocation and mission, the Eucharist as *epiklesis* establishes a deep rapport by virtue of which it can be said that every act of mission arises from the Eucharistic giving of thanks and tends toward it. The entire ecclesial life thus becomes, by the power of the Spirit, the Eucharist in history. And the bond between the announced Word and the sacramental event is offered in all its profundity. The unity of the mystery, proclaimed, celebrated and lived, is created by the Holy Spirit!

This "epiklectic" nature of the mission also reveals its eschatological quality. The Spirit coming through Christ from the Father draws the Eucharistic Church through Christ to the Father. The Eucharistic community is projected toward the future of God, all in all, nourished by the "bread of hope," a pilgrim people who proclaim with their lives the promises of the Lord. The Eucharist is, in the Spirit of God's coming, the viaticum, the food of wayfarers who are on their way to their promised home in heaven and who sing "the songs of the Lord in a foreign land" (Ps 137).

This pledge of the promised tomorrow cannot but fill the Church with joy and make it possible for people to live every day with a festive heart. In the Eucharistic invocation of the Spirit, the Church is given a foretaste of Glory and is sent forth as a witness of hope and peace.

4.3   THE TRINITARIAN FUTURE
OF HISTORY

a) *The Trinitarian Homeland*

In the transforming experience of Easter, the budding Church reread not only the present and the past but also the future of history. To the consciousness and the memory of Easter was added a Trinitarian hope. In the same way in which the fullness acknowledged in the event of the "third day" could not be absent in the beginning, so too it could not be absent in the end. The beginning and the end of the human experience are unlocked by Easter. The "fullness of time" (cf. Gal 4:4; Ep 1:10) is reflected, looking back, in creation and, looking forward, in the eternal Easter. In the Trinitarian event of love, narrated in the paschal event, beginning and end, protology and eschatology are brought together. The Trinity is the point of departure and the point of arrival, the first and the last. [80] That is why, in the initial Christian witness, the end-time is talked about in terms of Trinitarian history:

"Christ has indeed been raised from the dead, the first-fruits of those who have fallen asleep. . . . For as in Adam all die, so in Christ all will be made alive. But each in his own turn: Christ, the first fruits; then, when he comes, those who belong to him. Then the end will come, when he hands over the kingdom to God the Father after he has destroyed all dominion, power, and authority. . . . When he has done this, then the Son himself will be made subject to him who put everything under him, so that God may be all in all'' (1 Cor 15:20, 22-24, 28).

The Spirit will be present with the Father and the Son in that hour: "In the last days, says the Lord, I will pour out my Spirit on all people'' (Ac 2:17; cf. Jl 3:1ff).

The end-time will be especially the history of the *Father*. In him from whom everything has come, everything will come to rest. He will be the one who will subject everything to the Son so that the Son, pure response of love, may hand creation over to him when it is finally ready to receive the eternal glory of love, that is, the absolute and endless wellspring of God who will shine forth in giving fullness of life to everything and to all.

Then, in this universal welcoming of the dominion of the Father's love, "God will be all in all'' (1 Cor 15:28) and "the entire world will be the homeland of God.''[81] Then the longing expectation proper to exile will be satisfied and he, who is the eternal power of love, will create a "new heavens and a new earth'' where "there will always be joy . . . and no longer will there be heard tear-filled voices or shouts of anguish,'' and nature itself will be filled with gladness (Is 49:13), so much so that "the wolf and the lamb will lie down together'' (cf. Is 65:17-19, 25). Such will be the "dwelling place of God with men, and he will live with them. They will be his people and God himself will be their Emmanuel, their God with them'' (Rv 21:3; cf. Ezk 37:27).

For those who have refused love, however, he who is the eternal source of love will be, in that hour, Father in judgment. It is the "day of the Lord'' (cf. Am 5:18ff; Ac 17:13, etc.), the hour in which all will be judged on love and, depending on how the judgment goes, will be blessed or cursed by the Father of the "Son of Man coming in glory'' (cf. Mt 25:31-34).

Nevertheless, in that hour the eternal Lover will be the source of life or of condemnation only in the eternal Beloved, in whom he is well pleased. It is in the reception of the *Son* that the universe will derive the final glory of God, the eternal epiphany of his love. Just as in the supreme welcoming of love, all that is created, united to the Son, will be consigned by the Son to the Father. In this sense this hour will also be the day of our Lord Jesus Christ (cf. 1 Cor 1:8; 5:5, etc.), the time of his second coming (cf. Ac 1:11; Mt 25:31ff, etc.).

Gathered into the eternal receptivity of love, history will become perfect joy for those who loved and will bring eternal sadness for those who, not having loved even though having been eternally loved, will no longer be able to love: "You, fathers and teachers, what is hell? I think it is the suffering of not being able to love any more" (Dostoevski)

History of the Father, history of the Son, the end-time will be no less the history of the *Spirit*. Then he will be poured out on every person (Jl 3:1ff; Ac 2:16) in a fullness without end. And those future goods, of which he has been the pledge, will finally be fully unveiled (cf. Rm 8:23; 2 Cor 1:22; 5:5; Ep 1:14). Spirit of unity, he will unite heaven to earth forever, the world to the infinitely transcendent divine life, bringing to completion the eternal covenant. Spirit of freedom and openness, he will keep God and the world in their mutual otherness, such that the end will not be the dissolution of history in God or of God in history, but the communion of eternal love between the Creator and the creature, supreme reception, without confusion, of human history in the divine history of love.

He will thus celebrate the glory of love as "unity of life and death in favor of life."[82] Just as Christ was glorified in him by the Father through the resurrection from the dead, so too in him the whole universe will be glorified through the gift of life which conquers death (cf. Rm 8:11). This supreme epiphany of Trinitarian love will be the glory of God in man and of man in God, "the glorious ministry of the Spirit" (2 Cor 3:8), the glory promised and revealed in Christ (cf. Jn 1:14; Rm 8:17; Ph 3:21; Col 3:4; Tt 2:13).[83]

The unity of the Trinitarian mystery will thus shine forth in the glory of the end — the glory of the Father, who will pour out his love on all creatures forever; the glory of the Son, to whom all creatures will be united so as to receive this love in a hymn of praise that knows no end; the glory of the Spirit, who will celebrate their obvious unity, loving and welcoming, in the eternal alliance of the universe with God.

This glory will be the final victory, the dominion of love without end! What began "in the name of the Father and of the Son and of the Spirit" will then be fulfilled in "glory to the Father, to the Son, and to the Spirit." From love to love, eternity to eternity, across the journey of time, the universe will come to rest in the Trinitarian homeland of God (cf. Ph 3:20 and Heb 11:13-16). Inasmuch as it came from the Father, through the Son, in the Spirit, in the unity and the freedom of the same Spirit, by means of the reception of the Son, so will it return to the Father.

b) *Toward the Trinitarian Homeland*

In this vision of the Trinity as origin and goal of history, it appears as the adorably transcendent bosom in which the history of the world is nurtured, the placeless place in which it takes place, the timeless time in which it unfolds. The paschal event, the story of God in human history, shows how that history is intertwined with the Trinitarian history of God.

The future of mankind, the laborious march toward that future which, from the beginning has marked man's experience on earth, is not suspended in a void. It is caught up *in* God.

In the distinction between Lover and Beloved, the world was created by the First Principle, the Father, in view of and by means of him in whom he will eternally love his creation.

In the boundless welcome of the Beloved, the creature draws being and life in order to be handed over to the Father at the end of time until love's dominion conquers everything and "God is all in all" (1 Cor 15:28).

In the unifying force of the Spirit, the world is one with its God, kept by him in being and in motion.

By virtue of the freedom of the same Spirit, the world is other than its God, a finite creature in relation to the infinity of the Creator. Temporal history is thus linked with eternal history — without confusion or admixture, because God is God and man is not God and the world remains the *"opus ad extra"* of divine Love; but also without separation or division because the world is always the creature of God, loved in the Son and recapitulated in him (cf. Ep 1:10), pervaded by the creating and vivifying Spirit.

This unity of otherness and communion between universe and Creator, this identity of divine immanence and transcendence, are understandable only in a Trinitarian mediation. The relationship between the separation of the world *from* God, proper to mono-theistic religions, and the confusion of the world *with* God, found in various historical forms of pantheism, is overcome in the Trinitarian faith of the twofold confession of the life of the world *in* God and of the life of God *in* the world.

The consequence is decisive for a comprehension of the *meaning of history*. History is not the unfolding of human experi-ence in a separate and foreign way on earth in relation to a distant heavenly spectator, in a kind of glacial solitude with everyone under the sword of divine justice: "God in heaven and man on earth!" Nor is its meaning defined by the titanic progress of man, who makes himself like God, in a history of time confused with that of eternity, in an emancipation of the world which imprisons in itself any kind of ultraterrestrial horizon: *hidden God, hidden man* (Bloch)!

The Christian sense of history lies rather in an acknowledg-ment of the divinity of God and of the worldliness of the world, respecting the sovereign transcendence of the one and the profound dignity of the other.

It also lies in the joyous confession of the communion which exists between the Creator and the creature who, from the Father in the Son, receives being and life by virtue of the life-giving Spirit, in a relationship so profound as to justify beyond every limit the affirmed dignity of the world, because the whole of history is *in* God.

And finally, and above all, the meaning of history is to be found in the good paschal news of the creature's participation in the very life of God, made possible by the divine missions, through which God comes to pitch his tent *in* the world and to make his own the history of men so as to manifest in it, with them and for them, the eternal glory of his love.

In this light nothing in human experience is ever lost. In union with the living God, everything can be lived and transformed in love. The burden of the day and the obscurity of the future become meaningful in the challenge and the promise of God with us. The limitations and the sorrows of the present are made understandable by the sorrow that touches the Trinitarian love of God itself and can be supported with love, thanks to the Spirit whom the Father gives us in communion with his Christ crucified.

In a world where the hardest question seems to be that of meaning, of the profound significance, that is, of personal and collective undertakings which may give men the "courage to exist,"[84] the "Trinitarian homeland" offers itself as the good news, the goal of our journey which lights up the way, the companion of our present, which gives energy en route, the recollection of our beginnings, which makes us feel rooted and founded in love (cf. Ep 3:17).

In this — his being origin, presence, and homeland — the Trinitarian God reveals a side which could be called *maternal*.[85] His tender and encircling love evokes a mother's "visceral" kind of love. The Bible itself often speaks of the maternal tenderness of God (*rabem, rahamin*: maternal womb, visceral love):

"Sion has said: 'The Lord has abandoned me, the Lord has forgotten me.' Can a mother forget her infant, be without tenderness for the child of her womb? Even should she forget, I will never forget you'' (Is 49:14-15). ''As a mother comforts her son, so will I comfort you'' (Is 66:13). ''Is Ephraim not my favored son, the child in whom I delight? . . . My heart stirs for him, I must show him mercy, says the Lord'' (Jr 31:20; cf. also Ho 11:1-4, 8).

These texts refer to the God of Israel in whom Easter faith recognizes the Father of the Lord Jesus and, in the light of the cross of the Risen One, acknowledges as Love (cf. Jn 4:8, 16).

From the Father the maternity of love extends, however, also to the Son in whom the creature is welcomed and becomes a welcomer of love[86] and to the Spirit, whose very name, feminine in Hebrew (*ruach*), seems to do more than imply the maternal love which gives life and opens up to it.[87]

This divine maternity shines through in that creature who, more than any other, made herself a vessel of the Father, allowing herself to be overshadowed by the Spirit, to the point of conceiving in herself the Son of God in the flesh and giving him to the world — the Virgin Mother Mary. Her virginal maternity is the historical, concrete site of the covenant between the Trinity and time in which the infinite tenderness of divine love for men shines through. The eternal maternity of love is recounted in her temporal maternity.

Wrapped in the tenderness of Trinitarian love, history therefore makes strong and profound sense. Like a baby in its mother's womb, it lives to prepare itself for its eternal birth. *Death*[88] in this perspective is not a leap into a dark and hopeless void, nor is it the pure rending of the communion of love, which is also always life. As the faith of every era has proclaimed, death is the *''dies natalis,''* the day on which by dying one is born to life in the light and peace of the divine Trinity.

The measure of the truth of life, insofar as it is the measure of the truth of love (''since love in every time does not know how deep it is right up to the moment of separation,''[89]), death, a sorrowful rending even for him who has loved little or was loved little — ''who, in fact, without regret will leave his pain and solitude?''[90] — is the access to the hour of eternal love. It is the ''gateway of the humble'' (Bloy), the judgment of love: "In the evening of life we will be judged on love'' (St. John of the Cross).

For him who has lived in love, accepting the gift and giving it back to the Father in a life of love and works of charity and justice, death is the passage of love into love, from the life of the Trinity in time to the endless life of the Trinitarian joy of God: love conquers death (cf. 1 Jn 3:14).

For all, death is a harking back to the "eternal Sabbath," the watchman at the gates of the absolute future in which the whole history will be judged on love and every tear will be wiped away and every injustice righted and the winners will finally sing the song of triumph (cf. the vision of Rv 14:1ff).

Then the victory that Christ won over death (cf. Rm 6:8; 8:2; 1 Cor 15:26) will be extended to all of creation: "When the corruptible clothes itself with incorruptibility, and the mortal with immortality, then the saying that is written will come true: 'Death has been swallowed up in victory' " (1 Cor 15:54). Then the entire universe will be the homeland of God.

Man on earth and the people of God in history are on the march toward this "Trinitarian homeland." It is the greatest of all goals, proving the shortsightedness of the quest for worldly goods, inviting all to poverty of spirit and a perennial newness of heart and life. This homeland is the beyond which reminds people of their condition as pilgrims in love, "*on the way home but not yet there*," and urges them to be perennial wayfarers, "for whom the day does not begin where the other ended and no dawn finds them where the sunset left them."[91] It is the horizon of hope which sustains expectation and already fills the heart with confidence and joy. It is the power and the measure of love enabling the present task to "organize the hope," and the days to nurture the works of justice and peace.

EPILOGUE

A HISTORY THAT CONTINUES

In narrating a history, this book is itself a history.

The history it recounts is that of the Christian God and of people called to communion with him — the history of the event of Easter, which reveals the eternal event of the Love of the Father, of the Son and of the Spirit. It is the eternal history of this Love itself and our history, the history of those who have been gathered in the womb of Trinitarian life and called to receive in our existence, "entangled in stories," the eternal account of Love so as to give sense, force and hope to the hard work of living and to the sufferings of the world.

The history that this book is in itself could be described as a pilgrimage of thought and life toward the "Trinitarian homeland." Starting from the exile, which is the estrangement of the Trinity from the existence of so many Christians, the profound symbol of the estrangement of Love from the existence of so many, the journey took us back to the original account, that of Easter, where Trinitarian love was most fully revealed and offered to us. From there it moved toward the eternal wellsprings where the divine history of love was told. And from this eternal account, "homeland glimpsed but not possessed," it returned to the works of time in order to narrate in human history the history of God and to insert ever more into the life of the eternal Trinity the many humble stories which make up the human experience, giving them life and hope. The book's itinerary has thus gone from history to Glory, the epiphany of Love, in order to return anew to history and make the future of the glimpsed homeland its leaven.

The Hasidim, the Hebrew sages dispersed in the exile, have a story which describes this journey:

"A man inspired by God traveled into a great void until he reached the threshold of the mystery. Having arrived, he knocked. 'Whom do you seek?' a Voice asked him. He answered: 'I have announced Your Word to the deafness of the dying and they did not listen to me. So I have come here so that You may hear me and answer.' 'Go back,' the Voice said to him, 'there's no listening here: I have hidden my listening in the deafness of the dying.' "

The history that this book tells, and that this book is, requires that it continue to be narrated in the life of each of those who have encountered it. Story gives rise to story: *here*, not elsewhere; *today*, not tomorrow; with our own people, in the actual unfolding of time; beyond the word, in history lived out of love, where one steps over the threshold of the mystery:

Hic incipit mysterium Dei, sanctae Trinitatis, aeterni Amoris.

"Here the mystery of God, of the Holy Trinity, of eternal Love begins."[1]

Footnotes

1. TRINITY AND HISTORY

1. K. Rahner, *Il dio Trino come fondamento originario e trascendente della storia della salvezza*, in *Mysterium Salutis* 3, Brescia 1969, 404.
2. E. Kant, *Il conflitto delle facoltà*, tr. A. Poggi, Genoa 1953, 47.
3. J. Moltmann, *Trinità e regno di Dio*, Brescia 1983, 11.
4. Whence the lively interest of modern theology in the Trinity. Cf. among other things (besides the corresponding entries in the most recent dictionaries): J. Auer, *Il mistero di Dio*, Assisi 1982; G. Baget-Bozzo, *La Trinità*, Florence 1980; K. Barth, *Die kirchliche Dogmatik*, I/1, Munich 1932 and II/1, Zürich 1940; F. Bourassa, *Questions de théologie trinitaire*, Rome 1970; J.A. Bracken, *The Holy Trinity as a Community of Divine Persons*, in *The Heythrop Journal* 15 (1974) 167-182, 257-271; E. Brunner, *Dogmatik*, I, *Die christliche Lehre von Gott*, Zürich, 1960 (3); B. de Margerie, *La Trinité chrétienne dans l'histoire*, Paris 1975; A. Dumas, *Dieu unique et trine*, in *Initiation à la pratique de la théologie*, III, Paris 1983, 725-776; C. Duquoc, *Un Dio diverso*, Brescia 1978; E.J. Fortmann, *The Triune God: A Historical Study of the Doctrine of the Trinity*, Philadelphia-London 1972; K. Hemmerle, *Thesen zu einer trinitarischen Ontologie*, Einsiedeln 1976; E. Jungel, *Dio mistero del mondo*, Brescia 1982; W. Kasper, *Il Dio di Gesù Cristo*, Brescia 1984; G. Lafont, *Peut-on connaître Dieu en Jésus-Christ?*, Paris 1969; P. Lapide - J. Moltmann, *Monoteismo ebraico— dottrina trinitaria cristiana. Un dialogo*, Brescia 1982; B. Lonergan, *De Deo Trino*, I, Rome 1964 (2), II, 1964 (3); J. Moltmann, *Trinità e Regno di Dio*, Brescia 1983; C. Nigro, *Dio più grande del nostro cuore*, Rome 1974; K. Rahner, *Il Dio trino come fondamento originario e trascendente della storia della salvezza*, in *Mysterium Salutis* 3, Brescia 1969, 401-507; L. Scheffczk, *Il Dio che verrà*, Turin 1975; M. Schmaus, *Dogmatica cattolica*, I, Turin 1966 (3); D. Staniloae, *Dieu est Amour*, Geneva 1980; G.H. Tavard, *The Vision of Trinity*, Washington 1981; S. Verges - J.M. Dalmau, *Dio rivelato in Cristo*, Rome 1972.

On a more popular level, consult, for example: P. Aubin, *Dio-Padre, Figlio-Spirito*. *La Trinità alla luce della Bibbia*, Turin 1978; J. Danielou, *La Trinité et la mystère de l'existence*, Bruges 1968; *Il Dio di Gesù Cristo*, Rome 1982; P. Ferlay, *Père et Fils dans l'Esprit. Le mystère trinitiare de Dieu*, Paris 1979; L. Melotti, *Introduzione al mistero di Dio*, Leumann 1978; J.L. Segundo, *Il Nostro concetto di Dio*, Brescia 1974.

On modern Trinitarian theology, consult, among others: E. Bailleux, *Chronique: La Dogmatique de la Trinité*, in *Mélanges de Sciences religieuses* 29 (1972) 101-108; *Bibliografia Trinitaria*, edited by the Segretariado Trinitario, Salamanca 1978; F. Bourassa, *La Trinità*, in *Problemi e prospettive di Teologia Dogmatica*, ed. K.H. Neufeld, Brescia 1983, 337-372; J.A. Bracken, *What are They Saying About the Trinity?* New York 1979; W. Breuning, *La dottrina trinitaria*, in *Bilancio della teologia del XX secolo*, III, Rome 1972, 26-43; P. Coda, *Evento pasquale. Trinità e storia*, Rome 1984; *El misterio trinitario a la luz del Vaticano II*, Salamanca 1970; C.

Schutz, *Gegenwärtige Tendenzen in der Gottes- und Trinitätslehre*, in *Mysterium Salutis. Ergänzungsband*, Zürich 1981, 264-322; B. Sesboüé, *Theologie dogmatique. Trinité et Pneumatologie*, in *Recherches de Science Religieuse* 66 (1978) 417-460, 70 (1982) 379-413; P. Siller, *Il Dio uno*, in *Bilancio della teologia del XX secolo*, III, *op. cit.*, 13-25; *La Trinidad hoy*, Salamanca 1973.

5. Cf. the observations of C. Duquoc, *Un Dio diverso*, *op. cit.*, 30ff.

6. Cf. K. Rahner, *Theos nel Nuovo Testamento*, in *Saggi theologici*, Rome 1965, 467-585.

7. A. Stolz, *De SS. Trinitate*, Freiburg i. Br. 1939.

8. M. Schmaus, *Dogmatica cattolica*, I, *op. cit.*

9. Cf. K. Rahner, *Il Dio Trino . . . , op. cit.*, 435f.

10. I. Mancini, *Dio*, in *Nuovo Dizionario di Teologia*, Rome 1977, 331.

11. E. Jüngel, *Dio, mistero del mondo*, *op. cit.*, 372 (cf. 367: "The Gospel as Analogic Discourse About God.")

12. In the light of the "analogy of Advent," do not the "analogia entis" and the "analogia fidei" perhaps get reconciled? Cf. H.U. von Balthasar, *Karl Barth. Darstellung und Deutung seiner Theologie*, Einsideln 1976 (4).

13. K. Rahner, *Il Dio Trino . . . , op. cit.*, 414. On the "vice versa" which Rahner adds to the axiom, cf. below. The formula was drawn up precisely by the International Theological Commission, *Teologia - Cristologia - Anthropologia*, in *La Civiltà Cattolica* 134 (1983) n. 3181, I C 2,3.

14. K. Barth, *Die kirchliche Dogmatik*, I/1, *op. cit.*, 503.

15. Cf. J. Moltmann, *La storia trinitaria di Dio*, in Id., *Futuro della creazione*, Brescia 1980, 95.

16. G. Baget-Bozzo, *La Trinità, op. cit.*, 1s.

17. A. Milano, *Trinità*, in *Dizionario Teologico Interdisciplinare* 3, Turin, 1977, 495.

18. B. Forte, *La chiesa icona della Trinità*, Brescia 1984.

19. Cf. the text of E. Peterson, *Il monoteismo come problema politico*, Brescia 1983 (the German original dates back to 1935) and the debate connected with it: cf. the editorial of G. Ruggieri, *Resistenza e dogma*, 5-26.

20. G. Baget-Bozzo, *La Trinità, op. cit.*, 237.

21. Kahlil Gibran, *Il Profeta*, Milan 1983 (3), 30.

22. A position against the "vice versa" which K. Rahner adds to the axiom "the economic Trinity is the immanent Trinity" is thus taken. Cf. the criticism of G. Lafont, *Peut-on connaître Dieu en Jésus-Christ?*, *op. cit.*, 220, 226f. and Y. Congar, *Credo nello Spirito Santo*, 3, Brescia 1983, 25ff.

23. St. Thomas Aquinas, *In Boet. de Trinitate, Proem*, q. 2, a. 1, ad 6.

24. St. Augustine, *De Trinitate*, 1, 3, 5.

25. Cf. W. Pannenberg, *Analogia e dossologia*, in Id., *Strutture fondamentali della teologia*, Bologna 1970.

26. J. Moltmann, *Trinità e Regno di Dio*, *op. cit.*, 167.

27. Fourth Lateran Council (1215): DS 806.

28. Cf. *Summa Theologica* 1 q. 58 a. 6 (regarding the awareness of angels) which refers to Augustine, *De Genesi ad litteram* 1. 4, c. 22, PL 34, 312 and *De Civitate Dei*, 1. II, c. 7, PL 41, 322.

Footnotes 233

1. THE TRINITY IN HISTORY

1. Cf. B. Forte, *Gesù di Nazaret, storia di Dio, Dio della storia*, Rome 1984 (4), 88ff. ("The Starting Point: The Resurrection").
2. On the relation between the paschal event and the Trinity in contemporary theology, cf. P. Coda, *Evento pasquale. Trinità e storia*, Rome 1984.
3. Cf. how much it follows the proposal of the theological narrative of the paschal mystery of H.U. von Balthasar, *Mysterium paschale*, in *Mysterium Salutis* 6, Brescia 1971, 171-412.
4. Cf. E. Schillebeeckx, *Gesù, la storia di un vivente*, Brescia 1976 and *Il Cristo, la storia di una nuova prassi*, Brescia 1980.
5. For the history and the evaluation of the "liberal" research on Jesus, see the classical work by A. Schweitzer, *Geschichte der Leben-Jesu-Forschung*, Tübingen 1913 (2). Cf. also B. Forte, *Gesù di Nazaret, op.cit.*, 97 and 103ff. ("The HistoricalProblem of the Relation Between the Pre-Easter Jesus and the Post-Easter Christ").
6. Cf. *ibid.*, 96-102.
7. See among others: A. Ammassari, *La resurrezione*, 2 vols., Rome 1976; P. Benoit, *Passione e resurrezione del Signore. Il mistero pasquale nei quattro evangeli*, Turin 1967; *Dibattito sulla risurrezione di Gesù*, Brescia 1969; G. Giavini, *La risurrezione di Gesù*, Milan 1973; X. Léon-Dufour, *Resurezzione di Gesù e messaggio pasquale*, Rome 1973; W. Marxsen, *La resurrezione di Gesù di Nazaret*, Bologna 1970; G. O'Collins, *Il Gesù pasquale*, Assisi 1975; *La résurrection de Jésus et l'exégèse moderne*, Paris 1969; *Resurrexit, Actes du Symposium international sur la Résurrection de Jésus* (1970), Rome 1974; B. Rigaux, *Dio l'ha risuscitato. Esegesi e teologia biblica*, Milan 1976; P. Zarrella, *La risurrezione di Gesù. Storia a messaggio*, Assisi 1973. A systematic reading of the Resurrection-Trinity relationship is attempted in B. Forte, *Gesù di Nazaret . . . , op. cit.*, 180ff. ("The Human History of God: The Relation Between Jesus and God from an Historical Perspective"). Cf. also W. Pannenberg, *Cristologia: Lineamenti fondamentali*, Brescia 1974.
8. Cf. Acts 2:24; 3:15; 4:10; 5:30, etc. Cf. also 1 Th 1:10; 1 Cor 6:14; 15:15; 2 Cor 4:14; Gal 1:1; Rm 4:24; 10:9; 1 P 1:21. Elsewhere it is said that Jesus rose: cf. below. It seems that the oldest form is the one indicating the raising up of Jesus on the part of God. However, there are those who say that this formulation would have been drawn up in a second moment so as not to contrast with the rigid Hebrew monotheism which recognized God as the exclusive master of life and death. Cf., e.g., X. Léon-Dufour, *Resurrezione di Gesù a messaggio pasquale, op. cit.*, 37ff.
9. The equivalence in the NT between "God" and "the Father" is practically total. Cf. K. Rahner, *Theos nel Nuovo Testamento*, in *Saggi teologici*, Rome 1965, 549ff.
10. Cf. B. Forte, *Gesù di Nazaret . . . , op. cit.*, 92f.
11. H.U. von Balthasar, *Mysterium paschale, op. cit.*, 346.
12. Cf. H.U. von Balthasar, *Mysterium paschale, op. cit.*, 284ff. ("Cross and Trinity"); M. Flick-Z. Alszeghy, *Il mistero della Croce. Saggio di teologia sistematica*, Brescia 1978; B. Forte, *Gesù di Nazaret . . . , op. cit.*, 266ff. ("The Cross"); E. Jüngel, *Dio, mistero del mondo. Per una fondazione della teologia del Crocifisso nella disputa fra teismo e ateismo*, Brescia 1982; X. Léon-Dufour, *Di fronte alla morte. Gesù e Paolo*, Turin 1982; J. Moltmann, *Il Dio crocifisso*, Brescia 1973; id., *Trinità e Regno di Dio*, Brescia 1983, 30ff. ("The Passion of God") and 86ff. ("The Handing over of the Son"); M. Salvati, *Trinità e Croce. Saggio di lettura trinitaria della Croce di Cristo* (doctoral diss.), Angelicum, Rome 1984; H. Schürmann, *Jesu ureigener Tod*, Leipzig

234 THE TRINITY AS HISTORY

1975. Cf. also N. Hoffmann, *Kreuz und Trinität. Zur Theologie der Sühne*, Einsiedeln 1982.
13. Cf. W. Popkes, *Christus traditus. Eine Untersuchung zum Begriff der Dahingabe im Neuen Testament*, Zurich 1967.
14. Cf. the exegetical and theological panorama traced out by G. Rossé, *Jésus Abandonné: Approches du mystère*, Paris 1983.
15. In the intertestamentary texts the exile is the time of the Spirit's absence, spent from the expectation of the messianic outpouring of the Spirit himself. Cf. *Psalms of Solomon*, 17:42; *Ethiopian Enoch* 49:2; 62:2; *Testament of Judah*, 24:2; *Testament of Levi*, 18:7. The paschal account shows a Messiah who enters into the exile of the absence of the Spirit in order to later fill up this exile with the new effusion of the gift of the Spirit. On Heb 9:14 cf. A. Vanhoye, *L'azione dello Spirito Santo nella passione di Cristo secondo l'epistola agli Ebrei*, in *Credo in Spiritum Sanctum*, Acts of the International Congress on Pneumatology, Vatican City 1983, I, 759-773.
16. Cf. K. Rahner, in *Sacramentum Mundi*, 4, Brescia 1975, 215f. ("The Death of Jesus as Death of God").
17. International Theological Commission, *Alcune questioni riguardanti la cristologia*, in *La Civiltà Cattolica* 131 (1980) n. 3129, IV D.8.
18. J. Moltmann, *Trinità e Regno di Dio, op. cit.*, 258.
19. H.U. von Balthasar, *Mysterium paschale, op. cit.*, 258.
20. ITC, *Alcune questioni . . . , op. cit.*, IV C, 3.5.
21. J. Moltmann, *Il Dio crocifisso, op. cit.*, 287; cf. also 281 and E. Jüngel, *Dio, mistero del mondo, op. cit.*, 447: "In the concept of the triune God" faith reflects on and professes the history of the Lord's cross.
22. Is not the greatest limit of the so-called "atheistic theology" or "theology of the death of God" in its absolute lack of Trinitarian thought? The theme of the "death of God" can be Christianly understood only Trinitarily as "death in God": cf. E. Jüngel, *ibid.*, 288.
23. J. Moltmann, *Il Dio crocifisso, op. cit.*, 288.
24. H.U. von Balthasar, *Mysterium paschale, op. cit.*, 341f.
25. G. Lafont, *Peut-on connaître Dieu en Jésus-Christ?* Paris 1969, 261.
26. Cf. G. von Rad, *Teologia dell'Antico Testamento*, I, Brescia 1972, 165ff., 406ff., 502ff.
27. Cf. R. Brown, *Il problema della concezione verginale di Gesù*, in Id., *La concezione verginale e la risurrezione corporea di Gesù*, Brescia 1977, 37ff.
28. Cf. *ib.*, 89.
29. Cf. J. Jeremias, *Teologia del Nuovo Testament*, I, *La predicazione di Gesù*, Brescia 1976 (2), 63, and E. Schillebeeckx, *Gesù, storia di un vivente, op. cit.*, 135.
30. F.J. Schierse, *Rivelazione neotestamentaria della Trinità*, in *Mysterium Salutis* 3, *op. cit.*, 130f. Cf. the whole study: 111-168.
31. J. Moltmann, *Trinità e Regno di Dio, op. cit.*, 86.
32. J. Jeremias, *Abbà*, Brescia 1968 and W. Marchel, *Abba, Père. La prière du Christ et des chrétiens*, Rome 1971 (2).
33. W. Marchel, *Abba, Père, op. cit.*, 122f.
34. J. Jeremias, *Abbà, op. cit.*, 65.
35. Cf. B. Forte, *Gesù di Nazaret, op. cit.*, 200ff. ("The Awareness that Jesus Has of His History").
36. F.J. Schierse, *Rivelazione . . . , op. cit.*, 125.

37. Cf. J.-M. van Cangh, *La Bible de Mathieu: les citations d'acomplissement*, in *Revue Théologique de Louvain*, 6 (1975) 205-211.
38. Cf. the significant analysis of V. Maag, "Malkut Jhwh," in *Vetus Testamentum*, Suppl. VII, 1960. Cf. also my *Gesù di Nazaret*, *op. cit.*, 70ff.
39. Cf. G. von Rad, *Teologia dell'Antico Testamento*, I, *op. cit.*, 212. The name is met about 680 times in the OT in the complete form and 25 times in the abbreviated form of Jah.
40. R. Schulte, *La preparazione della rivelazione trinitaria*, in *Mysterium Salutis*, 3, *op. cit.*, 77 (cf. also the whole study [63-110]). Cf. also A. Deissler, *L'autorivelazione di Dio nell' Antico Testamento*, *ib.*, 285-344.
41. A. Gelin, *Messianisme*, in *Dictionnaire de la Bible*, V. 1166.
42. Cf. G. von Rad, *Teologia dell'Antico Testamento*, *op. cit.*, 165ff.
43. Cf. A. Milano, *Trinità*, in *Dizionario Teologico Interdisciplinare*, III, Turin 1977, 477ff.
44. Cf. on all this R. Schnackenburg, *La chiesa del Nuovo Testamento*, Brescia 1968 (2).
45. Cf. W. Pannenberg, *Cristologia: Lineamenti fondamentali*, *op. cit.*, 164ff.
46. On the history of the confession and of the Trinitarian reflection, cf.: A. Adam, *Lehrbuch der Dogmengeschichte*, I, Gütersloh 1965; G. Baget-Bozzo, *La Trinità*, Florence 1980; B. de Margerie, *La Trinité chrétienne dans l'histoire*, Paris 1975; Th. de Regnon, *Etudes de théologie positive sur la Sainte Trinité*, 5 vols., Paris 1892-1900; E.J. Fortmann, *The Triune God: An Historical Study of the Doctrine of the Trinity*, Philadelphia-London 1972; A. Grillmeier, *Gesù il Cristo nella fede della chiesa*, Brescia 1982; J.N.D. Kelly, *Il pensiero cristiano delle origini*, Bologna 1972; G. Kretschmar, *Studien sur früh-christlichen Trinitätstheolgie*, Tübingen 1956; J. Lebreton, *Histoire du dogme de la Trinité*, 2 vols., Paris 1927, 1928; I. Ortiz de Urbina, *Nicée et Constantinople*, Paris 1963; G.L. Prestige, *Dio nel pensiero dei Padri*, Bologna 969; L. Scheffczyk, *Dichiarazioni del magistero e storia del dogma della Trinità*, in *Mysterium Salutis*, 3, *op. cit.*, 187-278; M. Simonetti, *La crisi ariana nel IV secolo*, Rome 1975; *(La) Trinidad en la tradición prenicena*, Segretariado Trinitario, Salamanca 1974.
47. L. Scheffczyk, *Dichiarazioni* . . . , *op. cit.*, 194.
48. Cf. J. Lebreton, *Histoire du dogme de la Trinité*, II, *op. cit.*, 141-173; P.-T. Camelot, *Recherches récentes sur le symbole des Apôtres et leur portée théologique*, in *Recherches de Science Religieuse* 39 (1952) 323-337; B. de Mergerie, *La Trinité chrétienne dans l'histoire*, *op. cit.*, 92ff.
49. Cf. the oldest texts (already from the second half of the second century) in DS 1ff.
50. Cf. P. Nautin, *Je crois à l'Esprit Saint dans la Sainte Eglise pour la Résurrection de la chair. Etude sur l'histoire et la théologie du Symbole*, Paris 1947.
51. St. Cyprian, *De Oratione Dominica*, 23; PL 4,553.
52. DS 10: it is the text of the *Traditio Apostolica* of Hippolytus of Rome (beginning of third century).
53. Cf. A. von Harnack, *Manuale di storia dei dogmi*, I, Mendrisio 1912; F. Loofs, *Leitfaden sum Studium der Dogmengeschichte*, Tübingen 1959 (6); M. Werner, *Die Entstehung des Christlichen Dogmas*, Bern-Leipzig 1941.
54. Cf. the presentation of J. Moltmann, *Trinità e Regno di Dio*, *op. cit.*, 141-150.
55. Cf. C. Duquoc, *Un Dio diverso*, Brescia 1978, 30ff.
56. L. Scheffczyk, *Dichiarazioni* . . . , *op. cit.*, 237f.
57. C. Duquoc, *Un Dio diverso*, *op. cit.*, 37.

236   THE TRINITY AS HISTORY

58. F. Ricken, *Das Homoousios von Nikaia als Krisis des altchristlichen Platonismus*, in *Zur Frühgeschichte der Christologie*, Freiburg i. Br. 1970, 99.
59. I. Ortiz de Urbina, *Nicée et Constantinople*, Paris 1963, 87.
60. DS 125.
61. Cf. R. Cantalamessa, *Dal Cristo del Nuovo Testamento al Cristo della Chiesa: Tentativa di interpretazione della cristologia patristica*, in *Il problema cristologico oggi*, Assisi 1973, 143-197. Cf. also my *Gesù di Nazaret, op. cit.*, 133-156.
62. Cf. DS 150. Cf. then A.M. Ritter, *Das Konzil von Konstantinopel und sein Symbol. Studien zur Geschichte und Theologie des 2. Okumenischen Konzils*, Göttingen 1965.
63. The Second Council of Constantinople (553) will explicitly profess, combining the theological language of East and West, that "one is the nature and substance of the Father and of the Son and of the Holy Spirit, and one the authority and power. Consubstantial Trinity, one divinity which is to be adored in the three subsistencies or persons. Since there is only one God and Father, from whom everything is, and only one Lord Jesus Christ, through whom everything is, and only one Holy Spirit, in whom everything is": DS 421. Cf. also the more important formulas of Trinitarian faith: the Pseudo-Athanasian Symbol *Quicumque* (430-500?): DS 75; the elaborate Symbol of the Eleventh Council of Toledo of 675, which summarizes the Trinitarian speculation of St. Augustine and of Fulgentius of Ruspe: DS 525-532; the Creed of the Fourth Lateran Council of 1215: DS 800; the Credo of the Second Council of Lyons of 1274, handed to the delegates of Emperor Michael Paleologus: DS 851-853; the Decree for the Jacobites of the Council of Florence of 1442: DS 1330-1332.
64. L. Scheffczyk, *Dichiarazioni . . . , op. cit.*, 232.
65. *Ib.*, 207.
66. The expression is from G. Kretchmar, *Studien . . . , op. cit.*, and refers to the short duration of the formal discussion of the Trinitarian controversy (between Nicea and Constantinople: 325-381).
67. Cf. J. Moltmann, *Trinità e Regno di Dio, op. cit.*, 19ff.
68. Cf. A. Trapé-M.F. Sciacca, *Introduzione a S. Agostino, La Trinità*, Rome 1973, 1-127 (for the theology, especially 1-55), with bibliography.
69. R. Seeberg, *Lehrbuch der Dogmengeschichte*, II, Erlangen 1923 (3), 159.
70. Cf. the objection in G. Lafont, *Peut-on connaître Dieu en Jésus-Christ?, op. cit.*, 84ff. On Augustine: 72-105.
71. Cf. M. Schmaus, *Die psychologische Trinitätslehre des hl. Augustinus*, Münster, 1927.
72. Cf. M. Schmaus, *Die Spannung von Metaphysik und Heilsgeschichte in der Trinitätslehr Augustins*, in *Studia Patristica*, VI, Berlin 1962, 503-418. Cf. the reservations about this thesis of A. Trapé, *Introduzione, op. cit.*, 63f.
73. Cf. *Summa Theologica*, I, qq. 27-43 (qq. 2-26 deal with the One God). Next cf. H.F. Dondaine, *S. Thomas d'Aquin. Somme Theologique. La Trinité*, 2 vols., Paris 1943-1946; G. Lafont, *Peut-on connaître Dieu en Jésus-Christ?, op. cit.*, 107ff.; A. Malet, *Personne et amour dans la théologie trinitaire de S. Thomas d'Aquin*, Paris 1956.
74. G. Lafont, *Peut-on . . . , op. cit.*, 124.
75. New evidence of this affirmation is had, for example, in the hypothesis, admitted by Thomas, of the Incarnation of any divine Person or actually of the final assumption of human nature on the part of concretely signified divine nature, done abstracting from the Persons, or on the part of the different divine Persons together, done abstracting from their correlativity. Cf. *Summa Theol.*, III, qq. 3, 5, 6 and the reasoned criticism of G. Lafont, *op. cit.*, 146ff.

76. A. Milano, *Trinità, op. cit.*, 493. Cf. L. Bouyer's observation in *Il Padre invisibile: Approcci al mistero della divinità*, Rome 1979, 262: "We must recognize that starting from the divine essence, considered anteriorly to the persons and as if, in whatever way, their source, means rendering their distinction beyond a latent modalism almost impossible to explain, and even more, giving to differentiated relations between them and us a meaning which cannot be reduced to an empty formula."

77. A. Milano, *Trinità, op. cit.*, 494.

78. "In Deo omnia sunt unum, ubi non obviat relationis oppositio": DS 1330. Cf. H. Muhlen, *Person und Appropriation. Zum Verständnis des Axioms: In Deo omnia* . . . , in *Münchener Theologische Zeitschrift* 16 (1965) 37-57.

79. Cf., for example, J. Lortz, *Storia della Chiesa nello sviluppo delle sue idee*, II, Alba 1967, 12.

80. Cf. especially the *Lezioni sulla filosofia della religione*, it.tr. by E. Oberti and G. Borruso, 2 vols., Bologna 1973. On the doctrine of the Trinity, cf: *Hegel et la théogie contemporaine. L'absolu dans l'histoire*, Neuchatel-Paris 1977; E. Brito, *Hegel et la tâche actuelle de la christologie*, Paris 1979; C. Bruaire, *Logique et religion chrétienne dans la philosophie de Hegel*, Paris 1964; A. Chapelle, *Hegel et la religion*, 3 vols., Paris 1963-1971; C. Greco, *La mediazione trinitaria dell'unità di Dio nella Filosofia della Religione di G.W.F. Hegel*, in *Ecclesiologia e cultura moderna. Saggi teologici*, Rome 1979, 299-351; H. Küng, *Incarnazione di Dio. Introduzione al pensiero teologico di Hegel, prolegomeni ad una futura cristologia*, Brescia 1972; L. Oeing-Hanoff, *Hegels Trinitätslehre*, in *Theologie und Philosophie*, 52 (1977) 378-407; J. Splett, *Die Trinitätslehre G.W.F. Hegel*, Freiburg-München 1965.

81. G.W.F. Hegel, *Lezioni sulla filosofia della religione, op. cit.*, I, 97f.

82. *Ib.*, II, 369 (modified translation).

83. *Ib.*, II, 366f.

84. *Ib.*, II, 285.

85. W. Pannenberg, *Cristologia, op. cit.*, 231.

86. Cf. e.g., J. Splett, *Die Trinitätslehre* . . . , *op. cit.*, 145-150 and J. Moltmann, *Trinità e Regno di Dio, op. cit.*, 27f.

87. Cf. *Die christliche Dogmatik im Entwurf*, Munich 1927; *Die kirchliche Dogmatik*, I/I, Munich 1932 and II/I, Zürich 1940.

88. Cf. K. Barth's study of Hegel in *La teologia protestante nel XIX secolo*, 1, Milan 1979, 429-465.

89. A limited analogy may be found also in K. Rahner's proposal which speaks of a unique divine subject in three "distinct modes of subsistence"; cf. *Il Dio Trino come fondamento originario e trascendente della storia della salvezza*, in *Mysterium Salutis*, 3, *op. cit.*, 401-507. Cf. J. Moltmann's observations on Barth and Rahner in *Trinità e Regno di Dio, op. cit.*, 151-163 and W. Kasper, *Il Dio di Gesù Cristo*, Brescia 1984, 400-404. The revelation is taken in Rahner as *self-communication of God* in Christ and in the Spirit. If the divine unity is safeguarded thus, is there not the risk of leaving the personal reality, especially of the Second and the Third Persons, in the shadows? Is not the dialectic with which the movement of the intradivine life comes to be understood too weak? Cf. G. Lafont, *Peut-on* . . . , *op. cit.*, 171-228 (on K. Rahner). However, the force of the concept of subsistence in the formula "Subsistenzweise" must be acknowledged; rightly understood, it tends to exclude every possible Trinitarian modalism.

90. W. Kasper, *Il Dio di Gesù Cristo, op. cit.*, 400f.

91. Cf. the excessively simplified classical thesis on the two different definitions of East

and West in Th. de Régnon, *Etudes de théologie positive sur la Sainte Trinité, op. cit.*
The synthesis of the two conceptions is explained in I, 333-340; 428-435. On the
closeness of the two perspectives, on the other hand, cf., e.g., G. Lafont, *Peut-on
. . . , op. cit.*, 70.

92. St. Athanasius, *Lettera I a Serapione* 28: PG 26, 594f. 599.

93. St. John Damascene, *De Fide Orthodoxa* I 14: PG 94, 860.

94. Cf. H. de Lubac, *La posterità spirituale di Gioacchino da Fiore*, 2 vols., Milan 1981
and 1984; cf. next A. Crocco, *La teologia trinitaria di Gioacchino*, in Id.,
Gioacchino da Fiore e il gioachinismo, Naples 1976 (2), 115-146; G. DiNapoli, *La
teologia trinitaria di Gioacchino da Fiore*, in *Divinitas*, 23 (1979) 281-312; H.
Mottu, *La manifestazione dello spirito secondo Gioacchino da Fiore*, Turin 1983
(with bibliography; 293-305); J. Moltmann, *Trinità e Regno di Dio, op. cit.*, 218ff.
Cf. finally *Storia e messaggio in Gioacchino da Fiore* 1980.

95. Cf. the beautiful text of the *Liber Concordiae Novi ac Veteris Testamenti*, Venice
1519 (photomechanically reprinted Frankfurt, 1964), Lib. V, 84, 112.

96. *Tractatus super quatuour Evangelia*, ed. E. Buonaiuti, Rome 1930, 24, 21-27.

97. *Ib.*, 24, 7-16.

98. *Liber Figurarum*, ed. L. Tondelli, M. Reeves, B. Hirsch-Reich, *Il libro delle Figure
dell'Abate Gioacchino da Fiore*, 2 vols., Turin 1953 (2), II, XI tables. Unity is shown
by three interlooped circles.

99. *Tractatus, op. cit.*, 198, 18-27.

100. *Liber Concordiae, op. cit.*, V, 77, 105.

101. *Psalterium Decem Chordarum*, Venice 1527 (photomechanically reprinted Frankfurt
1965), I, dist. 1a, f. 229a.

102. *Tractatus, op. cit.*, 124, 20-22.

103. *Psalterium, op. cit.*, 230c.

104. This is Croce's thesis in *La teologia trinitaria, op. cit.*, held also by H. Mottu, *La
manifestazione, op. cit.*, 245.

105. Cf. E. Bloch, *Filosofia del Rinascimento*, Bologna 1981, 27.

106. "Tria tempra ista ad similitudinem trium Personarum": *Liber Concordiae Novi ac
Veteris Testamenti, op. cit.*, lib. IV, 2, 44a.

107. "Tres status mundi propter tres Personas divinitatis assignare curavimus": *ib.*, lib. II,
1, 6, 9a.

108. *Liber Concordiae, op. cit.*, lib. V, 84, 112. Also the classification of the various
"ordines" of human society is modeled on the Trinity: lib. II, 1, 8, 9c (spouses:
Father; clerics: Son; monks: Spirit).

109. Cf. *Summa Theol.* Ia IIae q. 106 a.4 ad 3um. Cf. also Thomas' hard judgment in
Expositio secundae Decretalis, in *Opuscula Theologica*, I, Rome 1954, 428:
"Joachim the Abbot . . . unskilled in the subtle dogmas of the faith." Cf. also J.
Moltmann, *Speranza cristiana: messianica o trascendentale? Un dibattito teologico
con Gioacchino da Fiore e Tommaso d'Aquino* in *Asprenas* 30 (1983) 23-46.

110. H. Mottu, *La manifestazione, op. cit.*, 253.

111. *Tractatus, op. cit.*, 31, 2-7.

112. H. Mottu, *La manifestazione, op. cit.*, 249.

113. Cf. e.g., E. Buonaiuti, *Giocchino da Fiore, i tempi, la vita, il messaggio*, Rome
1931.

114. K. Barth, *Die Kirchliche Dogmatik*, I/I, *op. cit.*, 360.

115. The Fourth Lateran Council (1215) condemned the lost work of Joachim, *De unitate
et essentia Trinitatis*, because in it the Calabrian abbot accused Peter Lombard of

admitting, not a Trinity, but a quaternity in God (persons and essence). It is this interpretation of Lombard that was declared false. Joachim's attachment to the Catholic faith is even explicitly affirmed: cf. DS 803-807. To label him a "heretic" on the basis of this Council's stand is therefore inexact. Cf. A. Crocco, *Gioacchino da Fiore, op. cit.*, 62-74.

116. *Trinità e Regno di Dio. La dottrina su Dio, op. cit.* Pp. 218-224 deal with Joachim. The latter's view would be a modalistic attempt: 224.
117. *Ib.*, 29.
118. *Ib.*, 203.
119. *Ib.*, 19.
120. Cf. E. Peterson, *Il monoteismo come problema politico*, Brescia 1983 and G. Ruggeri's editorial, *Resistenza e dogma*, ib., 5-26.
121. J. Moltmann, *Trinità e Regno di Dio. op. cit.*, 211.
122. G. Ruggier, *Resistenza e dogma, op. cit.*, 21.
123. J. Moltmann, *Trinità e Regno di Dio. op. cit.*, 29.
124. *Ib.*, 233.
125. *Ib.*, 227.

3. THE TRINITY AS HISTORY

1. On the biblical idea of "mystery," cf. G. Bornkamm, *Mysterion* in *Grande Lessico del Nuovo Testamento* 7, Brescia 1971, 645-716. Next cf. E. Jungel, *Dio, mistero del mondo*, Brescia 1982, 327ff. ("God as Mystery").
2. L. Wittgenstein, *Tractatus logico-philosophicus*, 7, ed. R. Rhees, Frankfurt 1969, 83.
3. St. Augustine, *De Trinitate*, 1, 13, 31.
4. Cf. K. Rahner, *Theòs nel Nuovo Testamento*, in *Saggi Teologici*, Rome 1965, 467-585. For the steps by which Christ gets to be called God, cf. below.
5. *Ib.*, 577.
6. On the theology of the Father, besides the general works on Trinitarian theology, cf. L. Bouyer, *Il Padre invisibile. Approcci al mistero della divinità*, Rome 1979; M.-J. LeGuillou, *Il mistero del Padre*, Milan 1979; A. Milano, *Padre*, in *Nuovo Dizionario di Teologia*, Rome 1977, 1067-1096.
7. Eleventh Council of Toledo (675): DS 525.
8. Origen, *In Joan.* II 10, 75: PG 14, 128.
9. St. Basil, *Epist.* 128,3: PG 32, 549; cf. *Epist.* 38,4; PG 32, 329; *Adv. Eunom.* I 15: PG 545; St. Gregory Nazianzen, *Or.* 25,16: PG 35,1221; *Or.* 39,12: PG 36,348, etc.
10. *De Trinitate* 4, 20, 29.
11. *Summa Theol.* I q. 32 a. 3c.
12. *Ib.*, q.33, a.1.
13. E. Jüngel, *Dio, mistero del mondo, op. cit.*, 426.
14. A. Nygren, *Eros und Agape. Gestaltwandlungen der christlichen Liebe*, 2 vols., Gutersloh 1937 (2), here II, 551. Notwithstanding the radicalness of the opposing views, this work remains the monumental book on Christian love. Cf. J. Pieper, *Sull'amore*, Brescia 1974, 104ff., for an evaluation.
15. Characteristics of "agàpe": cf. A. Nygren, *Eros und Agape, op. cit.*, II, 548; 551; I, 185f.; 60.

16. Eleventh Council of Toledo (675): DS 525.
17. *Summa Theol.*, I q. 33 a. 2c.
18. Cf. *Summa Theol.* I q. 33 a. 3, on "spiration": Cf. q. 36: "De persona Spiritus Sancti."
19. It is the Augustinian line: Cf. F. Bourasse, *Quéstions de theologie trinitaire*, Rome 1970, especially 58ff. (the Spirit "unity of love of the Father and the Son").
20. This is Richard of St. Victor's interpretation in *De Trinitate* (Sources Chrétiennes 63, Paris 1959), especially lib. III, 22ff.; V, 7ff.
21. E. Júngel, *Dio Mistero del mondo, op. cit.*, 427.
22. Cf. F. Bourassa, *Quéstions . . . op. cit.*, 191-238 ("The Gift of God").
23. Cf. e.g., the Nicene-Constantinopolitan Symbol: DS 150. On the ideal of the Father *Pantocrator*, cf. among others Irenaeus, *Adv. Haer.* I, 10,1:PG 7, 549.
24. Cf. what will be said afterward on the Trinitarian origin of history. St. Thomas, *Summa Theol.* I q. 33 a. 3, distinguishes the analogical articulations of the paternity of God in relation to all creatures, to the human creature made in his image, to men adopted in grace, to the blessed in the glory of the eternal Word.
25. Cf. W. Kasper, *Il Dio di Gesù Cristo*, Brescia 1984, 185ff. ("The Problem of a God Omnipotent Father").
26. Cf. G. Mendel, *La révolte contre le père*, Paris 1968; A. Mitscherlich, *Vers la société sans pères*, Paris 1969. Cf. also A. Milano, *Padre*, in *Nuovo Dizionario di Teologia*, Rome 1977, 1067ff.
27. Cf. P. Schoonenberg, *Un Dio di uomini*, Brescia 1971.
28. A. Milano, *Paternità di Dio e liberazione dell'uomo*, in *Asprenas* 26 (1979) 178-204.
29. M. Moltmann, *Trinità e Regno di Dio*, Brescia 1983, 1977.
30. Cf. my *Gesù di Nazaret, storia di Dio, Dio della storia*, 1981, 228ff. (the history of Jesus as history of freedom).
32. Cf. *ib.*, the whole of Part III.
33. On what follows, cf.: F. Hahn, *Christologische Hoheitstitel, ihre Geschichte im fruhen Christentum*, Göttingen 1966 (3); cf. also O. Cullmann, *Cristologia del Nuovo Testamento*, Bologna 1970 and L. Sabourin, *Les noms et les titres de Jésus*, Bruges-Paris 1963.
34. On the theology of the Son, besides the general works on the Trinity, cf. among the more recent Christological approaches those of a more markedly Trinitarian bent: H.U. von Balthasar, *Verbum Caro*, Brescia 1970 (2), Id., *Mysterium paschale*, in *Mysterium Salutis* 6, Brescia 1971, 171-412; Id., *Gloria. Un'esetetica teologica*, III/2: *Nuovo Patto*, Milan 1978; L. Bouyer, *Il Figlio sterno*, Alba 1977; B. Forte, *Gesù di Nazaret, storia di Dio, Dio della storia. Saggio di una cristologia come storia*, Rome 1981; W. Kasper, *Gesù di Cristo*, Brescia 1975; J. Moltmann, *Il Dio crocifisso*, Brescia 1973; W. Pannenberg, *Cristologia. Leneamenti fondamentali*, Brescia 1974.
35. Eleventh Council of Toledo (675): DS 526.
36. Cf. *Summa Theol.* I q. 32, a. 3c.
37. Cf. *Ib.*, q. 27 a. 2: "Utrum aliqua processio in divinis generatio dici possit." "Generatio significat originem alicuius viventis a principio vivente a principio viventi coniuncto."
38. DS 526.
39. It is here that St. Thomas, developing Augustine, bases the generation of the second divine Person as Word by way of the intellect, starting from the analogy of the production of the intellectual word in the human spirit: "Verbum proprie dictum in divinis personaliter accipitur, et est proprium nomen personae Filii. Significat enim

quandam emanationem intellectus: persona autem quale procedit in divinis secundum emanationem intellectus dicitur Filus, et ḥuiusmodi processio dicitur generatio . . . Unde relinquitur quod solus Filius proprie dicatur Verbum in divinis'': I q. 34 a. 2c. cf. *Summa Theol*. I q. 27 a. 2.

40. K. Rahner, *Il Dio trino come fondamento, originario e trascendente della storia della salvezza*, in *Mysterium Salutis* 3, Brescia 1969, 452.

41. God the Father creates and knows his creatures in the Word: *Summa Theol*. I q. 34 a. 3; *De Veritate* q. 4 a. 5.

42. W. Kasper, *Il Dio di Gesù Cristo, op. cit.*, 266.

43. *Ib.*, 266f.

44. Much has already been written on the theme of divine suffering. Cf. e.g., J. Galot, *Il Mistero della sofferenza di Dio*, Assisi 1975; K. Kitamori, *Teologia del dolore di Dio*, Brescia 1975; J.Y. Lee, *God Suffers for Us: A Systematic Inquiry into a Concept of Divine Passibility*, La Haye 1974; F. Varillon, *La souffrance de Dieu*, Paris 1975. For a Trinitarian reading of the mystery of God's suffering, cf.: J. Moltmann, *Il Dio crocifisso*, Brescia 1973; E. Jüngel, *Dio, mistero del mondo, op. cit.*,; W. Kasper, *Il Dio di Gesù Cristo, op. cit.*, and the chapter on the finitude of Jesus and the cross in my *Gesù di Nazaret, op. cit.*, 260ff.

45. Cf. DS 125 (Nicea) and 150 (the Nicene-Constantinopolitan Symbol).

46. Eleventh Council of Toledo (675): DS 526.

47. Cf. Duquoc, *Un Dio diverso. Saggio sulla simbolica trinitaria*, Brescia 1978, 101.

48. *Ib.*, 117.

49. On biblical pneumatology, cf. A. Milano, *Considerazioni metodologiche sulla pneumatologia del Nuovo Testamento*, in *Augustinianum* 20 (1980) 429-469 and Y. Congar, *Credo nello Spirito Santo*, 1. *Revelazione e esperienza dello Spirito*, Brescia 1982, Part I.

50. Cf. my *Gesù di Nazaret, op. cit.*, 289f.

51. H.U. von Balthasar, *Lo Spirito come Amore*, in Id., *Spiritus Creator*, Brescia 1972, 101 (cf. the whole article 101-116).

52. On the theology of the Holy Spirit, besides the general works on Trinitarian theology, cf., among others: H.U. von Balthasar, *Spiritus Creator, op. cit.*; L. Bouyer, *Il Consolatore. Spirito Santo e vita di grazia*, Rome 1983; S. Boulgakov, *Il Paraclito*, Bologna 1971; Y. Congar, *Credo nello Spirito Santo*, 3 vols., Brescia 1982-3; *(L')esperienza dello Spirito. In onore di E. Schillebeeckx*, Brescia 1974; P. Evdokimov, *Lo Spirito nella tradizione ortodossa*, Rome 1971; *Gegenwart des Geistes. Aspekte der Pneumatologie*, hrsg. v. W. Kasper, Freigurg-Basel-Wien 1979; H. Mühlen, *Der Heilige Geist als Person*, Münster 1963; Id., *Una mystica persona*, Rome 1968.

53. Cf. the *Memorandum* of the colloquies promoted by the Faith and Constitution Commission of the World Council of Churches: *La théologie du Saint-Esprit dans le dialogue entre l'Orient et l'Occident*, under the direction of L. Vischer, Paris 1981. Cf. also *Istina* 3-4/1972: *Orient et Occident. La procession du Saint-Esprit*.

54. Cf. V. Lossky, *La teologia mistica della Chiesa d'Oriente*, Bologna 1967. Cf. also M.A. Orphanos, *La procession du Saint-Esprit selon certains pères grecs postérieurs au VIIIe siècle* in *La thèologie du Saint-Esprit, op. cit.*, 29ff.

55. Cf. *La teologia mistica, op. cit.* A. de Halleux has synthesized these theses, taking them from Lossky's work: *Revue Théologique de Louvain* 6 (1975) 13f.

56. S. Boulgakov, *Il Paraclito, op. cit.*, 231.

57. *Ib.*, 230. An analogous position is held by P. Evdokimov, *Lo Spirito Santo nella tradizione ortodossa, op. cit.*
58. *Il Paraclito, op. cit.*, 230.
59. *Thesen uber das Filioque. Von sinem russischen Theologe* in *Revue Internationale de Théologie*, 6 (1898) 681-712, reproduced in French translation in *Istina* 1972, 261-289.
60. M.A. Orphanos, *La procession du Saint-Esprit, op. cit.*, 38ff. A rediscovery of the creative overtures of Palamism is due to J. Meyendorff, *Introduction à l'étude de Grégoire Palamas*, Paris 1959.
61. K. Barth, *Die kirchliche Dogmatik* I/1 500-511. Barth adopts Anselm's theses.
62. *Ib.*, I/2 273.
63. Besides *Die kirchliche Dogmatik* II/1, the text is in W. Niesel, *Bekenntsnisschriften und Kirchenordnungen der nach Gottes Wort reformierten Kirche*, Munich 1938, 2d ed. Zollikon-Zürich, n.d., 235-337.
64. Cf. for example A. Heron, *Le "Filioque" dans la théologie réformée récente*, in *La théologie du Saint-Esprit, op. cit.*, 125-132.
65. Cf. e.g., G.S. Hendry's criticism of Barth in *The Holy Spirit in Christian Theology*, London 1965, 45-52.
66. T.F. Torrance, *Theology in Reconstruction*, London 1965, 231, where, however, it is shown that these consequences are owed to an obscuring of the original intention of the formula which came about in the West.
67. Cf. *Memorandum*, V, in *La théologie du Saint-Esprit, op. cit.*, 23.
68. On the history of the insertion: H.B. Swete, *On the History of the Doctrine of the Procession of the Holy Spirit from the Apostolic Age to the Death of Charlemagne*, Cambridge 1876, 196-226 (documentation: 227-237); M. Jugie, *De Processione Spiritus Sancti ex Fontibus Revelationis et secundum Orientales dissidentes*, Rome 1936, 243-258; Id., *Origine de la controverse sur l'addition du Filioque au Symbole. Photius en a-t-il parlé?* in *Revue de Sciences Phil. et Théologiques* 28 (1939) 369-395.
69. Think of Cyril of Alexandria: PG 71, 377D; 75, 1093 A; 76, 1189A, etc.
70. Cf. *De Trinitate*, especially Chap. IV, 20; XV, 26-27.
71. Cf. Y. Congar's synthesis in *Credo nello Spirito Santo*, 3. *La teologia dello Spirito Santo, op. cit.*, 88-103.
72. *Ib.*, 97.
73. *De Trinitate*, VI, 5, 7.
74. Cf. PL 102, 971-976.
75. PG 91, 136.
76. Cf. A de Halleux, *Pour un accord oecuménique sur la procession de l'Esprit Saint et l'addition du Filioque au Symbole*, in *La théologie du Saint-Esprit, op. cit.*, 86-87. Cf. DS 850 and 1300-1302.
77. Cf. DS 265; *heteran pistin* — another faith.
78. Cf. M.-A. Chevallier, *L'évangile de Jean et le "Filioque"* in *Revue des Sciences religieuses* 57 (1983), 93-111.
79. Cf. Y. Congar, *Pneumatologie ou "christomonisme" dans la Tradition latine?* in *Ecclesia a Spiritu Sancto edocta. Mélange théol. G. Philips*, Gembloux 1970, 41-63.
80. *Esposizione della fede ortodossa*, I, 12: PG 94, 849B. Cf. also synodal letter of Patriarch Tarasius to the Seventh Ecumenical Council of Nicea in 787: Mansi, *Collectio conciliorum*, XII, 1122.
81. Cf. Y. Congar, *Credo nello Spirito Santo*, 3, *op. cit.*, 192ff, 196.
82. Cf. K. Barth, *Die kirchliche Dogmatik* I/1 500ff.

83. DS 150.
84. Cf. F. Hauck and S. Schulz, in *Grande Lessico del Nuovo Testamento*, 10, 1416-1446.
85. Döllinger had already called attention to this difference at the Second Conference of Union at Bonn between Orthodox and Old Catholics: cf. K. Stalder, *Le Filioque dans les Eglise vieilles-catholiques et dans leur théologie*, in *La théologie du Saint-Esprit*, *op. cit.*, 117.
86. *De Potentia* q. 10, a. 1 ad 8.
87. Cf. Y. Congar, *op. cit.*, 57.
88. Cf. F. Rouleau, *A propos du "Filioque." Document: Instruction pastorale de l'Episcopat catholique de Grèce*, in *Les quatre fleuves* 9 (1979) 73-78. The document dates from 1973.
89. *Summa Theol.*, IIa IIae q. 1 a. 2 ad 2.
90. J. Moltmann, *Propositions dogmatiques en vue d'une solution à la querelle du "Filioque,"* in *La théologie du Saint-Esprit, op. cit.*, 189 (cf. the whole article 179-189, reproduced also in Id., *Trinità e Regno di Dio*, 1983, 191ff.). Moltmann proposes — through an interpretation of the Symbol — the form: "I believe in the Holy Spirit who proceeds from the Father of the Son and receives his form from the Father and from the Son." The proposal evokes in some way the Palamite distinction of the two planes of existence (to proceed) and of the energies (to receive form).
91. D. Ritschl, *Remarques sur l'histoire de la controverse du "Filioque" et ses implication théologiques*, in *La théologie du Saint-Esprit, op. cit.*, 69. The diversity between the two theological statements has been marked by the excessively simplified classical thesis of Th. de Régnon, *Etudes de théologie positive sur la sainte Trinité*, Paris, I-II 1892, III-IV 1898.
92. S. Chr. 28, Paris 1951.
93. S. Chr. 1, Paris 1955.
94. Cf. my essay, *L'universo dionisiano nel Prologo della "Mistica Teologia,"* in *Medioevo* 4 (1978) 1-57.
95. D. Ritschl, *Remarques . . . , op. cit.*, 70.
96. Cf., e.g., *Il Dio Trino . . . , op. cit.*, 401-502, especially 413ff.
97. Y. Congar, *Credo nello Spirito Santo*, 3, *op. cit.*, 23ff.
98. D. Ritschl, *Remarques . . . , op. cit.*, 75.
99. Y. Congar, *Credo nello Spirito Santo*, 3, *op. cit.*, 8.
100. *Ib.*, 209.
101. The suppression of the *Filioque* was accepted by the Old Catholics and the Anglicans (Lambeth Conference 1978).
102. The *Tesi sul Filioque*, elaborated at the Congress of the Italian Theological Association of 1983, reported in *Rassegna di Teologia* 25 (1984) 87f. invite this deeper understanding and development. After an hermeneutical premise (Thesis 1: On the Trinity and History) and a theological premise (Thesis 2: The Relation between the Trinity and History is led back to the Son-Spirit relation about which the Nicene-Constantinopolitan Symbol is silent), these theses show how the starting point of every Trinitarian reflection must be Easter (Thesis 3) in whose light is elaborated the relation of reciprocity and complementarity between the Son and the Spirit in the movement from the past to the present of the faith (Thesis 4: The Problem of Tradition), in its present (Thesis 5: Ecclesial Existence), and in its opening to the future (Thesis 6: Church-Kingdom), to conclude with the immanent reflection on this relation itself (Thesis 7). This last thesis underlines the dual role of the Spirit in Trinitarian communion — overture (The Spirit pleroma or future of the Son) and of

bond of unity (the Son, repose or present of the Spirit): "The reflection of this reciprocity and complementarity in the formulas relative to the intratrinitarian life leads to the affirmation of a possible twofold integrative thesis of the *Filioque*: the Spirit is related to the Father as source and to the Son as pleroma or the future of the Son; the latter is related to the Father as to his source and to the Spirit as repose or present of the Spirit. This reciprocity — wrapped in the silence of the Symbol — is the unfathomable, albeit undeniable, foundation of the preceding theses." (88).

103. Eleventh Council of Toledo (675): DS 527.

104. This is the affirmation of Nicea-Constantinople: DS 150.

105. This is the thesis of H. Mühlen, *Der Heilige Geist als Person, op. cit.*, 156 for example.

106. St. Augustine, *De Trinitate*, 5, 11, 12.

107. *Ib.*, 15, 17, 27.

108. *Ib.*, 6, 5, 7.

109. *Ib.*, 6, 9, 10.

110. *Ib.*, 15, 26, 47; cf. also, e.g., 4, 20, 29; 5, 14, 15. The Spirit proceeds from the Son for St. Thomas as love proceeds from the word: "Non enim aliquid amamus, nisi secundum quod conceptionem mentis apprendimus" ("For we do not love anything unless we apprehend it by a mental conception."): *Summa Theol.*, I q. 36 a. 2c.

111. Cf. *De Trinitate*, 15, 17, 27ff.: the whole Trinity is love. However, it is the Spirit, who, in relation to the Father and the Son of whom he is communion, is properly called love: 15, 17, 29f.

112. The distinction is clearly made by St. Thomas: I q. 37 a. 1: "Nomen amoris in divinis sumi potest et essentialiter et personaliter." ("The name Love in God can be taken essentially and personally.")

113. E. Jüngel, *Dio, mistero del mondo, op. cit.*, 485f.

114. Cf. the Nicene-Constantinopolitan Symbol: DS 150.

115. Eleventh Council of Toledo (675): DS 527.

116. Cf. *De Trinitate* 15, 19, 33. Also for St. Thomas Aquinas "donum" is the proper name of the Holy Spirit: *Summa Theol.*, I q. 38.

117. Y. Congar, *Credo nello Spirito Santo*, 3, *op. cit.*, 154f., with numerous texts (cf. 150ff.).

118. Cf. W. Kasper, *Il Dio di Gesù Cristo, op. cit.*, 303.

119. Cf. St. Cyril of Jerusalem: PG 33,953; St. Athanasius: PG 26,663; St. Basil: PG 32, 133C. Cf. Y. Congar, *op. cit.*, 152.

120. It is significant that St. Thomas accepts the procession of the Spirit "a Patre per Filium" ("from the Father through the Son"): *Summa Theol.* I q. 36 a. 3.

121. E. Jüngel, *Dio, mistero del mondo, op. cit.*, 429.

122. C. Duquoc, *Un Dio Diverso, op. cit.*, 103.

123. Cf. E. Jüngel, *Dio, mistero del mondo, op. cit.*, 502ff.

124. Eleventh Council of Toledo (675): DS 528.

125. Cf. J. Pieper, *Sull'amore, op. cit.*, 30f.

126. Cf. DS 125.

127. Cf. DS 150.

128. Of Western origin since the second half of the fifth century: DS 75.

129. Eleventh Council of Toledo (675): DS 528.

130. Cf. *Summa Theol.*, I q. 39 a. 2.

131. Cf. *ib.*, q. 29, a. 4. Cf. also below the reflection on the "persons" in God.

132. Cf. *De Trinitate*, 15, 6, 10: "When one reaches the love that in Holy Scripture is

called God, the mystery is cleared up a bit with the trinity of lover, beloved, and love. But, since that ineffable light dazzled our spirit and we noted that the weakness of our mind could not yet attain it . . . we turned to the consideration of our spirit, according to which man has been made *to God's image.*"
133. *Ib.*, 8, 8, 12.
134. *Ib.*, 8, 10, 14.
135. *Ib.*, 6, 5, 7.
136. E. Jüngel, *Dio mistero del mondo, op. cit.*, 409.
137. *Ib.*, 427.
138. *Ib.*, 486.
139. Cf. *ib.*, 503.
140. John Damascene, *De Fide Orthodoxa* I 14: PG 94, 860.
141. Cf. St. Hilary of Poitiers, *De Trinitate* 3, 4:PL 10, 78 a; St. Augustine, *De Trinitate* 6, 10, 12; St. Thomas, *Summa Theol.*, 1 q. 42 a. 5; St. Bonaventure, *Sent.* I d. 19p. I 1. 4, etc. Cf. also the *Decretum pro Iacobitis* of the Council of Florence (1442): DS 1331.
142. Cf. DS 1330 and St. Anselm, *De processione Spiritus Sancti* 2D PL 158, 288 C.
143. Cf. e.g., *Summa Theol.*, I q. 30 a. 7.
144. Cf. A Deissler, *L'autorivelazione di Dio nell'Antico Testamento*, in *Mysterium Salutis*, 3, *op. cit.*, 285-344; B. de Margerie, *Les perfections du Dieu de Jésus Christ*, Paris 1981; M. Löhrer, *Riflessioni dommatiche sugli attributi e sui modi di agire di Dio*, in *Mysterium Salutis*, 3, *op. cit.*, 370-400; J. Pfammater, *Attributi a modi di agire di Dio nel Nuovo Testamento, ib.*, 345-369.
145. Cf. St. Thomas' classical treatment, *Summa Theol.*, I qq. 2-26 which, after the question of the existence of God (q.2), is divided into two parts: qq. 3-13 (simplicity, perfection, goodness, infinity, omnipresence, immutability, eternity, unity, and names of God) and 14-26 (divine knowledge, will, and power).
146. L. Scheffczk, *Il Dio che verrà*, Turin 1975, 155.
147. Vatican I, *Constitutio dogmatica Dei Filius* (1870): DS 3001. The Symbol *Quicumque* affirms the various divine attributes in equal measure of the three Persons: cf. DS 75.
148. Lateran IV (1215): DS 806. CF. also DS 800.
149. *Summa Theol.*, I q. 8 a. 3c.
150. Cf., e.g., K. Barth, *Die kirchliche Dogmatik*, II/1, 544.
151. Cf. H. Muhlen, *La mutabilità di Dio*, Brescia 1974; W. Maas, *Unveränderlichkeit Gottes. Zum Verhältnis von griechisch-philosophicher und christlicher Gotteslehre*, Munich-Paderborn-Vienna 1974.
152. Cf. G. von Rad, *Teologia dell'Antico Testamento*, I, Brescia 1972, 212.
153. M. Lohrer, *Riflessioni dogmatiche sugli attributi e sui modi di agire di Dio, op. cit.*, 388f.
154. F. Rosenzweig, *Der Stern der Erlosung*, III, Heidelberg 1954 (3), 192f.
155. P. Lapide in P. Lapide-J. Moltmann, *Monoteismo ebraico—dottrina trinitaria cristiana. Un dialogo*, Brescia 1982, 14. On monotheism, cf. S. Breton, *Unicité et monotheisme*, Paris 1981; *Concilium* 21 (1985) n. 1: *Il monoteismo*, edited by C. Geffré and J.P. Jossua.
156. Cf. DS 73, 75, 173, 528, 800, 803f., 1330, 1880. Next cf. C. Andresen, *Zur Entstehung und Geschichte des trinitarischen Personbegriffs*, in *Zeitschrift für die neutestamentliche Wissenschaft* 52 (1961), 1-39; J. Auer, *Person. Ihre theologische Struktur. Ein Schlüssel zum christlichen Mysterium*, Regensburg 1979; A. Milano, *Persona in teologia. Alle origini del significato di persona nel cristianesimo antico*,

Naples 1984; B. Studer, *Der Person-Begriff in der fruhnen kirchenamtlichen Trinitäslehre*, in *Theologie und Philosophie* 17 (1982) 161-177; J. Ratzinger, *Il significato di persona nella teologia*, in *Dogma e predicazione*, Brescia 1974, 173-189.

157. Cf. K. Rahner, *Il Dio Trino* . . . , *op. cit.*, 486ff. ("The Aporia of the Concept of Person in Trinitarian Doctrine").

158. *De Trinitate*, 5, 9, 10.

159. Cf. K. Barth, *Die Kirchliche Dogmatik*, I/1, 379f.

160. Cf. K. Rahner, *Il Dio Trino* . . . , *op. cit.*, 491ff.

161. Cf. A. Malet, *Personne et amour dans la theologie trinitaire de Saint Thomas d'Aquin*, Paris 1956. Cf. also G. Lafont, *Peut-on connaître Dieu en Jésus-Christ?* Paris 1969, 107ff.

162. Cf. *Summa Theol.*, I q. 29, a. 4. Cf. also above 2.3.d.

163. K. Rahner, *Il Dio Trino* . . . *op. cit.*, 456. Also K. Barth, *Die Kirchliche Dogmatik*, I/1, 384f. accepts this statement.

164. They are the three structural determinations of the person stressed, for example, by J. Auer, *Person. Ihre theologische Struktur, op. cit.*, and Id., *Il mistero di Dio*, Assisi 1982, 424ff.: *subsistence, existence, and communication*.

165. Cf. B. Lonergan, *De Deo Trino*, II, Rome 1964 (3), 186-193: "Et ideo relinquitur quod tria subjecta sunt ad invicem conscia per unam conscientiam aliter et aliter a tribus habetur" (193).

166. DS 1330.

4. HISTORY IN THE TRINITY

1. Cf. A. Hamman, *La Trinità nella liturgia e nella vita cristiana*, in *Mysterium Salutis* 3, Brescia 1969, 172.

2. This is the structure of Christian liturgy: cf. C. Vagaggini, *Il sense teologico della liturgia*, Rome 1968 (5).

3. J. Moltmann, *Futuro della creazione*, Brescia 1980, 93-109 ("The Trinitarian History of God").

4. Cf. G. von Rad, *Teologia dell'Antico Testamento*, I, Brescia 1972, 165ff., 406ff., 502ff.

5. Cf. what is said in 2.2a. Cf. also W. Kern, *Il creatore e il Dio Uno e Trino*, in *Mysterium Salutis* 4, Brescia 1970, 106-127.

6. Nicene-Constantinopolitan Symbol: DS 150.

7. Eleventh Council of Toledo (675): DS 525.

8. St. Thomas, *In I Sent., Prol.* cf. F. Marinelli, *Personalismo trinitario nella storia della salvezza. Rapporti tra la SS. Trinità e le opere ad extra nello Scriptum super Sententiis*, Rome-Paris 1969.

9. St. Thomas speaks of "ratio" and "causa": cf. *Scriptum super Sententiis*, in II, 20, 2, 1.

10. Origen, *Selecta in Ezechielem* 16: PG 13, 812A.

11. Id., *Homilia VI in Ezechielem* 6: PG 13, 715.

12. Fourth Lateran Council (1215): DS 800, and Vatican I (1870): DS 3001.

13. J. Moltmann, *Trinità e Regno di Dio*, Brescia 1983, 121.

14. St. Thomas, *Summa Theol.*, I q. 8 a. 1 c.

Footnotes

15. Cf. H.U. von Balthasar, *L'acceso alla realtà di Dio*, in *Mysterium Salutis* 3, *op. cit.*, 19-59 and W. Kasper, *Il Dio di Gesù Cristo*, Brescia 1984, 98ff. ("Experience and Awareness of God").
16. *Constitutio dogmatica Dei Filius*: DS 3004.
17. Cf. *Summa Theol.*, 1 q. 2 a, 3; *Contra Gentes* I 13, 15, 16, 44.
18. Presented by him in *Proslogion*, where he intends to sum up in one argument those given in *Monologion*: cf. K. Barth, *Fides quaerens intellectum. Anselms Beweis der Existenz Gottes im Zusammenhang seines theologischen Programms* (1931), ed. by E. Jüngel and I. U. Dalferth, Zürich 1981.
19. "Aliquid quo maius nihil cogitari potest": *Proslogion* c.2.
20. Cf. especially the *Lezioni sulla filosofia della religione*, It. tr. by E. Oberto and G. Borruso, 2 vols., Bologna 1973, and also *La fenomenologia dello spirito*, It. tr. by E. DeNegri, 2 vols., Florence 1973. On the ontological proof of the modern era, cf. D. Henrich, *La prova ontologica dell'esistenza di Dio. La sua problematica e la sua storia nell'età moderna*, Naples 1983.
21. One thinks of the beginnings of Neo-Scholasticism in the Neapolitan School: P. Orlando, *Il tomismo a Napoli nell secolo XIX. La scuola del Sanseverino*, Rome 1968.
22. Cf. W. Kasper, *Concezione della teologia ieri e oggi*, in Id., *Fede e storia*, Brescia 1975, 17-42.
23. Cf. for the value of narrative, experiential witness of God: J.B. Metz, *Breve apologie del narrare*, in *Concilium* 9 (1973) 860-878 (resumed in Id., *La fede, nella storia e nella società*, Brescia 1978, 197ff.).
24. As it is etymologically in the Latin *ex-perior* (whence *peritus* = one who knows directly, and *periculum* = test, risk) and in German *er-fahren* (to go out, to journey across a country, to have direct contact at one's own risk and danger).
25. Cf. C. Fabro, *L'uomo e il rischio di Dio*, Rome 1967.
26. DS 3005.
27. Cf. the work of Pseudo-Dionysius the Areopagite and his influence on the whole of Christian thought: B. Forte, *Universo dionisiano nel Prologo della "Mistica Teologia,"* in *Medioevo*, 4, 1978, 1-57.
28. Cf. L. Scheffczk, *Il Dio che verrà*, Turin, 1975.
29. See in this regard his argument with E. Brunner, *Nein: Antwort an Emil Brunner* (Theologische Existenz heute 14), Munich 1934. Cf. B. Forte, *Cristologia e politica. Su K¸ Barth*, in Id., *Cristologie del Novecento*, Brescia 1983, 63-104. Barth, however repeats Luther's "no" to every "theology of glory": cf. *Disputatio di Heidelberg*, Theses 18 and 19: *Wiemarer Ausgabe* 1, 354.
30. Cf. Barth's 1956 conference: *L'umanità di Dio*, Turin 1975.
31. Cf. J. Beumer, *Gratis supponit naturam. Zur Geschichte eines theologischen Prinzips*, in *Gregorianum* 20 (1919) 281-406; 535-552; E. Przywara, *Der Grunsatz "Gratia non destruit, sed supponit et perficit naturam." Eine ideengeschichtliche interpretation*, in *Scholastik* 17 (1942) 178-186; J. Ratzinger, *Gratia praesupponit naturam* in Id., *Dogma e predicazione*, Brescia 1974, 137-154; B. Stoekle, *Gratia supponit naturam. Geschichte und Analyse eines theologischen Axioms*, Rome 1962.
32. Cf. E. Jüngel, *Dio mistero del mondo*, Brescia 1982, 431ff., who sees in faith the place of the true encounter between the "two" loves.
33. Cf. e.g., St. Augustine, *De Trinitate* 12, 6, 6.
34. For theological anthropology, cf. *Mysterium Salutis*, 4, *op. cit.*; M. Flick-Z. Alszeghy, *Fondamenti di una antropologia teologica*, Florence 1970; D. Mongillo, *Anthropologie dogmatique*, in *Initiation à la pratique de la théologie*, III, Paris 1983,

577-609; J. Moltmann, *Uomo*, Brescia 1972; W. Pannenberg, *Che cosa è l'uomo?* Brescia 1974; O.H. Pesch, *Frei sein aus Gnade. Theologische Antropologie*, Freiberg 1983.

35. St. Alphonsus Maria de'Liguori, *Pratica di amare Gesù Cristo*, ch. 1, 2.
36. J. Pieper, *Sull'amore*, Brescia 1974, 80.
37. K. Rahner, *Il Dio Trino come fondamento originario e trascendente della storia della salvezza*, in *Mysterium Salutis* 3, *op. cit.*, 498ff.
38. St. Augustine, *De Trinitate*, 15, 23, 43.
39. Cf. *ib.*, 15, 22, 42.
40. *Ib.*, 14, 17, 23 (on the dynamism of the image).
41. It is the experience of modern atheism: cf. C. Fabro, *Introduzione all'ateismo moderno*, Rome 1969 (2).
42. F. Nietzsche, *La gaia scienza*, Milan 1978 (2), Aphorism 125.
43. Cf. M. Horkheimer - Th. W. Adorno, *Dialletica dell'Illuminismo*, Turin 1971.
44. Cf. M. Horkheimer, *La nostalgia del Totalmente Altro*, Brescia 1972.
45. St. Irenaeus, *Adversus Haereses* 4, 20, 7.
46. W. Hamilton, *Che cosa è la "morte di Dio,"* in *Dio è morto?* Milan 1967, 184. Cf. also R. Rubenstein, *After Auschwitz*, New York 1966 and *Concilium* 20 (1984), fasc. 5: "The Holocaust as Interruption: A Problem for Christian Theology."
47. On what follows, cf. E. Peterson, *Il Monoteismo come problema politico*, Brescia 1983; J. Moltmann, *Trinità e Regno di Dio*, 1983, 204ff. ("The Reign of Freedom"). Cf. also the *Tesi* (Theses) of the group with a "political" slant, elaborated at the Congress of the Italian Theological Association of 1983, in *Rassegna di Teologia* 25 (1984) 88.
48. *Tesi* 1, *op. cit.*
49. It is the citation of the *Iliad* with which Aristotle concludes Book XII of the *Metaphysics* and which Peterson holds is of great importance: *Il monoteismo . . . , op. cit.*, 31.
50. J. Moltmann, *Trinità e Regno di Dio*, *op. cit.*, 212.
51. *Tesi* 2, *op. cit.*
52. *Tesi* 4, *op. cit.*
53. *Tesi* 3, *op. cit.*
54. *Tesi* 5, *op. cit.* Thesis 6 is an invitation to discernment of the signs of the Spirit in the Word and in history, particularly through the contribution of Trinitarian theology.
55. This seems to be the risk not completely avoided by J. Moltmann, *Trinità e Regno di Dio*, *op. cit.*, 204-214.
56. Cf. B. de Margerie, *La Trinité chrétienne dans l'histoire*, Paris 1975, 367ff. ("Family, Church, human soul, imperfect complementary, and revealed analogies of the divine Trinity"). Cf., however, St. Augustine's hesitations about the family as image of the Trinity: *De Trinitate*, 12, 5, 5.
57. Cf. on what follows H.U. von Balthasar, *Teologia della storia*, Brescia 1969; Id., *Il tutto nel frammento*, Milan 1970; M. Bordoni, *Il tempo. Valore filosofico e mistero teologico*, Rome 1965; O. Cullmann, *Cristo e il tempo*, Bologna 1969 (4); W. Kasper, *Fede e storia*, Brescia 1975; H.-I. Marrou, *Teologia della storia*, Milan 1979 (2); J. Mouroux, *Il mistero del tempo*, Brescia 1967; G. Ruggeri, *Sapienza e storia*, Milan 1971; *Spirito Santo e storia*, edited by L. Sartori, Rome 1977.
58. Cf. E. Jüngel, *Dio, mistero del mondo*, Brescia 1982, 503.
59. Cf. O. Cullmann, *Cristo e il tempo*, *op. cit.*, 61ff.
60. Cf. A. Hamman, *La Trinità nella liturgia e nella vita cristiana*, *op. cit.*, 173f. (169-185), as well as C. Vagaggini's fundamental work, *Il senso teologico della*

liturgia, op. cit. Cf. also the document on ecumenical consensus about baptism in the Faith and Constitution Commission's *Battesimo, Eucaristia, Ministero*, Turin-Leumann 1982.

61. Faith and Constitution, *Battesimo, cit.*, n. 2.
62. Cf. *ib.*, nn. 3-7.
63. Cf. E. Jüngel, *Dio, mistero del mondo, op. cit.*, 505ff.
64. Cf. H.U. von Balthasar, *Fides Christi*, in Id., *Sponsa Verbi*, Brescia 1972 (2), 41-72; J. Guillet, *La foi de Jésus-Christ*, Paris 1980.
65. Cf. A. Hamman, *La Trinità . . . , op. cit.*, 172f. and 176 and C. Vagaggini, *Il senso teologico . . . , op. cit.* 196-209. Cf. also on prayer G. Moioli, *Preghiera*, in *Nuovo Dizionario di Teologia*, Rome 1977, 1198-1213 (with bibliography).
66. Cf., e.g., P. Galtier, *Le Saint-Esprit en nous d'après les Pères grecs*, Rome 1946; P. Evdokimov, *Lo Spirito Santo nella tradizione ortodossa*, Rome 1971.
67. The mystics' experience confirms this twofold movement of love. Think, for example, of the famous prayer of Elizabeth of the Trinity, *Ecrits spirituels*, presented by M.M Philipon, Paris 1949, 80f. (Nov. 21, 1904): "My God, Trinity I adore." Cf. the recent critical edition edited by C. de Meester: Elisabeth de la Trinité: *J'ai trouvé Dieu. Oeuvres complètes*, 3 vols. (2 tomes), Paris 1979-1980.
68. Cf. on what follows B. Forte, *La chiesa icona della Trinità. Breve ecclesiologia*, Brescia 1984.
69. 1983 Congress of the ITA, *Tesi sul "Filioque," Tesi* 4, in *Rassegna di Teologia*, 25 (1984) 87.
70. Id., *Tesi* 5, 87.
71. Id., *Tesi* 6, 87f.
72. Cf. in particular M. Thurian, *L'eucaristia, memoriale del Signore, sacrificio di azione di grazie e d'intercessione*, Rome 1967. Next cf. on all that follows the Document of Monaco of the official Catholic-Orthodox dialogue *Il mistero della Chiesa e dell'Eucaristia alla luce del mistero della Santa Trinità*, 1982, as well as B. Forte, *La chiesa nell'eucaristia. Per un'ecclesiologia eucaristica alla luce del Vaticano II*, Naples 1975 and Id., *Corpus Christi*, Naples 1983 (2).
73. Cf. A. Hamman, *La Trinità, op. cit.*, 174ff.
74. Faith and Constitution, *Eucaristia, cit.*, n.4.
75. Cf. H. de Lubac, *Corpus Mysticum. L'eucaristia e la chiesa nel Medio Evo*, Turin 1968.
76. Y. Congar, *Pneumatologie ou "Christomonisme" dans la tradition latine?* in *Ephemerides Theologicae Lovanienses* 45 (1969) 394-416.
77. Faith and Constitution, *Eucaristia, op. cit.*, n. 14.
78. Cf. B. Forte, *La chiesa come icona della Trinità, op. cit.*, 44ff.
79. *Ad Gentes* 2-4; *Gaudium et Spes* 40.
80. On eschatology as dimension of all Christian being and action, cf., among others: J. Alfaro, *Speranza cristiana e liberazione dell'uomo*, Brescia 1972; V. Boublik, *L'uomo nell'attesa di Cristo*, Bari 1972; W.D. Marsch, *Futuro*, Brescia 1972; J. Moltmann, *Teologia della speranza*, Brescia 1970.
81. J. Moltmann, *Trinità e Regno di Dio, op. cit.*, 116.
82. Cf. E. Jüngel, *Dio, mistero del mondo, op. cit.*, 414.
83. Cf. B. Maggioni - G. Ruggeri, *Gloria*, in *Nuovo Dizionario di Teologia, op. cit.*, 575-593.
84. Cf. P. Tillich, *Il coraggio di esistere*, Rome 1968, with its penetrating analysis of human anguish, tied in with the fear of death, the sense of guilt, and the lack of

meaning, and with a perspicacious statement that this third root is the one proper to modern times after the collapse of all possible securities.

85. On the theme of the "maternity" of God, proposed today with insistence, even in "reaction to an overwhelming and secular primacy of the masculine," cf. Y. Congar, *Credo nello Spirito Santo*, III, Brescia 1983, 161-171 ("On the maternity in God and on the Femininity of the Holy Spirit"). Cf. also C. Schutz, *Gegenwärtige Tendenzen in der Fottesund Trinitätslehre*, in *Mysterium Salutis. Ergänzungsband*, Zürich 1981, 314-317 ("Gottvater?").

86. Think of the curious medieval devotion to Christ-Mother and the monastic ideal of the paternal and maternal abbot: Cf. A. Cabassut, *Une dévotion médiévale peu connue, la dévotion à "Jésus notre Mère,"* in *Revue d'Ascétique et de Mystique* 25 (1949) 234-245; C.W. Bynum, *Jesus as Mother and Abbot as Mother. Some Themes in Twelfth-Century Cistercian Writings*, in *The Harvard Theological Review* 70 (1977) 257-284.

87. Cf. Y. Congar, *Credo nello Spirito Santo*, III, *op. cit.*, 164ff.

88. On the theme of death, cf., among others: M. Bordoni, *Dimensioni antropologiche della morte*, Rome 1969; L. Boros, *Mysterium Mortis*, Brescia 1969; E. Jüngel, *Morte*, Brescia 1972.

89. G. Kahlil Gibran, *Il profeta*, Milan 1983 (3), 27.

90. *Ib.*, 19.

91. *Ib.*, 135.

EPILOGUE

1. "I sought a land, a very beautiful land, where bread and work were not lacking: the land of heaven! I sought a land, a very beautiful land, where there is no sorrow and misery: the land of heaven! Seeking this land, this very beautiful land, I went to knock, praying and crying, at the door of heaven . . . A Voice said to me from behind this door: Go away, go away, because I have hidden myself in the poor. Seeking this land, this very beautiful land, together with the poor, we have found the door of heaven." I wanted to transcribe into dialect [the original text contains a version of the above in Italian dialect. - Tr.] the words of the *Hasidim* on my return from a trip to various countries of Latin America, where I found a church which celebrates and sings of the liberating Trinity in words and works with its people. Philip Strofaldi, my brother in the priesthood and in daily life, has composed beautiful music for these words, fashioning a song for them, *'A terra d'o cielo* (To earth from heaven), now used in different Christian communities in Italy.

An Interesting Thought

The publication you have just finished reading is part of the apostolic efforts of the Society of St. Paul of the American Province. The Society of St. Paul is an international religious community located in 23 countries, whose particular call and ministry is to bring the message of Christ to all people through the communications media.

Following in the footsteps of their patron, St. Paul the Apostle, priests and brothers blend a life of prayer and technology as writers, editors, marketing directors, graphic designers, bookstore managers, pressmen, sound engineers, etc. in the various fields of the mass media, to announce the message of Jesus.

If you know a young man who might be interested in a religious vocation as a brother or priest and who shows talent and skill in the communications arts, ask him to consider our life and ministry. For more information at no cost or obligation write:

Vocation Office
2187 Victory Blvd.
Staten Island, NY 10314-6603
Telephone: (718) 698-3698